MONTY

AN AUTOBIOGRAPHY

MONTY

AN AUTOBIOGRAPHY

COLIN MONTGOMERIE

First published in Great Britain in 2012 by Orion Books
An imprint of the Orion Publishing Group Ltd
Orion House, 5 Upper St Martin's Lane,
London, WC2H 9EA
An Hachette Livre Company

1 3 5 7 9 10 8 6 4 2

A CIP catalogue record for this book
is available from the British Library.

Hardback ISBN 978 1 4091 4095 5

Typeset in Nexus Serif TF

Printed and bound by CPI Group (UK) Ltd, Croydon, CR0 4YY

The Orion Publishing Group's policy is to use papers that are natural,
renewable and recyclable products and made from wood grown in sustainable
forests. The logging and manufacturing processes are expected to conform to
the environmental regulations of the country of origin.

www.orionbooks.co.uk

For Gaynor

CONTENTS

ACKNOWLEGEMENTS

To my wonderful family, children and step children who are my inspiration. To my father and brother – James and Douglas – who are a constant source of support. To my step daughter Lynsey and her cousin Lauren who are working tirelessly raising funds and awareness for my late mother's charity, The Elizabeth Montgomerie Foundation, and to all those at the Maggie Cancer Caring Centres – thank you.

To my Ryder Cup team – the players, caddies, wives, girlfriends and the entire backroom staff – the best team in sport. To my friends on the tour and above all the caddies as a whole (whatever their collective term is) who have allowed me to share so many bacon sandwiches and endless discussions about Leeds United. To my best man Guy Kinnings, Sarah Casey, David Jebb, Michelle Mair, Sarah Wooldridge, and the entire team at IMG Golf and IMG Media who have been there for me throughout. To everyone at The European Tour, the PGA and the R&A – thank you for your help and support. To Martin Gilbert at Aberdeen Asset Management for his support. To the Callaway team on tour who have welcomed me back so well, to Rolex for their meticulous eye for detail and to all my other sponsors and supporters. To the team at Sky Sports, who have allowed me to venture into the commentary box. To all my friends at Gleneagles, Royal Troon and Turnberry – all of whom manage to make me feel very much at home. To the sponsorship team and all the staff globally at HSBC with whom I have so enjoyed working, and to my good friends Tim Abbott and Peter Walker at BMW UK who allow me to drive the best cars in the world. To Alfred Dunhill, Diageo and all the other outstanding sponsors of golf, without whom we would have nothing to compete for. To the members of the Association of Golf Writers who have been there for my highs and lows and with whom I have enjoyed some cathartic post-round banter.

Thanks, too, to everyone at Orion who have been so understanding, particularly Alan Samson and Lucinda McNeile.

And finally, my thanks to the golfing public who have supported me through thick and thin every week on tour but especially at Celtic Manor – without whose enthusiastic support my team would have found it difficult to achieve what they did.

FOREWORD

by George O'Grady, Chief Executive, The European Tour

Golf has been blessed, decade after decade, with admirable champions and, surveyed from any angle, scrutinised how you like, Colin Montgomerie's achievement in being Europe's Number One golfer eight times – including a remarkable seven years in succession – is a benchmark unlikely to be surpassed.

Great sportsmen are inspired to ascend unprecedented heights by courtesy of prodigious talent, raw courage, instinctive self-belief, innate ambition and sheer motivation. Colin possessed all these qualities and much, much more in becoming the most consistent golfer of his generation in the world, winning 40 titles, and during a 20-year association with The Ryder Cup he superbly demonstrated not only as a player but also as a captain his unique leadership attributes.

Colin represented Europe eight times as a player, winning 23 ½ points from 36 matches, remaining unbeaten in the singles, finishing on the winning team five times, but the greatest, proudest moment of his illustrious career came when as the captain he led his team to a glorious victory in the famous biennial contest on that memorable blue-sky Monday in Wales in 2010.

For Colin the love of golf triggered an exhilarating, triumphant journey and one which I and millions around the world have been proud to admire, appreciate and celebrate.

1 | THE GREATEST HONOUR

The proudest moment of my career.

That is what being captain of the European Ryder Cup team meant to me. Were I to win the Open, or any one of the Majors – something which is perhaps becoming a bit improbable at this stage of my career – I'd be thrilled. So would my family. But it wouldn't come close to how I felt when I was presented with the Ryder Cup in 2010 at Celtic Manor. It wouldn't come close. The Ryder Cup will always have pride of place in my trophy cabinet regardless of what impressive piece of silverware might be sitting next to it.

People will almost certainly read this and say to themselves, 'Oh, he's just saying that because he has never won a Major.' But, were you to ask a couple of our Major winners for their take on a Ryder Cup win versus a Major, it would not surprise me one bit were they to see things in much the same light as I do myself.

Not too long ago, I came across Graeme McDowell's comments at the post-match press conference when he was asked to compare the Ryder Cup triumph with his US Open win at Pebble Beach: 'It was a different level of pressure to Pebble Beach and this is why this match is extremely special and will continue to be one of the greatest – possibly *the* greatest – event on the planet.'

The Ryder Cup really is that big a deal.

The denouement of the 2010 match was virtually unwatchable as everything came down to the final single, the one between

Graeme and Hunter Mahan. The American, who needed a half-point if the US were to hang on to the trophy, had clawed his way back from three down after eleven to be only one to the bad with three to play ...

From a European point of view, the situation was becoming more excruciating by the minute.

That, though, was when Graeme showed all the qualities which paved the way for his US Open triumph. When it came to the 16th, he holed a 25-footer – it was as pressure packed as any 25-footer can have been in the game's history – for the birdie which took him back to two ahead. As his putt fell so, by all accounts, the smile on my face grew proportionally bigger.

But there was still a lot of work to be done ... Holding himself together on the par-three 17th, he hit a shot which flirted with the bunker but pulled up on the fringe.

When poor Hunter came up short from the tee and then fluffed his chip, Graeme's steely nerves did the rest. He putted to within five feet of the hole and happily accepted his opponent's proffered hand when the American's par putt failed to find the hole.

Europe had won the Ryder Cup, with the result a nail-biting 14½ points to 13½.

Half Europe converged on the green and a roar carried through the Usk Valley. When I returned in 2011, it was as if the echoes had never gone away.

In the winter, I took the trophy to the Wales–Ireland rugby match at the Millennium Stadium in Cardiff. I was due to have lunch with some friends and, as I walked into the hospitality suite carrying the metal trophy case, the place came to a standstill. It was almost as if there was some kind of halo around the case.

And it is not just across Europe that the magic has spread. I took the trophy on a tour in Tokyo, Shanghai, Singapore and Australia, followed by Dubai, Abu Dhabi, Qatar, Oman and Bahrain, and the reaction in those faraway parts was similarly astonishing. Even going through security, the place would go nuts. People were stuck in queues, patiently waiting as the airport staff took photographs. I don't think my fellow travellers minded – at least I hope they didn't.

As with the FA Cup, or the Open championship's Claret Jug, the Ryder Cup knocks people for six.

*

After all the hugs and tears in the immediate aftermath of our victory, I went on some kind of mental walkabout. At least to my ears, the yelps of delight and the cheers suddenly faded to a background buzz. I was in one hell of a state, an out and out wreck. The emotion of the previous four days had well and truly caught up with me.

Once back at the Twenty-Ten clubhouse, I found myself a quiet corner in the locker room. And, at a time when I should have been going over and over the captain's closing ceremony speech (my friends had kindly advised that it would be heard by an audience of some 160 million), my thoughts were all over the place.

They darted back and forth, from my wife, Gaynor, to my vice-captains, to my winning team – and to what it all meant to the European Tour.

Heaven knows how long I was like that but there came a point where Jamie Spence, a former player and a Tour official who had been helping non-stop throughout the week, happened upon me and said, firmly, 'You need something to eat.'

The cheers and the singing, this time from the balcony, were beginning to register with me once more as Jamie returned with an industrial quantity of bacon rolls and a Diet Coke. As it came, so Darren Clarke and José Maria Olazábal, two of my vice-captains, escaped the mayhem of the balcony to follow the scent.

Together, the three of us ate that welcome sustenance and relived the events of the day. No one said very much but there were tears in our eyes and they spoke volumes. We were all equally overwhelmed.

Balcony scenes, I have to say, are not really up my street. I was aware of having looked out at the very beginning, but only to marvel at our endlessly loyal fans down below. This was the players' time, not mine.

I have always been happy to leave this kind of thing to others. I am not much of a drinker. No more, as my daughters would cheerfully testify, am I a singer or dancer.

Before too long, Darren and Ollie were hearing some cries or exhortations from the fans which they drew to my attention. There was an unmistakable chant of 'We want Monty. We want Monty.'

It was moving, it was incredible and it was insistent.

Darren and Ollie looked at me. 'On you go,' they said. 'You deserve it.'

So out I stepped into the evening sun and a racket that snatched my breath away.

To be standing out there as thousands of people, not all of them wholly inebriated, yelled 'We love you, Monty!' was one of the most extraordinary moments of my life – a personal moment which is almost too poignantly personal to record.

Yet you cannot afford to be self-indulgent for long in a team situation and, shortly after, when we were all back in the locker room and preparing for the closing ceremony, I noticed that all was not well with Ollie.

Spaniards show their emotions rather more than most and Ollie was weeping, openly, and saying he was sorry, but he would not be attending the ceremony. He could not face the public.

It turned out that he had telephoned his great friend Seve Ballesteros to tell him of the excitement and sense of achievement in the European camp, only to find that the health of this extraordinarily charismatic figure had taken a sad turn for the worse.

'This might be the last Ryder Cup Severiano ever knows,' he muttered.

I understood how he felt. The news was desperately distressing, but I still believed it was important for Ollie that he should be publicly acknowledged for the magnificent part he had played in our victory, with specific reference to the way he had helped the Molinari brothers out on the course. Also, there was the point that Seve, watching at home, would be expecting to see him out there.

I called for everyone's attention.

'Right, lads, quiet a minute,' I began. 'José Maria doesn't want to come on to the stage so I have decided we are all going to boycott the ceremony. Agreed?'

Everyone nodded in approval. 'Sorry, Ollie, either you join us out there or the whole thing gets cancelled. What do you say? Come on, let's go.' I had been desperate to hit the right note and, to my relief, there was a wry smile amid the sadness as Ollie came on board.

Seve came with us as well.

Lee Westwood's caddie, Billy Foster, who had also worked with Seve, came up with a brilliant idea.

There is a famous photograph of Ollie and Seve together at the 1991 Ryder Cup, one with Ollie bouncing up on his friend's shoulders in a bid to see something in the distance. It had been in our locker room all week and Billy suggested it should join us on stage. A couple of the caddies carried it down in advance of the ceremony and fended off a million questions along the way as to what on earth they were doing.

When I introduced Ollie to the fans the roar was already deafening and, as the framed photograph caught all eyes, it rose to a crescendo which told its own story of what Seve meant to the Ryder Cup.

Seve, who died on 7 May 2011, could not but have felt the vibes back in Santander.

*

It is because the 2010 Ryder Cup was the week and the win of my career that I recall the match at the start of this autobiography. I like the idea of having the details winking at me from the shelf and serving as inspiration for the years ahead.

On 23 June 2012, I will be embarking on my fiftieth year and, when I turn fifty, I will become eligible for the Senior Tour. I have always said that I have no interest in playing that circuit and I am not about to change my mind.

But I suppose I should confess to a slight crack in that cast-iron statement. I started off by admitting that if the Senior Open were to be played at one of my favourite Scottish courses – at Troon, Turnberry, St Andrews or Carnoustie – I would want to be there. I then went on to say I would enter the 2013 Senior Open at Birkdale and take it from there.

Now, as I consider that prospect, I am already chuckling over a question which would be bound to arise if I were ever to do as such great players as Gary Player, Tom Watson and Bernhard Langer in winning this premier event for the over fifties. Would it in any way make up for not winning a Major?

Of course it wouldn't but, then again, Player will tell you that he rates his Senior Majors every bit as highly as he does his nine regular Majors ...

It is a bit like how I used to talk about the PGA championship. I once described it as the least important of the four Majors before adding, tongue-in-cheek, that I would change my mind in a hurry were I to get my name on the trophy.

There is, of course, something else the Senior Tour has to offer. I have heard that the players spend plenty of time discussing the good old days.

If that is indeed the case, I can assure you that there would be plenty of occasions when I would waste no time in turning the conversation to 2010, the year we defeated the Americans at Celtic Manor.

2 | TEAM PLAYERS

Allow me, as I said at the opening ceremony, or words to that effect, to introduce my team ... They were twelve first-class golfers and twelve first-class individuals whose combined force was such that they were able to seize the moment against one more great US side. They won for Europe but, on another level, they won for their captain and for that I can never thank them enough.

LEE WESTWOOD

Quite simply, he was Europe's No. 1 and he played that way. I was thrilled to have him in my team. I had total confidence in Lee. There was talk in the lead-up to the event that he might still be carrying the calf injury which had kept him out of the game for six weeks, but I knew that if he was still struggling he would have been honest enough to say so. There was no way he would try to conceal anything.

If Lee said he was fit, he was fit.

My intention had always been to pace the team, giving each man at least one session off, but the weather put paid to that idea. With rain delays forcing the Friday fourballs to carry over into Saturday morning, it was clear there was no way we would be able to follow the traditional format of five sessions – two on Friday, two on Saturday and the singles on the Sunday.

Equally, though, no one wanted to cut the number of matches to squeeze them into the time available. Corey Pavin and I discussed the options with the Tour officials from both camps and we decided on what I thought was an excellent plan. Instead of the five sessions, we would have four; meaning that in Sessions Two, Three and Four (the singles) all the players would be out simultaneously. That suited me just fine.

The format, from start to finish, would look like this:

Session 1: Four fourballs
Session 2: Six foursomes
Session 3: Two foursomes and four fourballs
Session 4: Twelve singles.

I had complete confidence in every member of my team and had no worries whatsoever about having them all involved in the remaining three sessions. In Ryder Cups in the past, there have been eight or perhaps nine very strong players, with some weaker links making up the numbers. But that was not the case in this side of 2010 and I was at pains to make sure the players knew how I felt when I explained the changes.

In this way, what could conceivably have been a negative was transformed into a positive, further reinforcing our 'togetherness'.

But I was a bit concerned about Lee. Because of the adjustments, there would be no opportunity to rest him if it became necessary. All we could do was to ensure that he had the best possible treatment on tap in the way of icing and physiotherapy. It made me feel better about him and, rather more importantly, it was going to make him feel better about himself if he was experiencing the odd tweak.

RORY McILROY

It was back in 2009 that I was walking along the range in Abu Dhabi when one of the golf writers fell into step to ask which of my fellow players I would stop to watch, if I had time.

'Rory McIlroy,' I replied. 'Everyone wants to watch him because they think they could be looking at the next Major champion. He's that good.'

Well, he didn't win the next one, which would have been the Masters of 2009, but he did win six Majors later – the US Open at Congressional.

Rory is all about talent. In my view he is the second most talented golfing individual ever to come out of Europe behind Seve.

The twenty-one-year-old Rory brought a glorious rush of youthful enthusiasm to the locker room. I had watched him playing in the Vivendi Trophy (the rebranded Seve Trophy) with Graeme McDowell in 2009 when the two annihilated Søren Kjeldsen and Álvaro Quirós in the fourballs before putting paid to Henrik Stenson and Peter Hanson in the greensomes. It was impressive stuff.

Rory then followed those successes by leading out Great Britain and Ireland in the singles, where he beat Stenson again in a performance which was as magical as it was mature.

When it came to the Ryder Cup, I was tempted to follow suit and have Rory at the top of the line-up on the last day, but I decided against the idea for one very good reason. I suspected that Corey Pavin would put Tiger out top and I wanted to avoid a Rory–Tiger clash at all costs.

Not because I feared Rory couldn't handle Tiger; I had no worries about that at all. It was more because there had been an issue between them in the run-up to the tournament.

Rory had made some throwaway statement about wanting to play Tiger because he was sure he would beat him. 'I would love to face him,' Rory told the press. 'Unless his game rapidly improves, I think anyone in the European team would love to face him.'

I was dead against that sort of thing. You don't go riling Tiger Woods like that – and I think most players in the age group above Rory's had learned as much from that famous occasion in the 2006 Accenture Match Play championship in Carlsbad when Tiger was due to play Stephen Ames in the first round.

The press had gone to Ames for a quote on how he felt he would do against the World No. 1 and Ames, not wanting to sound beaten before he set out, endeavoured to give the impression that he had hope.

'Anything can happen in match play,' he volunteered, cheerfully, before adding an ill-advised 'given the way Tiger's hitting it'.

Tiger being Tiger, he won by 9 & 8 (that was over eighteen holes) and more or less admitted at the end that Ames's comments had contributed to the scoreline.

My feeling about Rory was that, if he were to play Tiger, it could prove too much of an all-round distraction.

As things worked out, Woods played Francesco Molinari in the eighth match out of the twelve and Rory and Tiger missed each other, as they had all week. Enticing contest though it would have been for everyone, I was massively relieved that it did not come about. My whole approach to the captaincy was that we were a team as opposed to a group of individuals and the last thing I wanted was for personal issues, which the press are bound to play up in a Ryder Cup week, to get in the way.

Now Rory, as Jack Nicklaus has said, is 'as smart as a whip', and he knew that he had made a mistake in saying what he had. His worry once he got to Celtic Manor was that it might have a negative impact on our chances.

He was down on himself when he spoke to me about it and all I could do was to offer as much reassurance as I could. Somehow, I had to unearth the inner, carefree Rory, the golfer who, as a teenager, had so amazing a handle on our Royal and Ancient game that he was at one point playing to a handicap of plus six.

As the two of us were talking things through, Graeme McDowell's caddie, Ken Comboy, was standing nearby and must have heard snippets of our conversation. Comboy decided to take matters into his own hands. He had his own idea as to how to get that McIlroy smile back in place …

On the Wednesday evening he went into Newport and found six Rory-style wigs – something which, to my way of thinking, was akin to finding the proverbial needle in a haystack.

The next morning, before our first practice session, Ken sidled over to me and explained what he had in mind and I was delighted to become an accomplice.

My role was to hold Rory back on the putting green before he headed out for his round. I was singularly well suited to that task, requiring as it did the ability to keep talking. I did as instructed while Ken scampered away with the wigs.

When Rory politely excused himself and said the others would be waiting, we crossed the bridge to the tee – and it was at this point that he spotted Martin Kaymer, Graeme McDowell, Luke Donald and the caddies all sporting the 'McIlroy look'.

It was a good laugh and just what Rory needed to make him feel that he was back in the thick of things. He was the only one to have been overly worried about his Tiger comments but it was important for him to see that no one else was holding them against him.

Those curly wigs straightened things out.

It was an inspired call by Ken. Out of a negative, we had found a positive, one which added an extra fillip to our team spirit. The photographers were giving us the thumbs-up and most of the newspapers went with the picture the following day.

There was another bit of fun – Rory described it as 'cool' – on the Thursday morning. I was on the tee of the par-three 17th along with two of my vice-captains, Thomas Björn and Darren Clarke, when Darren picked up Ian Poulter's club, and had a swing.

Someone from the packed gallery shouted, 'Go on then!' and I thought, why not? 'Come on lads,' I said, 'nearest the pin.'

I duffed mine, Darren pulled his and Thomas shanked his. I think it was fair to say everyone was glad that none of us was playing. It was one more amusing bit of nonsense but, at a different level, it also showed how tight – or do I mean loose? – we were as a group. I don't think the Americans had that.

The pairing of Rory with Graeme McDowell was obvious. They were both from Northern Ireland and are great friends. I had high hopes for the two of them and was slightly surprised when, after the second session, they had done no better than to halve one and lose the other.

Why? They are both fabulous talents but something wasn't quite right.

It could have had something to do with the way Rory had not quite understood what to expect. It wasn't a case of taking the event too lightly. Not a bit of it. In fact, I don't think any of us underestimated the strength of the American challenge, despite the fact that we were seen as hot favourites.

It had more to do with the way in which, when all the talking was done and the match was under way, the level of expectation soared off the scale. It's a scary atmosphere out there, especially playing at home when you are expected to win. If you haven't prepared yourself for it, the pressure can hit you like a tonne of bricks and that is how it was for Rory.

He took the second session foursomes' loss to Stewart Cink and Matt Kuchar badly and I had a tricky decision to make in order to lift his spirits. Did I break his partnership with Graeme or was it better to leave things as they were?

It turned out to be not such a very difficult decision after all. I decided that all they required was the vote of confidence which would be implicit in my leaving them together. They responded brilliantly, beating Zach Johnson and Hunter Mahan 3 & 1.

If I were a betting man, I'd have no hesitation in putting a few quid on Rory being Europe's top scorer in 2012. After the events of Celtic Manor, he now 'gets' the Ryder Cup. Boy, does he get it.

LUKE DONALD

Luke was one of my captain's picks and, with all due respect to Padraig Harrington and Edoardo Molinari, he was the first of the three. If there had been such a thing as the 'most valuable player in the team' award, Luke would have walked away with it. Somebody came up with the following quote which mirrored his performance to perfection – 'You can't even play PlayStation as well as Luke Donald performed in the Ryder Cup.'

Luke himself will tell you that his game has benefited, hugely, from the input of Dave Alred, the rugby-player-turned-performance-coach who taught England's Jonny Wilkinson to make the most seemingly impossible of goal-kicks.

Pat Goss, Donald's long-term technical man, had felt that Alred would be the man to help his player make the most of his potential by harnessing his organisational skills. For the past three or so years, Alred has encouraged Donald to put pressure on himself in his practice sessions by way of making them as similar to the real thing as possible.

If, say, he is practising his wedge play, he has to take note of how many shots from the 70–110-yard range land within a six-foot hoop he places around the hole. As I write, his percentage is probably even better than it was at the start of the year when he mentioned to the press that he expected to get 50 per cent of those shots inside that circle.

Moving on to the putting green, he monitors his progress with a daily exercise in which he arranges five putts of four, five, six and seven feet around four different holes. Here, he expects to report back to Alred that he has made a minimum of 17 out of the 20.

I used to do something similar when I was at Houston Baptist University ... It was the 100-putt routine in which Dave Mannen, the coach, called us to hole 100 two-footers in a row. You had to hole each in turn and, if you missed, you had to go back to the beginning and start all over again. It was, of course, all about muscle memory.

Luke has bulked up, as they say, in the last few years but, at five foot nine, he is never going to come across as a hugely powerful golfer. Yet anyone who thinks of him as a short hitter is stuck in a time warp. Alred apparently describes him as 'sneaky long and getting longer all the time'. As for Luke himself, he notes, quietly, that he is 'plenty long enough and I'm working on it'.

Luke never missed a shot at Celtic Manor and had a vital win against Jim Furyk in the singles. As a character he is quiet and unassuming. He gets on with the job and I was happy to leave him and his caddie, John McLaren, to it. He was brilliant and I couldn't have asked for more.

We all know what he went on to do in 2011 and none of it surprised me. To recap, he won twice in America – the Accenture and the Hospital Classic – and finished the year at the top of the PGA money list while winning the Vardon Trophy, the Byron Nelson Award and the PGA Player of the Year trophy. Back at home, he won the BMW at Wentworth, which was when he became the World No. 1 for a first time, and followed up by bagging the Scottish Open at Castle Stuart to reinforce his position at the top of the golfing globe.

What next for Luke?

A Major I would think.

MARTIN KAYMER

Martin was the most recent winner of a major championship, the 2010 PGA at the time of the Ryder Cup but, perhaps because he is such a reserved character, he came up on the rails in terms of public awareness.

Not, though, among his colleagues. None of us was surprised by his success in that we were all well aware of what a great player – not to mention a great man in the Bernhard Langer mould – we had in our midst. Back in 2008, Nick Faldo had so liked what he had seen of Kaymer that he took him out to Valhalla simply to give him a taste of what the match was about.

It was the best preparation he could have had yet, as applied with Rory, I don't think Martin quite performed to the best of his abilities at Celtic Manor. Although he did well in the fourballs and foursomes, his game never ignited in the way it could have done.

To peak for each of the big events in turn is not something that comes easily to even the best of players and, as likely as not, Martin simply did not click that week. There is also the point that the pressures attached to a home tie in the Ryder Cup are not necessarily going to bring out the best in someone at the first time of asking.

It was because I thought that he might be a little overawed by his first Ryder Cup experience that I paired him with Westwood on the first day. This was Lee's seventh match and he was well able to take a rookie-Ryder Cup man under his wing.

Having made that decision, my next move was an obvious one – that they were the perfect partnership to lead us out on the first morning. They were not necessarily the strongest pair but they were the best front-runners.

I have always gone big on the need to get off on the right foot, of giving yourself every chance to hit a good shot off the first tee in a medal context and of snatching the first hole in match play.

If you can get off to a flier in a Ryder Cup, it can build momentum which can feed through to everyone behind and I was confident that the combination of Martin's form and Lee's experience would make itself felt.

I was right on that score: they did their job magnificently but unfortunately, for whatever reason, their success did not filter down to the rest of the team and we ended that first session down 2½–1½. The best-laid plans …

It was during Lee and Martin's foursome that the only 'incident' of the whole competition occurred out on the course. It was a rules issue that demonstrated the sportsmanship and etiquette that lie at the very heart of the game.

They were up against the young Rickie Fowler and Jim Furyk and, on the 4th hole, Furyk hooked his drive into the cloying rough which was getting worse all the time because of the weather. They were given a free drop, but poor Rickie mistakenly used his own ball rather than Furyk's. The rules are quite clear on this point: you have to finish the hole with the ball you used from the tee unless, of course, you have lost it.

As soon as Rickie realised he had made a mistake he informed the officials himself and forfeited the hole. I would have expected nothing less, but I was still impressed. Rickie was a young man in a high-octane situation but he did not allow that to affect him. He acted superbly.

With Martin well and truly settled in after his two matches with Lee, I was able then to shift things around a bit. Ian Poulter is such a versatile character that he can play with just about anyone and I was comfortable that Martin's calm and his flamboyance would spell success.

It did. They had a memorable 2 & 1 victory over Fowler and Mickelson. But though I had precisely the same good feelings when I paired Poulter with Ross Fisher, that fell some-what flat.

IAN POULTER

You would pick Ian if he was anywhere in the top fifty in Europe. He is our 'Mr Ryder Cup'. I rated every member of my team, without question, and I stand by Luke Donald being the most valuable player in terms of golf. But when it came to heart, passion and pride in representing Europe, Ian Poulter led the field; he was the public face of the whole competition.

Ian is a very confident individual, one of the most assured people I have ever met. His ability to make waves is his greatest strength. On and off the course he is 100 per cent a team player and quite incredible at match play. It is in his DNA: he loves the sense of battle and competition that comes with the format, he feeds off the crowds, relishes the responsibility of playing with a partner. In fact, I would say Ian is simply made for the Ryder Cup.

As in plenty of good relationships, Ian and I have had our differences. We have both, at various times, done our best to play them down but they have all been well documented thanks to a press corps who, in fairness, do a first-class job in bringing the professional game to life for readers who want to know rather more than what clubs we took for our seconds at this hole and that.

I have vivid memories of Ian as he appeared at the Open at Troon in 2004. He was wearing a pair of Union Jack trousers, which weren't exactly my thing. Another time, he was kitted out in pink from head to toe. Me, I'm more of a plain navy man. In other words, on the surface we could not be more unalike when the truth is that we have more in common than most would believe. I think we share the same stubborn streak and precisely the same massive passion for the game.

One of our 'altercations' occurred at the 2005 Seve Trophy at the Wynyard.

I was the captain of the Great Britain and Ireland team against continental Europe and we were struggling on the first day, having gone down in three out of the four fourballs. Our hope was that Padraig Harrington and Paul McGinley would salvage something from the last match which was still out on the course.

Ian had lost his match with Nick Dougherty and was hitting some balls on the range as the last party arrived on the final green. As they contemplated their putts, Padraig and Paul could hear Ian hitting away.

I have no doubt that Ian would have stopped as the putts were about to be taken but the problem was that Harrington and McGinley could not be sure – and that in itself proved to be a distraction. They lost their match and we were 4–1 down.

Afterwards, I am perfectly happy to admit, I laid into Ian in the locker room for not holding his hand up and saying, 'Don't worry, I am watching you. Get on with it.' But it wasn't only Ian I gave a rollicking to, it was the whole team. We hadn't been good enough and it was my job as captain to try to sort it out. Ian knew he was in the wrong, I knew he was in the wrong, I said my piece and that was it. Or it should have been. I made an error in airing my frustration in public. I shouldn't have done that and I later apologised. There was nothing more to it than that.

For the record, my kick up the collective team backside seemed to work. We went on to win 16½–11½.

Another small spat to make the papers occurred when Nick Faldo had to sort out his wild cards for the 2008 Ryder Cup. He and Poulter were in each other's company a lot during the US PGA championship, which was fair enough given that they are good friends and live close to each other in Florida.

Other wild-card seekers such as myself were a bit put out at the time and, when we heard that Ian was not coming to the Johnnie Walker at Gleneagles for the last 'counting' tournament for the Ryder Cup points' list, there were a few cracks along the lines that Faldo had already told him that he could be sure of his team place. My own less than clever quip was that Ian had 'a hotline' to the captain.

That quote was duly relayed to Ian, who responded with the spot-on suggestion that I should mind my own business. 'Monty,' he advised the messenger, 'has got entirely enough to do this week to try and make the side himself. He should be getting his head down and trying to play good golf.'

The truth in this instance was that I was more irritated with Nick than Ian. Not because he went on to pick him and not me, because I think, in retrospect, that I would have done the same. It had more to do with the fact that Nick never asked me to be involved in any capacity, in spite of the fact that I had played in each of the eight previous matches.

I shall go into more detail later ...

Hardly surprisingly, the friction stories were given another airing in 2010 when it was reported that Ian criticised my course design in Bahrain during the Volvo Golf Champions event in January.

He was perfectly entitled to say what he said and I daresay that, if I had opened with a disappointing score on someone else's course, I would have found something to complain about as well. It would have been nothing personal directed at the designer and I am sure Ian was not simply having a go at me. Of course he wasn't. In fact, he said something similar about the changes Ernie Els made to Wentworth for the BMW PGA championship that May. As I remember it, he double-bogeyed the 18th in his second round and came away saying that the course was neither fun nor fair. Was that directed personally at Ernie? Of course not.

All it represented was a reflection of Ian's desire to win and his frustrations at not doing so. No one could understand that kind of reaction better than I can.

I respect Ian Poulter enormously and I would hope the feeling is mutual. I think we will remain friends for ever after what we went through at Celtic Manor. It was a privilege to have him on my team and we would not have won without him.

ROSS FISHER

Ross is a very talented individual, one of the best drivers of the ball around today, but his pairing with Poulter on the first day was one of the decisions I got wrong. It was done for all the right reasons, but, when it came to the bit, it didn't work. Where Martin Kaymer just got on and did his job, Ross seemed to shrink beneath Ian's Ryder Cup exuberance. That is not a criticism of either of them; it is merely an observation on how you can never fully predict how two people will interact. Ian's character can overwhelm some people and I think that's what happened with Ross. I've seen the same with Tiger Woods in foursomes – occasions when his playing partner doesn't shine because he is terrified of letting Tiger down.

Hitting on the right pairings, or trying to hit on them, was one of the most difficult aspects of my captaincy. As a player, I had always been happy to play with anyone. If I was told I'd be playing with Bernhard Langer, for instance, then great, that was no problem. In fact, it was an honour. As indeed it was to be lined up with any of the partners I had over my Ryder Cup career. I never actually thought about how the captain had arrived at his decisions until I had to do the arranging for myself.

To some extent, all I could do was put my team out there and hope for the best. They were all proven golfers but, if they didn't perform on the day, was it down to me? Well, yes, that's just how it works. As captain, it is your job to take that kind of heat.

The players were doing their best, so if things went wrong it was my fault. I had no problem with that and it was why I made the changes I did following the first session. I had the responsibility of reacting to the circumstances in order to give the players the best chance of turning the situation around.

All along, I felt it was vital that I talk to the players on an individual basis to make sure they were comfortable with what I was proposing.

Over the years I have seen some pairings that just haven't worked, even in cases where the players concerned were good friends. There simply wasn't any spark there; none of what it takes to make two heads better than one.

So I was very aware of this element of my job and, when it came to Fisher and Poulter I thought I had made a good move. I was wrong.

The fact that they had played in the World Cup together was the clincher for me, but, for whatever reason, there was no fire when the two of them got together on the Friday morning. No punching of the air, no buzz, no chemistry. After they lost to Steve Stricker and Woods, I decided to split them for the foursomes session, explaining to Ross that the reason I was partnering him with Harrington was because I felt that Padraig would help bring out the best in his game. Thank heavens it worked.

Before they went out, I said to Padraig, 'I need you to help get Ross. He's taken a bit of a knock in confidence in the first match and needs some help to bring him out of himself. I don't care which one of you sinks the putts but just make sure Ross doesn't retreat into his shell.'

I needn't have worried. From the moment they were together, Ross blossomed and began knocking the ball around brilliantly, holing the putts when it mattered and making a significant contribution to their victories over Phil Mickelson and Dustin Johnson and then Furyk and Johnson.

MIGUEL ÁNGEL JIMÉNEZ

I have never known anyone as comfortable in his own skin as Miguel Ángel. And it is some skin. He is amazing. At forty-six years old, to play in the Ryder Cup and win his single – it was the first time he had won a Ryder Cup single – was absolutely terrific. He played very steadily all week and was super in the team room, with his hugs and his gesticulations and his cigars setting off smoke alarms. He was thrilling to have around and never less than a reassuring presence.

He may not always have been consistent throughout his career but, just as he has a warm-up routine – it went out on YouTube at the 2011 Open – which looks like a circus routine, so he has this ability to be able to pull the equivalent of a rabbit out of a hat. The kind of flash of sheer genius that can turn a match.

However bleak a situation might look, you know that if you have someone like Jiménez around all is not lost.

There were so many wonderful moments during the 2010 Ryder Cup that it would be impossible for me to describe them all here, but one in particular, involving Miguel Ángel, must find its way on to these pages. Mainly because it illustrates how the Ryder Cup can affect even the most seasoned of professionals.

I knew exactly what I wanted from my vice-captains while they were out on the course. Clear, precise, level-headed information over the walkie-talkie (once Paul McGinley had worked out you needed to press one of the buttons in order to communicate).

'Okay, guys,' I told them, 'wait until the hole is finished and then give me the result. I am only interested in how each match stands. Whether we are up, down or halved. That way I will have an overall picture at all times of how we are doing. So please wait until everyone has finished putting – either that or the hole has been conceded – before supplying an update. Got it?'

And that is pretty well what happened, until the singles on the Monday when, finally, the sun burned off the early morning moisture to give us a belated look at Celtic Manor and the surrounding Welsh countryside at its supreme best. The heat was on in every sense and I needed to stay 100 per cent focused to juggle all the positions and permutations in my head.

My walkie-talkie was permanently attached to my ear that day and, even with those instructions to my vice-captains to keep messages short and simple, I went through three sets of batteries.

I wanted to be with every player on every hole but, since that was impossible, I tried to make myself as available as possible, covering the course in my buggy and offering support and encouragement where it was needed most. Sky TV helped in this. They provided me with a television in the buggy which had a four-way split screen, allowing me to choose different matches to watch live.

It was clear early on that the Americans were fighting back and Jiménez's ding-dong battle with Bubba Watson was going to be vital. The two of them were playing the 8th when a huge roar reached my ears. The match was all square at the time and, though it was clear that something good had just happened, it didn't necessarily mean we had won the hole.

I would have to wait for the call from my trusted lieutenant Sergio García who was out with Jiménez. But, seconds after the roar died down, my walkie-talkie crackled. It was Sergio. The hole must be ours. Or perhaps Jiménez had secured an unlikely half. I pressed the 'receive' button to find out.

'Jiménez chips in!!! Jiménez chips in!!!' yelled Sergio.

Then it went silent. Nothing more. No indication of the

score or whether the hole was won or halved. Just a very excited Spaniard thrilled at the genius of his compatriot. I saw the chip on television a little later and I think that I would have reacted like Sergio did. It was one of those key moments, if not *the* key moment. From there on in, Jiménez didn't lose another hole and closed Watson out 4 & 3.

It was at the 2011 Open that Jiménez, after his opening 66, gave the journalists a glorious glimpse of the Jiménez psyche. He had been talking of how he would be going back to his hotel for a glass of his favourite Rioja and, as he left the room, he had issued the kindly reminder, 'There is more to life than golfing the ball.'

EDOARDO MOLINARI

Edoardo has a strong personality and plays with tremendous passion. He is full of flair, courage and touch and demonstrated all of these qualities in abundance when he birdied the last three holes at Gleneagles to win the 2010 Johnnie Walker championship. He had been desperate to force his way into the Ryder Cup alongside his brother because he wanted to make his father – and his country – doubly proud. Under that kind of self-inflicted pressure, what he did was nothing short of sensational.

Before he teed up at the 16th, he had seen a board showing how Australia's Brett Rumford had signed off with two birdies to close at nine under par. Since he was only seven under at that stage, it was pretty obvious what he had to do to beat the Australian.

He caught the green in two at the par-five 16th on his way to making the first of his birdies. He then holed a 30-footer at the 17th and punched the air time and time again – at least that's what I've been told – as he thought of how he would have caught my attention which, of course, he had.

On to the last, the uphill, par-five 18th where we can expect so much of the action to be when the 2014 Ryder Cup comes round. Here, he was short of the green in two but chipped close and holed out for the most important hat-trick of birdies he will ever make. Rumford had second place to himself while Edoardo's brother, Francesco, after a closing 75, finished in a share of third.

That night, Edoardo marvelled at how, only twelve months earlier, he had been plying his trade on the Challenge Tour. 'This has been such a great day for me,' he said. 'To win and to get to play alongside my brother in the Ryder Cup is a dream come true.'

The Italian was exactly the type of character I wanted in my team and I had no hesitation in picking him. He was there on merit but there was an additional bonus to having him on board ...

I felt sure that Edoardo would help bring out the best in Francesco – and that is exactly what happened. The two of them lost their foursomes against Zach Johnson and Mahan by two holes but, when it came to their Session Three fourballs, they halved with Stewart Cink and Matt Kuchar. It was the best of half-points in that they had been one down with three to play.

Edoardo may have felt a sense of disappointment at letting Rickie Fowler snatch a half on the last day when he had been three up on the American with three to play but he shouldn't have felt like that at all. Rickie played brilliantly over those closing holes, as indeed Edoardo had done to go three up in the first place. With the fearlessness of youth, Rickie fought back; that's how golf goes.

Edoardo should not be kicking himself because of it. Instead, he should focus on the fact that, if he had lost the match, the US would have won the Ryder Cup. It was that simple.

FRANCESCO MOLINARI

Francesco is quieter than Edoardo, perhaps because he is the younger of the two, and that is one of the reasons I felt it was so important that I keep him and his brother together all week, even putting them out one after the other in the singles. (That ploy also guaranteed that their Italian supporters could do more to make their presence felt, which they certainly did.)

Edoardo could act as both a playing partner and a friend to Francesco, which I thought was vital.

Unfortunately, Francesco came up against a brick wall in Tiger Woods on the Monday. Tiger was the old Tiger that day – nine under par for his last eleven holes – and I'm not sure anyone could have beaten him. Francesco, though, gave it his best shot, winning the first two holes by way of giving the Americans something to think about.

It was quite an introduction to Francesco's first Ryder Cup, which I very much hope won't be his last.

I had, incidentally, been as relieved as anyone when word came that Tiger would be at Celtic Manor. His appearance made the event bigger and better.

I felt proud when spectators gave him such a cheer at the opening ceremony, while I think everyone was impressed at Tiger the team man that week.

On the final day, we were both there on the 17th, watching McDowell and Mahan tee off. Tiger was sitting on the grass and, as Graeme and Hunter strode off down the fairway, I helped him to his feet. 'Fantastic play today, Tiger,' I said. 'That was an incredible round of golf. It feels you are getting back to where you were. Good luck to you.'

He thanked me for my comments and I have to say that I was glad to have had that opportunity of saying something I felt so keenly. Golf is a better place when an in-form Tiger is around.

One of my highlights of the week came when Francesco and Edoardo secured their half-point against Cink and Kuchar. Francesco's putting had not been at its best but when he had to hole a clutch four-footer on the last to win the hole, halve the match and complete a fabulous 5½ out of six points for the session, he didn't buckle. That putt ensured that every member of the team contributed, which was critical and meant a lot to me personally.

When Francesco and Edoardo had lost their Session Two foursomes to Zach Johnson and Hunter Mahan, I had not even considered splitting them up. I was certain they would come good and to have separated them would have been to knock their confidence unnecessarily, which could in turn have had a damaging impact on their new pairings.

Confidence is a key part of both their games; they told me at the start of the week that they had never lost together and were sure they would deliver for me. They did – and they deserved to, given the way they played.

Mind you, they certainly made things hard for themselves when Francesco missed the putt on the 17th which would have put them all square with Cink and Kuchar going up the last. This was the only time I became involved in offering advice, much as I was tempted to on a number of prior occasions …

As the non-playing captain you live every shot, mentally deciding the best strategy and sometimes wishing the player on the course was thinking the same as you. But you can't say anything; at least, I didn't think I could. I felt it was my job to keep my mouth shut unless asked.

In 1997, Seve had adopted a very different approach but in a rather different situation. At forty-one, Seve not only wanted to play, he could have played – and would doubtless have manufactured some of the more demanding shots better than any of the rest of us. I wasn't quite in that position.

I've been asked before whether I should have advised Rory McIlroy, when he was on the 18th fairway of his singles against Stewart Cink, to lay up instead of going for the green.

In hindsight, he probably should have been more cautious, but he is an aggressive player, that's his style. Just imagine how it would have been had I offered some pearl of wisdom which had resulted in his defeat.

Not only would he have been livid, and rightly so, but it would have dealt a blow to the team's confidence in me. On this occasion, Rory found the bunker and took two to get out before holing the bravest of putts to halve the match. He did it his way and, anxious moments though it prompted, that was fine by me.

The situation with the Molinaris was slightly different. They were one down with two to play but with a putt to win the hole when, out of the blue, I had Harrington on my walkie-talkie.

Padraig had finished his match and had hurried to watch the brothers. 'Monty,' he screamed over the airwaves, 'you have got to come and tell Francesco that the ball breaks more than he thinks. I've just faced the exact same putt and I missed it.'

That was good enough for me. As the only person who could offer any advice on the course, I hopped into my buggy and Rhys Davies, my extraordinary driver and someone who in another life must have been a rally champion, whizzed me to the green in record time. I couldn't approach Francesco, who was by then bending over his ball and weighing up his options, but I spoke to his brother.

'Edoardo, does Francesco know that this putt breaks more than it appears to? Harrington's just had the same putt.' Edoardo assured me Francesco was well aware of the correct line and so I left it at that. There wasn't anything more to be done. As it was, he missed anyway.

His heroics were to come one hole later.

PETER HANSON

Peter is a quiet bloke for whom I have all the time in the world and any amount of respect. Who wouldn't have after the way he played his way on to the team?

He had planned on a week off prior to playing in the Johnnie Walker championship, where the team would be decided, but instead asked for a last-minute sponsors' invitation to play in the Czech Open. If he could win the tournament, he would be certain of his slot on the European team.

The sponsors gave him the thumbs-up on the Monday and, after rushing out to the Czech Republic, Hanson did not take too long to discover the form which had seen him winning in Mallorca in May.

There were a few hiccups for the player at the start of his fourth round and, though he recaptured his lead with a birdie at the 10th, there was more trouble in the offing at the 12th. After a good drive, he knocked his second into a bunker beyond the green. It cost him a six and saw him slipping behind Peter Lawrie and Gary Boyd. Once again, he fought back, making a birdie at the 16th which paved the way for his closing 74 and a place in the play-off alongside Lawrie and Boyd. He won that at the second play-off hole – a feat which took his play-off record to three wins in three starts.

Though the initial impression was that he had hauled himself into the ninth and last spot, he had in fact done better than that. With Jiménez having a series of last-day mishaps, he had overtaken the veteran Spaniard to head for Scotland and the Johnnie Walker in eighth place.

'What Peter did today was the stuff of champions,' said Robert Lee from the ranks of the television commentators. That just about summed him up.

Peter is an extremely good golfer and was the player who had probably improved the most over the two-year Ryder Cup span.

I was thinking along those lines when I put him out at number ten in the singles. He was on a roll. His game was really coming together, and, thinking back to what I had seen of his Czechoslovakian performance on TV, I felt that he could handle himself if things got tight towards the end.

Though he came up against an inspired Phil Mickelson and lost his singles, he was still great for us, winning with Jiménez against Bubba Watson and Jeff Overton.

Peter and Miguel Ángel got on fantastically well and formed a brilliant partnership. It wasn't quite a case of opposites attracting, but it wasn't far off. If I had one word to describe Peter, I would say 'solid'. It is a word with a wealth of different meanings – 'safe', 'sound', 'stable' and 'strong' to name but a few. You want a Peter Hanson on your side.

PADRAIG HARRINGTON

In terms of press opinion, Padraig was probably my riskiest pick but I didn't agree with that assessment at all. I believed it was essential we had someone with his three-Major status in the party, someone who had shown he could handle himself under severe pressure over and over again.

To be honest, I wasn't surprised at the outcry when I selected Padraig over Paul Casey, who was at that point ranked ninth in the world, and I strongly suspect it made it tough for Padraig to perform at his best.

On the day I announced the team – 29 August – I had gone to great lengths to explain my choice … Padraig had won three Majors in the last three years; his stature was such that no one would want to find themselves up against him in match play; and he was someone who knew everything there was to know about European golf.

I also mentioned his work ethic and the fact that he would give 110 per cent.

Some of the writers wanted to know whether I was concerned about his form in the 2010 season. 'Not at all,' I said. 'I think that when Padraig's back is up against the wall, he can produce fantastic performances and that's what I'm expecting at Celtic Manor.'

In normal circumstances I would have expected Padraig and Luke to have won comfortably over Bubba Watson and Jeff Overton in the opening fourballs, not least because the Americans were a rookie partnership. Yet, perhaps because Padraig felt under extra pressure to perform, they lost to the tune of 3 & 2.

But even after that defeat I never questioned my decision. I had total confidence in Padraig and he justified it in full when he rose to the challenge magnificently with Ross Fisher when the latter needed someone of Padraig's standing to take charge. He was also great in the team room, where his presence was critical. Who wouldn't want someone with that kind of background contributing to the overall feel-good factor?

The degree to which Padraig is a team man shone through at all times ...

After he had lost to Zach Johnson in the singles, he did not waste a moment worrying about himself and his record. As I have mentioned above, he had hurried to watch the Molinaris and was worried sick that Francesco that might not know the extent to which his putt would break at the 17th.

GRAEME McDOWELL

Graeme was riding high coming into the Ryder Cup, having followed a win in the Wales Open at Celtic Manor by capturing the US Open at Pebble Beach. It was an amazing crescendo in terms of achievements and it was fantastic from my point of view that the Ryder Cup came so soon after these twin performances. For me, Graeme's greatest strength lies in his confidence and it was gloriously and palpably intact.

He did get off to a slightly shaky start in the Ryder Cup but you could see that he was picking up all the time. By the Sunday evening, it was evident from his demeanour that he was back to his best, which is why I made the decision I did in relation to the singles draw.

After the team's incredible performance in Session Three, we went into Monday three points to the good, 9½–6½. Obviously I had no idea how the Americans would line up and, although I did try to anticipate to a degree – I certainly expected Woods and Mickelson to come out somewhere near the top rather than in eighth and tenth as they did – I decided in the main to play my own game. All too often in the past I had seen the dangers attached to trying to be too clever at this stage.

In the 2002 Ryder Cup, with the scores tied at eight apiece, captain Sam Torrance ignored the perceived wisdom of the time that you place your best players at the bottom of the draw, where the real business was likely to be conducted. Instead, he loaded the first seven berths with his in-form men of the moment.

In contrast, the US captain, Curtis Strange, held back Davis Love III, Phil Mickelson and Tiger Woods to tenth, eleventh and twelfth positions. A strong finish without doubt, but it proved academic. Mickelson fell to Phillip Price on the 16th and it was as the Love and Woods matches were still in full swing that Paul McGinley famously knocked in his putt from nine feet to secure the trophy for Europe. In other words, what happened to Love and Tiger did not matter. Their efforts were meaningless.

I remember thinking that I had never before seen a more rattled captain than Curtis at the conference where the singles' line-up was announced. He was as a man who had been thrown a curveball, one which put the Americans on the back foot before the matches even began. As for Sam, he just smiled.

All this had been going through my head as I discussed the order with my vice-captains and Harrington and Westwood. We decided that our plan was to try to close things out as quickly as possible, by placing Westwood, McIlroy, Donald, Kaymer and Poulter at the top of the order while keeping something up our sleeve should the matches not go as we hoped. That 'something' was Graeme McDowell, a proven winner and someone who would not buckle under any pressure, should it come to it. You couldn't guarantee he would win, but you could be certain he would not give his point away.

Initially, Graeme was not very happy about being in the anchor slot, concerned as he was that it might be a dead rubber. I think he had pictured himself as being in sixth, seventh or eighth slot, where he felt the Ryder Cup would be won.

I took him to one side to discuss it. 'Graeme, I understand what you are saying, but just look at this American team for a second. They have surprised us all week. They are bloody good. Woods isn't going to fall down. Mickelson isn't going to fall down. Do you really think this team is going to roll over and accept defeat? You know they aren't. This competition is far from over and this could, believe me, work out for you as much. I need you at number twelve if things go wrong elsewhere.'

He understood my reasoning and looked happy as he headed off to bed that evening, which is what I had hoped to achieve. I didn't want anyone in the team not feeling comfortable about the position he was in. Graeme McDowell was my insurance policy, and, as I will explain a little later, I place a lot of faith and importance in insurance policies.

And did it pay off?

Did it not ...

Ever since 4 October 2010, I only have to see Graeme to think of that 25-footer he holed on the 16th to return to two ahead. The cheers will ring through my ears – and his I suspect – for years to come.

Mahan, to recap, had fought back from three down to one down with three to play and Graeme knew by then that a halved match would not do the trick. He *had* to win.

Graeme talked afterwards about having been fighting his swing prior to that 16th hole where he hit what he described as 'the greatest second shot and the greatest putt of my career'.

On the subject of the attendant pressures, he said that he had been imagining winning and losing 'in the same breath'.

Everyone who witnessed his win of wins would understand.

3 | TEAM BUILDING

On the evening of 13 January 2009, a couple of days prior to the start of the Abu Dhabi championship, I walked into one of the meeting rooms in the Emirates Palace Hotel with the intention of backing Sandy Lyle as the next Ryder Cup captain. I was equally happy to support José Maria Olazábal if his name came up again. Ollie had been talked about before in this context, only when he had been sounded out he had been unable to promise anything. He had been assailed by arthritic problems for several years and, at that stage, he was not at all sure whether he would be up to the role.

It was the first meeting of the year of the European Tour committee and the issue of the captaincy was high on the agenda. The discussion was going to interest me from rather more than a committee angle. Whoever's team it was going to be, I planned to be in it. I had played in eight matches and, having missed out on the 2008 instalment, I was desperate to win my place back.

There were approximately thirty people around the table, twenty or so players, the chief executive of the Tour, George O'Grady, and eight or nine members of the Tour staff.

The discussion was wide-ranging, with all sorts of names being put forward. Sandy's duly came up and I gave him my support, but it was clear early on that his captaincy was not going to receive the endorsement of the committee, mainly because his age counted against him. I understood the concerns raised. The competition has become so big that it needs someone at the helm who is 100 per cent in touch. By September 2010, Sandy would be fifty-two, far from past it in the golfing sense but any player who has moved on to the Senior Tour is each week becoming further and further removed from the main Tour. Of course he is.

In a way, it is a bit like when you turn professional. Suddenly, the lists of scores in the amateur game no longer catch your eye. You struggle to keep up with who is going to make the next Scottish or Walker Cup side.

I felt bad for Sandy. As a player, he has contributed massively to European success. He was one of the stalwarts of the Tour, a double Major winner, a good colleague and a Scot into the bargain. His four peers, Langer, Seve, Woosnam and Faldo, had all had their turn at the captaincy but there was one too many of them in that little posse of champions. Nineteen ninety-nine would have worked for him but, after Mark James got the nod that year, there would be no further chances. It was just one of these things; not everyone can do it.

The same applies to people like Larry Nelson and Mark O'Meara in the US and Peter Alliss over here. Who would believe that Alliss never captained the team when he played in the match eight times?

It is probably always going to be this way. There are many superb candidates waiting in the wings even as I write. Thomas Björn, Paul McGinley, Darren Clarke and Lee Westwood all come to mind but I doubt there will be room for them all.

Other names to get a mention at our meeting were Ian Woosnam's and Miguel Ángel Jiménez's. Woosnam prompted quite a debate because the event was taking place at Celtic Manor in Wales but, while that was a huge point in his favour, there was the fact that he already had his turn – at the K Club in 2006.

Miguel Ángel Jiménez? The general consensus of opinion was that this great character's English was not quite up to the PR demands of a home tie. Thomas Björn was rejected as being too young and too good. He had every chance of playing his way on to the team.

Olazábal, as I say, had been picked out for the job some time before but things had not moved on. No one wanted to push him into making a decision but, at the same time, there was a strong feeling that we needed to get something sorted out. In such circumstances, it made sense to pencil him in for 2012. By then, he would be well and willing.

We were starting to go round in circles and people were beginning to wonder where – and when – it was all going to end. That was when Henrik Stenson, who was sitting next to me, spoke up.

Stenson, for the most part, does not waste words and when he does speak, people listen.

'This is crazy,' he said. 'We have an obvious captain in the room.' We all began looking at each other. I was staring from one to the other of Darren (Clarke), Thomas (Björn) and Paul (McGinley) when suddenly I heard Stenson delivering his punchline. 'Monty.'

Oh God, I thought. I'd had my eyes fixed on the possibility of 2014 at Gleneagles. That had seemed like the perfect fit. I lived there, I loved the place and I would just be young enough. And, hang on a minute, wasn't it just possible that I might be playing in 2010? (I didn't like to suggest as much but, in my heart, I genuinely thought that could happen.)

Though Henrik's little speech had thrown my dreams upside down, this was the Ryder Cup captaincy we were talking about and I wasn't going to dismiss anything hastily. 'Right, okay,' I said, a tad lamely and somewhat unconvincingly.

Thomas Björn, the committee chairman, intervened with a thoughtful, 'Whoa, hold on a second. Monty's set for 2014. Ignore Monty.'

But nobody did; they had all started to talk about me as if I wasn't there. It was becoming very strange indeed. George O'Grady then stepped in.

He suggested that they should get a handle on what I really thought of the idea. 'Colin,' he said, turning towards me, 'if you were offered this job, would you take it?'

It was an authoritative and pertinently worded question to which I found myself replying as follows: 'George, I know people have been thinking about me for 2014 but if you were to offer me the job of captain for 2010, I would be honoured and would gladly accept.'

Not bad, I thought, given how completely ill prepared I was.

'If you don't mind then, Colin,' said George, with a smile, 'I think we've got to a stage where you probably should leave the room.'

'Oh, okay, fine,' I said. 'I'll be off.'

I stepped outside, expecting to be greeted by nothing more than an empty, soulless corridor. Wrong. There must have been at least a dozen members of the press hanging around. They knew about the meeting and they were looking for a steer on the captaincy.

This was going to be awkward. It was going to look very odd, suspicious even, if I merely sat down outside the room as I had intended.

I wasn't sure how to play it and, given everything that had just happened, I wasn't exactly at my sharpest. There was only one thing I could think of to say: 'Do you know the way to the cloakroom?'

They sent me down one corridor and then another and, once there, I texted Peter Lawrie to tell him what was going on: 'Peter, before you start talking about me, you should know that there are twelve press guys outside the room. I am stuck in the cloakroom. I had to go somewhere or they would have twigged something was going on. Can you let me know when you are ready for me to come back!'

When, eventually, the call came, the committee were quick to bring me up to speed. Apparently the idea of my taking on the captaincy earlier than originally envisaged had been positively received, but they had decided that the best bet was to sit on the final decision for a couple of weeks, which would take us to the week of the Dubai Desert Classic.

I didn't really agree with this, to be honest; there didn't seem any benefit in putting things off, as all that would happen was the rumour mill would go into overdrive. But they stayed with their decision; they felt they needed time to let the idea percolate. What was critical, it was explained to everyone in the room, was that nothing was to be discussed outside those four walls.

There was a time, when things could be kept within four walls but, with tweets and twitters and texts, those days were long gone even then.

At that point, I felt I should probably remind everyone of the press presence outside. George agreed to deal with the writers, which he did, but I must say I didn't fancy our chances of keeping a lid on this for a fortnight.

No one, I was certain, would say anything intentionally, but whispers start and journalists have a nose for these things. They were bound to put two and two together soon enough. In fact, it only took only a couple of days. Having been 50-1 in the bookies to be the next captain, my price suddenly plummeted to something like 1-50. Now I am no gambling man, but even I know that is odds-on. What happened, I don't know, but the word was out.

As had been agreed, no formal announcement was made for two weeks, Decision Day being set for 28 January. The moment the meeting was convened, I was off again. 'Monty, can you leave the room please.' Fortunately I needed to go no further than the corridor, the press having been kept away this time.

I was nervous. The bookies may have felt differently, but I knew this was not a done deal because Olazábal seemed to be back in the reckoning. As much as anything, I just wanted a decision, to know where I stood.

As soon as I was recalled, Thomas Björn spoke up. 'Colin, the committee has unanimously decided to offer you the role of European Ryder Cup captain for the 2010 competition to be held at Celtic Manor. We want you to win us back the trophy.'

Wow. I learned later that there had been further discussion about Ollie but, given his questionable fitness and the fact that I was playing regularly on the Tour and was two and a half years older, they had returned to the idea of having me in 2010 and Ollie in 2012.

In answer to Thomas, I said I was extremely proud to have been selected: 'Becoming Ryder Cup captain is the greatest honour that can be bestowed on any European golfer and I promise I will leave no stone unturned to try to win back the Ryder Cup for Europe.'

That was pretty much it. Everyone shook my hand and we left the room. As we did so, I might as well have been passing through the wardrobe into Narnia; I was entering a new world.

What does the role of Ryder Cup captain entail? A couple of press conferences before the event itself then three days of practice and three days of competition? It's an honorary position, an incredible one without doubt, but it doesn't actually require you to do that much, surely?

Wrong, hugely wrong. Naively, I was shocked about the level of involvement required of the captain.

I should have known from that very first day when the announcement was made.

The moment I stepped out of that committee room, Mitchell Platts, our director of communications, was on to me:, 'Right, Colin, this is what we do from now on in ...' He proceeded to reel off a list of sponsors, partners and patrons of whom I needed to be aware, and informed me I had to change my tie and make sure I was appropriately attired for the various official functions. I had to wear the correct watch (Rolex) and I had to step out of the correct car (BMW). Suddenly I was not an individual; I represented the Ryder Cup team and, as such, had to respect the match sponsors, an obligation with which I was more than happy to comply.

Without the sponsors, the ongoing success of the competition would be in jeopardy.

Neither wearing a Rolex nor, for that matter, stepping out of a BMW is exactly hard work but there was a lot to remember.

Clothing and golf accessories were another aspect of my Ryder Cup role. Glenmuir were our official on-course sponsors and we had Level 4 golf bags, suit carriers and shoe bags, plus Proquip waterproofs, thank goodness. (I'll get into that later.) For our off-course wear, we had Canali which, mercifully, appealed to everyone.

All this was organised by the European Ryder Cup committee and had nothing to do with me. The US Ryder Cup committee do it very differently, leaving it to the captain to sort out his own deals. That can obviously work fine but I was more than happy to hand over that side of things to someone else.

I also found myself transported into a diplomatic world where I had to be extremely careful what I said. Over the years that has not exactly been my strong suit and I was very aware of not provoking any war of words with the Americans or, indeed, any of my fellow Europeans.

Understandably, the press are always looking for an angle and seizing their chance to rekindle any past controversy – Kiawah Island in 1991 or Faldo's letter at Brookline in 1999 – or pushing the current captain to pass comment on his predecessors. Practice can improve how you handle these questions which are designed to catch you out but a bit of early assistance would not have gone amiss.

In his book *Monty's Manor*, Ian Carter described me as 'quite simply the best interviewee in sport'. (In truth, most writers would want to add the rider that I am good on the Wednesday of a tournament week – i.e. before the event starts – but that it is in the lap of the gods as to what I am like thereafter.)

I felt that for the term of my captaincy I was anything but a good interviewee in that I kept things deliberately bland. It wasn't me at all but I understood the importance of this 'new Monty'. The Ryder Cup was not about me, it was about the team. I just happened to be the focal point. I was rolled out for everything – press days and charity days, etc., because there was no one else. It was knackering, but I was determined not to drop the ball.

Making a mess of being Ryder Cup captain would have lived with me for ever.

Prior to being appointed captain, as I mentioned previously, I truly believed I had a chance of making the team. But, once I accepted the role, that became irrelevant.

I sat down with the Tour officials and explained that even if I were to win a Major, I still wouldn't seek to play. I suggested that any Ryder Cup points I managed to accrue should be crossed out.

I was captain and I was thrilled to be captain. There was no room for me to be dreaming about holing the winning putt for Europe or whatever. One job was enough.

Tom Lehman and Mark James are two past captains who very nearly qualified to play in their respective teams (James in 1999 and Lehman in 2006) and I didn't want to have any such issue distracting me. As far as I was concerned, from January 2009 until September 2010 I didn't exist as a player.

And, frankly, given the way I turned out to be scoring, it was as if that was quite literally the case.

*

Appointing my vice-captains was my first concrete decision and I had strong views as to the role they should play. I didn't believe they should be there just as company; old friends with whom to have a couple of beers in the evening; instead I wanted my vice-captains to be truly involved, both in the event itself and in the matter of team selection. It was critical that, whoever they were, they wouldn't be going to Celtic Manor to be part of a team in which they had not had a hand. It was going to be our team, not my team. And that's how it worked. We spent a lot of time together discussing every aspect of the campaign and became very close in the process. Life-long friends in fact.

The reason I chose four current players – Paul McGinley, Thomas Björn, Darren Clarke and Sergio García – was because they were already emotionally engaged in the European Tour. We were all insiders, fighting for the same cause. All four were also strong characters with big opinions and definite personalities. Which was exactly what I wanted. I had no time for yes-men. If we were going to plot our way to victory, we needed to be able to listen to each other's points of view and bounce ideas to and fro. These guys were all going to speak up, have an input.

They were superb. Incredibly supportive, hard-working, knowledgeable and selfless.

I discussed with Darren the possibility of his becoming one of my vice-captains during the Open at St Andrews in 2010. I had already spoken to McGinley and Björn and was due to speak to García. Darren and I met in his hotel room and we had a great chat. I explained to him that, since he was unlikely to make the side, which was unfortunate since he has played some of his best golf in a Ryder Cup jersey, I really wanted him on board as a vice-captain.

Now, had he said, 'You're speaking to someone who's going to win the 2011 Open championship at Royal St George's', I might have omitted that line about how he was unlikely to make the side. As it was, he agreed immediately with what I was saying and was brilliant throughout. It was important for me to have the game's best and brightest citizens on board and Darren was a great contributor to the cause.

When it came to García, I wasn't considering him as a potential vice-captain at that stage. He was still in the mix as one of my captain's picks and I wanted to be totally up front with him.

'Forget about proving to me what you can do,' I told him. 'I know what you are capable of but you have got to show your peers what you can do. You've got three big tournaments, this Open, the Bridgestone Invitational and the US PGA. You've got to come up with the goods in those events to give me an option.'

Unfortunately that didn't happen. Sergio quite simply did not play well enough to force himself into the reckoning.

But something else very interesting happened during our conversation in St Andrews. After I had laid out how I saw the situation, Sergio looked me straight in the eye. 'I understand what you are saying, Monty, and I want you to know I'd love to be there, come what may.'

I sort of misunderstood what he was trying to say and thought he was talking about playing. In a slightly bumbling fashion I replied, 'Yes, I know you would. Of course you would. I understand that. Who wouldn't?'

'No, no,' he said. 'Even if I am not selected.'

'Sorry?'

'I want to help. Whatever happens, I want to be there.'

That got to me. Until that moment, I really hadn't been thinking along vice-captain lines, but this was something else. Here was a thirty-year-old superstar, who played the majority of his golf in the US, clearly stating where his heart lay. He wanted to win the Ryder Cup for Europe whether he was playing or not. His passion and commitment added up to a startling illustration of the strength of the European Tour family.

'Right, got you,' I said. 'I understand what you're saying.' And when it was clear after the US PGA that he wasn't going to make it, I had no hesitation in calling and asking if he was still available. I had my fourth vice-captain.

When we eventually arrived at Celtic Manor, I think Sergio found it hard initially. He couldn't quite accept his locker wasn't with the players'. That got to him and he was a wee bit down on the Tuesday at practice and, to a lesser extent, on the Wednesday.

But from Thursday onwards he had brushed all that aside and was outstanding. His Spanish zest for the competition was contagious. It was a joy to watch him in full cry.

I felt confident that I had made all the right choices and I hope, in turn, that the committee were happy with the one they had made that night in Abu Dhabi.

Initially, I had no idea how my appointment was going to be received and I suspected there would be some doubters. One accusation I anticipated was that I was a hothead who would be incapable of withstanding the pressure. I can be a hothead but, equally, I can be stubborn – and it was my stubborn streak which made me all the more determined to prove the naysayers wrong.

I was intent on winning back the Ryder Cup and, as I said to Björn, I would leave no stone unturned in that pursuit, the main reason being that I knew exactly how much a triumph would mean to the European Tour. A home victory is five times more valuable than an away win because there are more people watching and the buzz is so much greater. And that, in turn, brings in new sponsors and detonates a new enthusiasm for golf.

It might be harder to win on American soil, but in economic terms there is no contest. George O'Grady, the CEO of the European Tour, was already doing a magnificent job in keeping our circuit looking good in the midst of a recession and, to a man, everyone in the team knew that a good result at Celtic Manor would be the best possible boost we could give him.

So many reasons to win, so much heaping on the pressure ...

Professional golfers of a certain standard are used to personal disappointments, as I know only too well. They can be hugely disappointing for you and your family but they are not going to keep too many other people awake at night. The Ryder Cup, on the other hand, could not be more different.

If you lose your match, you are not only letting down your team-mates but everyone on Tour. Add in your family, your country and your continent and it doesn't bear thinking about. For heaven's sake, why do we put ourselves through such anguish?

Because it is an experience like no other. The event gets you in its grip and never lets go.

Perhaps you have to have played in eight Ryder Cups and captained the team to truly understand what I am trying to say. The match somehow changes you as a person as the atmosphere soaks into your very being. The pressure you have to withstand strengthens your resolve to succeed, while the electricity that courses through your veins becomes addictive.

All the players at Celtic Manor will have sensed something of this but, the more you play, the more you 'need' to play. Seve knew that feeling. Olazábal, Bernhard Langer, Sam Torrance are four more to have been in the Ryder Cup's grip to that extent but that's probably it. Going back a bit, I should perhaps include Tony Jacklin, because he was the captain responsible for upping the ante and taking the event to a new level.

4 | STICKY PICKS

At this stage I did not know there would be a fifth vice-captain in the mix. Suffice it to say I had selected the four I felt I needed and choosing them had been a cinch. Deciding on my three captain's picks, on the other hand, was anything but.

I have said in the past that twelve picks would make for the best possible team. Because of the way the qualification process works, those who qualify automatically are not necessarily the best nine or ten European players when the gun goes; some could have picked up most of their points at the start of the points-gathering campaign rather than in the months immediately preceding the contest. That said, I understand that a full team of picks would never work. The implications of qualifying for the team are too massive for the players, not only financially – through sponsorship and endorsements – but in terms of the various exemptions and privileges that can go with a team place.

It doesn't happen now, but there used to be an event in America to which only those who had made a Ryder Cup team were invited. To some, that kind of perk could mean a lot. So the players understandably have a vested interest in staying with the status quo rather than leaving the decision-making to one individual.

For the purposes of my captaincy, I did manage to push through a bit of a tweak by having three captain's picks rather than the traditional two.

I wanted my wild cards to have forced my hand through a level of play that could not be ignored and, accordingly, I was keen to see the various candidates up close and in action.

That is partly what drove my rather hasty comments back in August 2009 when I said that in the following year I would prefer, even expect, the top Europeans to be at the BMW PGA at Wentworth, the Wales Open and the Johnnie Walker championship.

Though the reason I said what I said was purely because I wanted to go into the Ryder Cup with the twelve strongest golfers, I should have phrased things a little differently. As it was, there were those who detected an implicit criticism in what I was saying about too many players spending too much time on the US Tour. That was never my intention. These top golfers are individuals and it is up to them where they ply their trade.

Yet there is an issue here which might need to be resolved. Because of the way the Ryder Cup points' system works, and because of the strides made by our American-based players over the last few years, we ended up in 2010 having too many men chasing too few places on the World Points' list.

To explain what is a complex system, there were nine automatic places on offer once I had decided that I would be handing out three wild cards. The first four slots were reserved for the best-placed Europeans on the Ryder Cup World Points' Table. And the next five for the leaders on the European Ryder Cup Points' Table.

In 2010, McDowell and Kaymer, both of whom were playing mainly in the States, won a Major apiece. In addition, you had Westwood and McIlroy amassing World Points galore on their US forays. All of which meant that the pickings were suddenly looking a bit thin for the other Europeans on that side of the

Atlantic. Both Paul Casey and Justin Rose fell into that category. They were doing very well but, in terms of ranking points, they had not accumulated enough to propel themselves into that all-important top four.

Again, since they had played only a handful of events in Europe and were not in a position to make the team via the European Tour Points' list, the only way they could get to Celtic Manor was via the wild-card route.

Almost all the Europeans had played the BMW PGA and I think more would have carried on from there to the Wales Open had not the Madrid Masters got in the way, requiring a trip to Spain between the two.

That said, I was still concerned about the European turnout in Wales, especially as the event was being played on the same course we would be playing the Ryder Cup. It would have been invaluable experience.

I had also hoped that some of the US-based players would return for the Johnnie Walker championship at Gleneagles in July in an attempt to give themselves the best chance of selection.

Unfortunately, that didn't happen and I must confess to a degree of disappointment.

As it transpired, Gleneagles proved pivotal in a manner I had not expected ...

As things stood, whatever the result of the Johnnie Walker, no one was going to play themselves into one of the automatic qualification spots. The top nine was by then set in stone; it was now down to my three picks and, my goodness, I felt the pressure.

They were to be announced following the conclusion of the tournament and it turned out to be a nightmare of a Sunday, not one I would want to relive in a hurry. In fact, I would go as far as to say that it was the worst day I have had in my twenty-five years on Tour. I was going to have to disappoint and upset friends and regular playing companions.

If I didn't pick someone who was pushing at the door, it was almost as though I was dropping them, sacking them even. And there was every chance I'd be sitting next to whoever it was in a locker room some time soon. Perhaps in an ideal world you wouldn't have a fellow player dictating who is in the team and who isn't, but that is the way things are for now. I knew what lay ahead when I took on the role and I had to deal with it. It wasn't something I could hand on to any company Human Resources department.

The first of my three picks was perhaps the easiest: Edoardo Molinari. As I had stated from the beginning, if someone forced themselves into the reckoning, I would respond.

Edoardo didn't just play his way into the reckoning, he charged into the fray as he birdied each of the last three holes to win the tournament. Peter Hanson had shown any amount of guts by annexing the Czech Open when he wanted to seal his place in the side and, a week later, Edoardo was rising to the challenge in much the same staggering style.

His was a fantastic, gutsy display of golf and one which fully deserved to be recognised. And, of course, the fact that his brother, Francesco, was already in the team made the situation even better.

Having made up my mind, I wanted to let Edoardo know my decision as quickly as possible. I was at Gleneagles with three of my vice-captains – Thomas Björn, Paul McGinley and Darren Clarke – who were assisting me in the decision-making process. I asked Thomas if he could pop out of the room we had commandeered at Gleneagles and intercept the Italian before his trophy presentation.

When Thomas brought Edoardo in, I asked him to take a seat.

'There is only one word to describe what you have just achieved, and that's *amazing*,' I began. 'That was one of the best finishes in golf that I have seen, anywhere in the world. The manner in which you dealt with the pressure of competing against your brother [Francesco had started the day one ahead of him] to win the tournament and to give yourself the chance of playing alongside him at the Ryder Cup was brilliant. Brilliant for your family, brilliant for Italy and brilliant for us.

'Edoardo, I am thrilled to say I want you in the team.' I could also have added that both brothers were a credit to Denis Pugh, the teacher-cum-commentator who has so often helped me with my game.

Though Denis never attempted to alter my relatively long and flowing action, he had encouraged the brothers to keep their backswings short and to use a minimum of wrist action. His explanation, here, is that their power emanates from their body turn or, to be more precise, from the spring in their core muscles. I think everyone agrees that they look very sound.

When I had wound up my little speech to Edoardo, the emotion hit him hard and tears began to flow. He must have been thinking of the bigger picture; of how he and Francesco, who had played since childhood days in Turin, were going to be standing shoulder to shoulder as members of Europe's Ryder Cup team with their proud parents looking on.

'Go and enjoy your evening,' I told him. 'Give your acceptance speech for winning today but, please, please, don't say anything

Possibly my first ever game of golf at The Troon Ladies' Golf Club with Mum

Holiday snap, with my brother Douglas

Thank goodness Mum's doing all the hard work

Mum's BMW 1602. My love affair with cars is just beginning

Sunningdale 1987 – Walker Cup. A lot younger and a lot slimmer

Above: It's always good to beat the best

Right: With my trusty caddy, Alastair McLean – all eight Orders of Merit as a team (Getty Images)

Left: I was a lot more flexible in the 1990s than I am now

One of the best days I've ever had in Ryder Cup play. To beat No. 1 and 2 in the world set us up for our record points total (Getty Images)

Below: 2004 Ryder Cup – 18th green, thanking Bernhard, our Captain, for picking me (Getty Images)

With Darren Clarke and Lee Westwood: thrilled to celebrate with my main competition (Getty Images)

Alfred Dunhill Links 2005 – this is what Stirling University produces (Getty Images)

about this. We are not making the formal announcement until six o'clock.'

He was walking on air as he left the room but, true to his word, he didn't say a word to anyone.

Since Edoardo was now the owner of one of the wild cards, there were only two left and, with Luke Donald a certainty in mind, it meant that I could only pick one player from among eight top-quality and experienced candidates: Robert Karlsson, Henrik Stenson, Álvaro Quirós, Simon Dyson, Ross McGowan, Justin Rose, Paul Casey and Padraig Harrington.

It came down to one out of Casey, Rose and Harrington, all of whom were playing The Barclays tournament in New Jersey and, thanks to the five-hour time difference, were either out on the course or about to tee off. Not something we had thought about in advance I have to say.

I ran into Karlsson and Quirós, both of whom were playing at Gleneagles, and was able to speak to them there and then and explain why they hadn't made it. (Wherever possible, I felt it was important to have such a discussion face to face.) I also called Stenson with the news but, where the US-based players were concerned, it was not so easy.

What do I do here? I decided to tackle Justin Rose first as he had yet to tee off but, as I reached for my phone, the doubts crept in. Would Justin really want to know before he set out on his crucial final round in the first play-off tournament for the season finale FedEx Cup? The last thing I wanted was jeopardise his chances. I knew he was doing okay up to that point. Would it be better to leave it until he'd finished? But if I did that, wasn't it likely that somebody would give him the news as word of my decisions spread across the course? What would be the fairest thing?

I made the decision to ring. It was never going to be the best of calls but it was harder, far harder, than I had anticipated. Justin was stunned and, though he made the very salient point that he had won twice in America over the summer and he had felt sure that would be enough, he didn't say too much else.

I wasn't getting a whole lot back and I certainly didn't blame him. He had played in one Ryder Cup already; he was a prominent figure on the USPGA Tour and he had expected to be picked. I understood that but, from my perspective, his performances towards the end of the season, from the Open really, had tailed off severely. If that hadn't been the case, he would have been in. We discussed all this and, to his credit, he sort of came round in the end and said the right things and ended up wishing us the best of luck. I appreciated that but I could not have felt for him more.

The other players who had to be informed were on the course, which meant I couldn't speak to them. I knew their phones would either be off or on silent, so it was down to voicemail and my texting abilities to pass on the news.

Luke Donald, of course, was easy. I left him a message and texted one word, 'Congratulations'. I don't know when he picked it up, but I did notice that after he had started with six straight birdies and had a total of seven in the front nine, he had five bogeys and a single birdie coming home. If he looked at the halfway point, it obviously wasn't the best for his concentration.

Having contacted Luke, I steeled myself for the second difficult call, the one to Paul Casey. He was the player who, having the highest ranking, would have expected to be in before the rest.

With more than a touch of irony, Padraig Harrington and Paul were paired in that final round. I texted both, the first with a 'yes', the second with a 'no'.

Caroline Harrington was out on the course armed with Padraig's phone, presumably on vibrate or silent. When she received my text – it came when they were playing the sixth – she gave Padraig a thumbs-up. Paul happened to look up just at that moment and must have known what it meant.

Caroline, meantime, had no idea what the situation was with any of the others and was in no position to enlighten Paul. He must have guessed that the news wasn't going to be good but he only had it confirmed when he was back at the clubhouse.

It was an appalling situation, one which makes me squirm to this day, but I couldn't see any other way to deal with it.

When I did eventually speak to Paul, he was excellent and has been ever since. A true professional. Whatever he may have thought privately, publicly he behaved impeccably, saying everything the Tour and I could have wished for. All I can add is that he, like Justin, is a credit to his family and to the game.

It was an extremely tough decision to make between Harrington and Casey. The vice-captains and I had debated it at length. In reality, you wanted both of them.

There was no question that Casey was among the top twelve players in Europe, even though he hadn't qualified, but Harrington had three Majors behind him. He was a proven force under the most extreme pressure and would bring significant prestige to the party. At one point, I had asked my vice-captains the following question: based on the scenario that if it boiled down to an eight-foot putt to win the Ryder Cup – yes, it was as close as that – who would they want standing over it? Harrington or Casey? It was 3–1 in Harrington's favour and their call was definitely something I took into account as I made my decision.

If my worries were over, there was one person whose headache was just beginning: the artist Ian Faulkner, whom I had commissioned to produce portraits of each member of the team, and the vice-captains, which I planned to present at the opening ceremony at Celtic Manor. Back in May or June I had given him a heads-up, based on who I knew was going to qualify – Kaymer, Westwood and McIlroy – and he started with them. In addition, there were other players at that stage who seemed to be making a charge and looked strong candidates. I don't know if it will be any comfort to Quirós, but Ian has a three-quarters finished portrait of him in his studio.

Ian had also looked at the sheet of 'possibles' I had passed on and he had decided to paint Sergio. I was delighted when I was able to use that one after all. As for Edoardo and Padraig, I left poor Ian very little time to start and finish their portraits, but he ended up making a great fist of both just the same

To me, those sixteen paintings, of which I have copies on display in my house, represent forged bonds that will never be broken. Every time I walk past them I smile.

5 | THE GREAT ESCAPE

What was my road to the Ryder Cup captaincy? It had much to do with getting off on the right golfing foot, of having a father, James, who was sufficiently steeped in the game to become the Secretary of Royal Troon. And then there was Troon itself, where I came by the first of my golfing memories.

It is a little Ayrshire town, between Prestwick and Ayr, where people walking down South Street are just as likely to be carrying a set of golf clubs as a shopping basket. As for the local gossip, that will probably concern the weather as it relates to playing golf or the condition of the various courses. In Open championship years, of course, it will be all about who is playing and where they are staying.

I was born on 23 June 1963 and, almost as soon as I could walk, I was pottering around on the little practice course next to the ladies' clubhouse at Troon. My idea of fun was to try and hit the ball over the dips bisecting the second and eighth holes. You could probably step across them but to me, at that stage of my golfing life, they presented much the same challenge as, say, the carry over the water on the long 18th at The Emirates, Dubai. I was obsessed with knocking my ball over these dips and the personal challenge drew me back again and again.

Other small children were similarly employed and it kept us out of trouble. Also, it did no harm that we were playing beneath the windows of the Troon Ladies' clubhouse because the members of that establishment were never going to stand for any nonsense.

Douglas, my brother, was six or seven and I was five when my father, by then the managing director of Fox's Biscuits, a company which is now 150 years old, moved down to Yorkshire. He and my mother, Elizabeth, joined Ilkley Golf Club, where my father served as the men's captain in 1979 and my mother as the ladies' equivalent in 1980.

It was at Ilkley that I had my first lesson from Bill Ferguson, a magnificent club professional of the old school.

His first observation – and I can remember him saying it to this day – was that my grip was 'very strong'. Like every other child of my age, I had discovered that a strong grip was the key to hitting further.

Bill would have been teaching an endless stream of small boys and girls and, though people said I showed promise, the game certainly did not dominate my childhood. No one spoke of me as a budding professional; my hobby was golf and I was quite good at it, especially when it came to keeping up with the rest of the family on holiday.

Our summer vacations tended to fall into one of two categories – package trips to the beaches of Spain and Portugal or caravan expeditions to Italy. The latter must have been something of a busman's holiday for Mum, having to look after her three boys, but I know she enjoyed those weeks away. She loved the family being together. Dad would hook up the caravan and off we'd go to Hull to catch the North Sea Ferries' crossing to Rotterdam, from where we would drive down through Germany, Austria and into northern Italy. Getting there was part of the fun, and it *was* fun – bloody good fun. We laughed a lot, the four of us.

Though the main attraction of these holidays was to get some sun and enjoy the local fare, we always packed our clubs. I treasure my memories of playing together as a family, and, with Dad involved, there was always a healthy air of competition, that's for sure.

Mum didn't have a competitive bone in her body, but the rest of us – we all wanted to beat each other like fury. We were there to enjoy ourselves and we did. Thinking about those rounds now takes me back to a very happy place.

My first school was called Ghyll Royd Prep School in Ilkley, which I loved. The sport was excellent as, indeed, it was at my secondary school, Strathallan in Perthshire, where I went in 1974, aged eleven. Dark blue uniform this time, as opposed to the red and grey stripes of Ghyll Royd – and kilts on a Sunday.

Wonderful reputation though Strathallan enjoys, and impressive establishment though it is, it was too far from home for me. (It certainly isn't now, in that I could almost walk to it from where Gaynor and I live today.)

Family has always meant everything to me and I was often homesick. It would start as the station master blew the whistle at York as we set off for Edinburgh. From Edinburgh, we would switch to another train to take us to Perth.

It was on the Edinburgh–Perth leg of the trip that we would change into the kilts in which we were expected to arrive. We would never have dreamed of setting off in them at York station.

Rugby, hockey and cricket were the main sports at Strathallan, just as they had been at Ghyll Royd. We played rugby for a term and a half, hockey for half a term and cricket in the summer. There was a rough golf course round the edge of the rugby pitch called Big Acre but the game was not encouraged as it is today.

I was a centre-half at hockey, a game I really enjoyed. I wasn't really nimble enough about the pitch, while my long swing – it wasn't quite as full as my golf swing – was a danger to all and sundry. My main strength was that I could read a game well – something which, I suppose, is roughly the equivalent of good course management, the ability to see further than the shot in hand.

Douglas and I would often combine to good effect: at short corners, he would stop the ball and move out of the way so that I could give it a whack. We scored a lot of goals and I injured a lot of goalkeepers who were probably not as sensibly or expensively padded as they are today.

Yet, much though I loved my hockey, cricket was my favourite pastime, the sport in which I made the most headway. I opened the bowling for Strathallan and came in to bat at four or five, by which time there were usually spinners to face. I hated them. I always believed that if I got to the ball just as it pitched, I could defy the spin, so off I would charge down the wicket, sledgehammer at the ready. How did I never learn? More often than not, the ball would escape my intended assault and I would continue my onward journey towards the pavilion in the knowledge that I had been stumped.

Fielding was fun. What appealed was the way you worked in collusion with your team-mates to find a way to get the batsman out. That I so loved the teamwork made it all the stranger that I would end up playing golf, a sport which you play for yourself – at least until the Ryder Cup comes round.

Back at home, I used to enjoy keeping score for Ilkley and, to this day, I'm glad that I got to grips with how to do it. I will happily sit all day watching a Test match on TV and mark down every delivery.

In time, I was on the fringe of the Yorkshire Under-18 side.

There was one never-to-be-forgotten occasion when I bowled to Geoff Boycott in the nets. Another time, Chris Old, who opened the Yorkshire attack, bowled to me in the indoor facility at Headingly, Leeds. That meant everything to a sport-smitten schoolboy such as myself.

I suspect that Montgomerie the cricketer did not look too dissimilar to Montgomerie the golfer. Years ago, in an old copy of the *Sunday Telegraph*, there was an article about Ted Dexter, the lordliest of stroke players, which was accompanied by a wonderful pair of photographs. The first caught him at the end of a tee shot and the second at the end of what looked as if it had been a full-blooded six. Save for the difference in clothing, they were, to all intents and purposes, identical, not least in terms of weight transference.

I departed Strathallan after my O-levels to study A-levels at Leeds Grammar School. I took Geography, Maths, Economics and Business Studies. Forget the grades. Let's just say I did the equivalent of making the cut and qualifying for a university place, should it be required.

When I left school, my golf handicap was six. (When Rory McIlroy turned professional, his handicap was a mind-boggling plus six!) But I had returned the odd sub-70 score and both Bill Ferguson and my father shared the view that, if I really got down to work, I might one day play for the Scotland amateur side. That really tickled me.

Having missed out on the Scottish Boys' scene, I decided to target the Scottish Youths, which meant that I was still spending as much time in Scotland as had been the case when I was at Strathallan. It would all have been easier had I decided to aim for an English cap but I was Scottish through and through and playing for England was not a consideration – and never mind that my Scottish golfing forays were hardly the merriest.

The Scottish golfing fraternity is close-knit and there was a section of the Scottish golfing contingent who, entirely understandably, saw me as a bit of an interloper; I was not obviously one of them. My English accent probably wouldn't have helped, any more than the fact that I was out to purloin a place in the Scottish Youths' team. Also, I was good, and getting better.

No one ever said anything to my face but, rightly or wrongly, I was conscious of a certain resentment and of how I had to do that bit better than the regular Scots when it came to being chosen for a team. My father was no less aware of what was going on than I was. If anything, he noticed it more than I did.

Dad had by then offered me two years in which to give golf a try but, by way of helping towards the cost, he suggested that I work part-time as a representative at Fox's in those weeks when there were no tournaments.

It was as if I had been gifted a couple of gap years to see where my future might lie. I jumped at the chance.

To deal with the job first. Well, I liked the biscuits, which was the best of starts.

Did other aspects of the job have a similar appeal? Not really. I tried hard and kept many a supermarket shelf well stocked but I am not sure if Fox's were sorry to see the back of me when the time came. The person responsible for looking after the fleet of company cars certainly wasn't, but I will come on to that later. For now, let's just say the excess on their insurance would have shot up while I was there.

On the golfing front, I was altogether less of a liability. Having long before modified that strong grip I had as an infant, I was as reliable as they come when it came to driving a golf ball. To be honest, straight hitting has always been a forte and, for a long time, I was virtually always playing my second shot from off the fairway.

Over that two-year period, my handicap came down from six to plus three and, perhaps more crucially, I met that target of winning my first Scottish Youths' cap in 1983. (In 1982, I had drawn attention to myself with a top-five finish at the British Youths' championship.)

Good though this progress was, I was still far from building a career – in golf and/or in business. Once again, my father stepped in with a solution.

It was part of his remit with Fox's Biscuits to travel regularly to the United States and it was on one of those trips that he passed through Roswell, New Mexico, supposed home of top-secret alien crash landings and autopsies. Having heard that the New Mexico Military Institute offered a college education in tandem with a first-class golf programme, he stopped off to have a look.

He went in the summer, when the campus was deserted, and everything he saw smacked of opportunity. He had a word with the golf coach, who seemed sufficiently impressed with my Scottish Youths' cap to consider my application.

On his arrival home, I received an enthusiastic account of the college, the golf programme and how impressed he had been with the coach and suggested I apply.

'What's the worst that can happen? Your golf doesn't improve sufficiently to consider a leap into professionalism? Well, so what if that's the case ... You'll have a college degree to fall back on, along with a wealth of experience.'

It all made sense. NMMI offers incredible opportunities on so many levels.

The only problem was that none of them suited me. I lasted two days.

A new place of education and a new uniform. Khaki this time, with a green cap, shining belt buckle and polished boots, all issued on day one of my arrival in September 1983. The cap looked a touch on the small side. 'That won't be a problem, Mr Montgomerie, not once we've shaved your hair. Now move along, son,' he said, or words to that effect.

Day two, 4 a.m. An hour before my group of new recruits had been instructed to be on parade, I threw my clubs out of the bedroom window before sliding down the drainpipe. I disappeared into the night, never to return.

My escape route – for in effect that is what it was – took the form of a Greyhound bus to Albuquerque Airport, followed by a call to my father. That was right up there with tough phone calls such as those I had to make to Justin Rose and Paul Casey prior to the Ryder Cup. How on earth was I going to tell my father, a man with a thoroughly distinguished military record, what I had done?

He was brilliant, if more than a little shocked. He instructed me to board the first plane, regardless of where it was heading. Houston was the place in question and, about three hours later, I was calling home again, this time from the Double Tree Hotel on the perimeter of Bush Airport, Houston.

Once I had explained where I was, my long-suffering parent told me to stay put while he tried to sort something out.

'We're going to make this work, Colin. You have got to give America another chance. If you don't, you'll regret it for the rest of your life.'

Before he put down the phone, he added a meaningful, 'And don't do anything else daft.'

The way things unravelled could not have been more fortunate. Heavens I was lucky.

A family friend in Ilkley, a minister by the name of Paddy, knew a chap called Ed Billings, the athletics' director at Houston Baptist University. Paddy made an introductory call to Ed and, a day later, I was meeting Dave Mannon, the university golf coach, in the hotel lobby.

Though I was shaking as I went down for that appointment, I needn't have been. Dave and I hit it off from the start. He had been very well briefed and I liked everything he had to say.

'Look,' he agreed, 'we'll have you at the university because your grades are good enough without having to sit any additional exams. You can enrol in the business course, and we'll try you out at golf.'

That was it. I was in. Dave was doing a friend a big favour to make this happen and I have been grateful to all concerned ever since.

Education in the US is not cheap and, as the term had already started, there was no hope in that first year of any kind of scholarship to ease the financial pain. Dad shelled out uncomplainingly because he believed in me and in the long-term benefit of a university degree. My brother, by this stage, was working his way up the career ladder as a banker and he supported that decision to the hilt. We were not a family in which it was necessary for everything to be apportioned evenly between the two of us to avoid friction. That was not how we had been brought up. If there was an opportunity for either one of us, the other would support it 100 per cent.

So there I was, a Business Studies freshman at Houston Baptist University and trying to make it on to the college golf programme. I was what's known as a 'walk on' for that first year, a regular academic student trying to break into the college team.

I felt a little awkward in that capacity. I was living in different accommodation from the rest of the golf scholarship students and, without a car, I was reliant on the goodwill of others to help me get around the place. But having let Mum and Dad down over the NMMI, or at least having the feeling that that is what I had done, I was determined to make this work.

I poured my all into my golf, while simultaneously doing more than enough to keep up with my studies. It wasn't too long before I made the golf team and I was soon battling it out with a guy called Daryl Henning (now a club pro in Houston) for the No. 1 position.

A significant benefit of my success on the golf course was that I was offered a scholarship for my sophomore, junior and senior years, all of which helped to the point where Dad lent me $2,000 to buy my first car – a second-hand (or probably even third-hand) Mazda GLC.

I loved that car, as I have loved almost all the cars I have owned since, and decided to go the whole hog and purchase a personalised registration plate. The $10 'MONTY' cost me was money well spent, in my view. I felt quite the thing, bombing around Houston with my clubs squeezed into the boot, or 'trunk' as I was calling it by then.

After that faltering start, I had settled into the American way of life ...

I got my degree – a BA in Business Studies and Law – at the

end of the four years, in 1987, and I am very proud to have that certificate. It is the reason I am writing this book today.

Why? Because it was my insurance policy. When I eventually turned professional in 1987 and went on to qualifying school, the putts didn't have to go in. If I failed as a golfer, I had my degree to fall back on. To no small extent, the pressure was not what it might have been had I had nothing in the way of a Plan B.

*

I played plenty of golf at home during the holiday breaks and, little by little, a game plan was beginning to form in my head. I was thinking of the results I needed to have under my belt for it to make sense for me to give professional golf a go.

One goal was the Amateur championship and, in 1984 at Formby, I found myself up against a young Spaniard in the final, the then eighteen-year-old José Maria Olazábal. Ollie thumped me 5 & 4, and I did well to keep the match going that long. As a measure of how I stood against the best amateurs in Europe, this was a wake-up call. I still had a lot of work to do.

As Ollie and I battled it out – 'hung on' would be a more accurate description of things from my point of view – there may well have been those in the gallery who thought we had good futures ahead of us. However, I doubt if it occurred to anyone that either of us, let alone both of us, would one day captain Europe in the Ryder Cup.

The harsh truth, of course, is that any number of gifted amateurs don't make the grade for one reason or another. It is impossible to predict. The jump between amateur and professional is huge. You go from being top of the class to bottom and it is easy to let that destroy your game. It takes a lot more than just a decent swing to become a professional golfer. Ninety per cent is in the mind.

I remember reading an article some years ago in which the writer was comparing Sam Torrance with a fellow professional who was one of Sam's peers. My recall will not be exactly accurate but the gist of the story is what matters. The journalist had set out to compare Sam's average score with this other chap's. (I am not deliberately hiding his name, by the way. I have honestly forgotten.) Over, let's say, a five-year period during which they were both on the Tour, Sam had a scoring average of something like 70.02, the other 70.30. That's how close they were in ability over eighteen holes, but only Sam had the stellar career.

Why? Because Sam knew how to make the putts that counted, the ones that gave him the chance to win. It is highly possible that the player with whom Sam was being compared had the more natural ability but that is not what it is all about. It's only a small part of the equation. Professional golf has more to do with how you handle pressure. It is a thin line.

It was a bitter blow to lose out on that Amateur title at Formby, not least because a place in the Open awaited the winner and that year's Open was at St Andrews. Furthermore, there was a place in the following year's Masters. Yet there was a plus side ...

I had proved to myself I was near the top, if not actually at the summit, of the amateur game. The natural progression I had charted out for myself was not a million miles off track.

Also, my performance at Formby led to two further markers being reached: I was selected to represent Scotland against England at Royal Troon and I was also picked for the Great Britain and Ireland team for the Eisenhower Trophy in Hong Kong in November.

We tied with the auld enemy at Troon but fared considerably worse in the Far East. This was my first trip to the incredible city of Hong Kong and, although I am a far from enthusiastic flier, this glimpse of another world gave me a thirst for travel that has never gone away.

If the location was a highlight, the golf was less satisfying, with GB&I coming in fourth behind Japan, the US and the Philippines.

The following year, 1985, marked another significant milestone in my golfing apprenticeship. That was when I was selected for the GB&I Walker Cup team to take on the Americans at Pine Valley, a course which was then – and is still – regarded as one of the best in the world.

Playing Walker Cup golf is every amateur's dream. It is a competition with a distinguished history, having originally been established in 1922 by a member of the Bush family of US presidential fame. In fact, the 'W' in George W. Bush stands for Walker.

This is a powerful connection across the Atlantic and is mirrored by the seriousness with which the Americans take the contest. Over the years they have established a fabulous record, having won thirty-four times to GB&I's eight. I am afraid to say my two excursions in the competition did not help redress that balance.

In 1985 we lost by 13–11, with my contribution a paltry half-point. Two years later, at Sunningdale, my personal performance was much improved, with two wins in the singles, but we failed to stem the run of seven straight American victories and lost by 16½–7½.

While I was hugely disappointed to be on two beaten

sides, playing in those teams had been a genuine honour and privilege. There is little in the sporting world to compare with representing your country and there is no doubt that my Walker Cup experiences had a significant impact on my later career. My appetite for golf at the highest level, and international team events in particular, had been well and truly whetted.

*

Sandwiched in between those two Walker Cups I played nine holes of golf that would change my life.

In the summer of 1986 I was home from university, with a year to go at Houston, and my thoughts turned to what I might do once I had graduated. Professional golf was still high on the agenda, but I was also aware of the fragility of such a career path. It would be folly to assume I would make the grade when so many others did not.

Yes, I was well on my way to pinning down a degree, but I felt the need to take it a bit further. Was there a job which would allow me to combine my knowledge and love of sport with my business studies?

Over my three years at Houston, moving within a golf-orientated world, one name repeatedly cropped up – IMG: Mark McCormack's International Management Group, the home of Arnold Palmer, Jack Nicklaus, Nick Faldo and many other greats of the game. Sport and business, business and sport. It seemed the logical place to start looking for a job.

I wrote a letter of application, on spec, and was more than a little surprised to receive a swift response. Ian Todd and Peter German, two company executives no less, were up in Scotland and wanted me to join them on the back nine – I clearly was not deemed important or interesting enough to warrant a full round – at Turnberry.

This must have been in late July because the grandstands were still in situ after the Open which had been held earlier in the month. (Greg Norman was the winner.)

To my mind this was no social outing but a serious interview for the role of trainee client manager, whatever that was. I was nervous but prepared. My father and I had discussed the questions I should ask, and the likely questions they might put to me. My mind was fixed firmly on impressing these two prospective employers and my golf was of secondary importance.

I was therefore every bit as surprised as Ian and Peter when I walked from the 18th green having birdied seven of the nine holes.

I felt I had done myself justice with regard to the interview, and as we sat in the clubhouse afterwards I had high hopes for being offered a position. How wrong I was. 'Colin,' Ian said to me once we had settled, 'why work for us when we could work for you.'

This was not one of the possible scenarios I had considered. I was taken aback, but their faith in me gave me the boost I needed to make up my mind. Yes, I still had to complete my degree, while I also had unfinished business on the amateur circuit. Overall, though, my mind was set. I was going to give it a go in the professional world and see where the adventure took me.

The unfinished business was my desire to win an individual national match play title. In 1985 I had claimed the Scottish Stroke Play championship but, since my 'near' miss in the Amateur at Formby, I had not been challenging in the head-to-head format.

My chance came in 1987 at Nairn, following the award of my degree from Houston and the Walker Cup exploits at Sunningdale.

Although we had lost that match with room to spare, my personal performance had left me in good heart as I set out to win the Scottish Amateur title.

It was one of those weeks when the putts dropped, and they needed to as I was up against stiff competition. On my route to the final I was twice pushed very hard. In the second round, Chris Cowan took me to the 17th and, in the third, Jim Milligan and I had a tussle which went all the way to the home green.

The final, however, was a different story. Over thirty-six holes I was too strong for the twenty-year-old Alasdair Watt who, I think, just ran out of steam after what was otherwise a great week's play. The final score was resounding, 9 & 8, though that wasn't a fair reflection on Alasdair's ability. Regardless of how talented you are, golf can decide to bite you hard for no apparent reason. As I know myself.

My victory at Nairn was a watershed moment.

I had achieved almost all I had set out to achieve on the amateur circuit. I'd loved it and, crucially, I had learned how to win. Looking back, that mattered a lot and I would recommend that today's youngsters should take aim on packing as many good results as they can into their amateur careers.

It obviously did Padraig Harrington no harm that he played in three Walker Cups prior to turning professional, while Luke Donald, Simon Dyson, Paul Casey, Rory McIlroy and Tom Lewis have all one Walker Cup or more on their CVs. Luke, for the record, played on two winning sides, in 1999 and 2001.

As I said, I felt 'qualified' to take the next step or, rather, the plunge.

6 | INTO THE UNKNOWN

It is was all very well making the grand statement that I was now a 'pro', but without any tournaments to play in I was like a singer without an audience. That's where having IMG on my side was a significant advantage. They worked their magic and I received an invitation to the 1987 Ebel European Masters Swiss Open, five thousand feet up the Alps at Crans-sur Sierre.

As a venue, Crans-sur-Sierre is stunning beyond belief, with mountain views all around. But, though I managed to win out there in 1996, that first trip was an out and out disaster from the moment I left Heathrow. When I went to collect my clubs in Geneva, all the other players on my flight picked up their luggage and hurried down to the station to catch the train to Sierre while I was left standing. My clubs, and with them my golf shoes, had never left the UK.

Things would get worse. Because I had to hang around filling in forms, I didn't arrive in Crans until well after midnight. I had made sensible arrangements to stay in a small, reasonably priced B&B but, with everyone else in that little mountain town in their beds, there was no one to point me in the right direction. I had no idea where to go.

After an hour or so pacing the streets, I walked into the Rhodania Hotel. It was one of the more glamorous establishments in the town. The lights were on and the front door ajar.

To my relief, they had a room and, at that time of the night, I really couldn't quibble at the price of £150 – yes, £150 back in the 1980s. I couldn't begin to afford it but what else could I do?

There was no sign of the clubs the next day and, though I could have borrowed some, I was still going to be stuck on the shoe front. Borrowing shoes has never worked for me because one of my feet is a size larger than the other. (The corresponding shoes nowadays go to one of the charity shops in Perth.)

On the plus side, this was probably as good a time as any to learn my lesson about packing for a golf tournament. Ever since that first week, I have always carried my shoes in my hand luggage.

Everything was finally delivered on the Wednesday evening, just twelve hours or so before I was due to embark on my professional career from the tenth tee.

I was neither relaxed nor well prepared but, as luck would have it, I hit a first shot which was bang out of the middle and went for miles. This was the life for me. Simply by turning professional I seemed to have acquired a handful of extra yards.

I strode proudly down the fairway and decided on an eight-iron for my 145 yards' second. This shot, too, felt 100 per cent as it left the club face, only there was a problem. The ball was still soaring as it cleared the green and pitched among the trees beyond.

That was the first I knew of balls travelling 10 per cent further in the mountain air.

I ran up a six and finished with a 77 which, on that course, was the equivalent of an 87. The next day's 70 was rather better but not good enough to make the cut.

By the time I arrived back in Troon, I was £1,000 the poorer and Lyle, Faldo and the rest had not exactly been given cause for alarm.

My degree was a great source of comfort in such a week – and has remained as much ever since. True, I relaxed a bit when I won the 1989 Portuguese Open, but even after that there was still the thought that it might help me in the matter of finding something else to do if I were to be injured at any point.

In golf, as in any other sport, there is always the possibility of physical damage which could spell the end of your career. Indeed, with golf being an individual game, the prospect is arguably greater than it might be in a team sport where the other players can in certain circumstances take the pressure off you.

In this respect I have been lucky. I can honestly say that I have never had a 'golfing' injury in all the years I have played. By that I mean an injury sustained because of the sport I play. Footballers pull hamstrings, runners snap Achilles tendons, rugby players crack collar bones, all in the pursuit of their chosen activity. For golfers, the main concern is the repetitive motion of swinging a golf club and the strain it can put on joints and tendons.

Seve was an unfortunate victim towards the end of his playing days and even Tiger Woods, with all the conditioning and medical advice he has on tap, has suffered endless knee problems. Four operations on the same joint ...

I have mostly managed to avoid anything more than the odd tweak. I am only careful about my fitness regime to the extent that I don't overdo things. I did practise hard in my college days, and when I first started out on Tour but I have never been a Vijay Singh among workers.

The reality is that my genetic make-up has served me well. Even now, I am pretty flexible.

I do have good intentions where my fitness is concerned. My gym at home is filled with shiny new equipment – at least it was shiny until it gathered dust. It's a sad admission but I don't suppose I am alone in finding that my fitness fads seldom last for long.

Usually, as I abandon ship on my latest set of good resolutions, I remind myself of the litany of players who have injured themselves overdoing things in the gym. They become like greyhounds, highly tuned but with the risk that at any moment something might give. With me, that was never really an issue and I am happy to leave it like that. Touching wood is probably the safest exercise for me at this juncture.

The odd injury fright I have had has never been down to golf itself. Towards the end of 2001, when I thought I had the beginnings of a bad back, the problem turned out to be more mental than physical. I woke on the Saturday morning of the Volvo Masters in Jerez and found I couldn't move. After I had managed to get out of bed and crawl to the phone, a hotel porter got hold of Dale Richardson, an ace physiotherapist who works for a handful of Tour players. He wasted no time in answering my call for help and soon had me lying on the floor, arching my back and then slowly sitting up to touch my toes to stretch the muscles. It was painful in the extreme.

'There is no way you can play today, Colin,' he said. 'Look at the state you're in. You'll be lucky to make it downstairs on your own, let alone get round the course.'

I was not to be persuaded. 'Please keep working on me, Dale. Please. I can't just pull out. I've got to play.'

He stuck with me for the next few hours, overseeing stretches and massages until, against all the odds, I was able to take the tee.

It was strange. Once my circulation got going, the back

improved and I played okay, handing in a 71. Come the next day and I had to go through the same routine all over again before posting an eminently respectable 69.

On the Saturday, I had a stroke of luck as the round was cut short because of high winds and the tournament reduced to fifty-four holes. Thanks to Dale giving my back one more pounding, I was able to hand in a 68 on the Sunday and finish as high as seventh. But the improvement to my back was only short-term.

I called my management company soon after my return to the UK and we decided that I should head for the Mayo Clinic in Rochester, Minnesota, to have some MRI scans and find out what was at the root of my problems.

Normally, of course, you are delighted when one of these scans gives you the all-clear; on this occasion, I wanted them to find something that could be fixed.

No such luck.

Because I was still not walking properly and they could not come up with any answers, they sent me to another department – the psychological unit. Inevitably I thought of that old cliché about men in white coats coming to take you away when the reality was that I was introduced to this lady psychologist who was outstanding. One of those people who is absolutely on top of her job. I told her about everything that was going on in my life and the impending break-up of my marriage and, instead of producing some unpronounceable condition with a Latin tag, she gave me a simple six-letter word – stress.

She explained that the mind is a very powerful thing. It finds the weakest point in your body and, for most golfers, that is the lower back. 'There may not be anything particularly wrong with your lower back,' she advised, 'but it will be weaker than in normal blokes, just because of what you do for a living. It's all to do with wear and tear.'

Since my everyday circumstances were not going to improve overnight, that particular back condition impinged on my life and my golf for the next couple of years.

Some time later, I spent three days in traction after going on a rollercoaster in Australia. I was so incredibly tense – okay, terrified – at not being in control, that my back couldn't cope.

More recently, I dislocated my shoulder and missed a tournament as a result. That was sore, I can tell you. Was it the result of a dramatic rescue of a child from an on-rushing lorry? Or from a 50-foot tumble as I attempted to climb Kilimanjaro? Not quite. I fell off a small milk crate. I was doing a photoshoot for Yonex. They wanted to see the bottom of the club and the only way for this to happen was for the photographer to be lower than me. So here I was, standing on a table with this chap stretched out below, snapping away.

As he finished, I stepped off the table and on to the crate that doubled as a step. It collapsed. Either the plastic was too fragile or I was too heavy. Take your pick ...

*

At the end of 1987, I had to go to Qualifying School. And what torture it is – six rounds in which the pressure has 108 holes to build rather than the usual seventy-two. In which connection, you have to admire players like Rory McIlroy, Matteo Manassero and, most recently, Tom Lewis, all of whom managed to escape the week. Lewis, the latest of this trio to turn professional, did so by the simple expedient of winning the Portugal Open – it used to be called the Portuguese Open – in what was only his third start on Tour.

I fought my way through the UK leg of the school and, in November, decamped to La Manga in Spain along with 150-odd others all looking for an all-important place in the top thirty. My mum came along to look after me and made sure I ate properly. Between us, we made a success of the exercise. I finished twenty-first and was a professional golfer in possession of a Tour card. The grand plan, as sketchy as it had been, was moving forward.

My first full year on the professional Tour, 1988, was an eye-opener if ever there was one. Not least financially. I did okay in terms of my golf, making fifteen cuts out of the twenty-two tournaments I entered, with my best-placed finish a tie for third in the PLM Open at Falsterbo in Sweden. I also won Rookie of the Year honours. Yet, in spite of that relative promise, the precariousness of my career choice hit me hard.

As a young, almost unknown golfer, the sponsors were hardly beating a path to my door. Clubs, bag, shoes and balls were supplied but, in terms of travel and accommodation, I was on my own. And when you look at the locations of my twenty-two events – ranging from Mallorca (missed cut), Biarritz (missed cut) and Cannes (missed cut) to Belgium, Monte Carlo, the Netherlands and Stuttgart – it was expensive. If you didn't play, you didn't get paid: there are no salaries to fall back on in professional golf. Your wages are your winnings.

This is no hard-luck story, not at all. I loved that first year, and I knew I was in a privileged position, but money was tight. On average I had to shell out around £1,500–£2,000 a week for the flights, hotel and a caddie. Where the caddie is concerned, you pay expenses plus a percentage of your winnings – 5 per cent basic, rising to 7.5 per cent for a top-ten finish and 10 per cent for first or second. In other words, I had to make about £3,000 a week simply to break even. With the prize money as it was back then, that meant finishing in the top twenty.

For the larger tournaments, the money was greater but that merely meant that the Faldos, Woosnams, Langers and Lyles of this world would fly into town and you could safely assume they would claim the bulk of the loot. Add to that players like Sam Torrance, Ken Brown, Gordon Brand Jnr, Eamonn Darcy, Christy O'Connor Jnr, José Rivero and Barry Lane, all of whom had won their share of big events, and you could forget the top ten.

The rest of us were in effect fighting for positions fifteen to thirty and there was not a lot of cash down there.

What this really boiled down to was that about twenty guys were making any money, while another hundred, of whom I was one, were in effect gambling £2,000 to make £3,000.

I stayed in cheap hotels and ate a lot of junk food but, for me, there were plenty of factors to balance the ledger, notably the thrill of competing. That has always been my driving force. I thrived on it in those early years and I still thrive on it today.

I have never had a romantic, misty-eyed view of the game. For me it is about nailing a seven-iron to within a foot of the pin. I want to get near, have a chance for a birdie, and I want to win. I am like a horse in blinkers – at least until I am distracted!

I would be competitive in any job. If I were a postman, I'd want to be the best in the world. So while all those trips down to A. T. Mays to book flights and buses and B&Bs were not a lot of fun, I never minded. As far as I was concerned, it was necessary to get me to a place where I could compete.

This attitude was reflected in how I practise. I've always had the feeling that practice days hold me back from that moment when I can play for real. That's when my game kicks in. For some reason, my swing has always been at its best when the pressure is on and I need it most.

*

For me, 1989 holds three significant memories. The first is the Catalan Open in March, played at Pals, near Girona, in Spain. With one hole to play I was two shots ahead. A certain first victory, surely? Unfortunately not. I am not saying I deliberately three-putted the final green to let Mark Roe claim victory – of course I didn't – but something inside me rebelled.

It was almost as if the opportunity had come too early and was disrupting my learning curve. I know it sounds daft but, subconsciously, it was as if I willed myself to miss those putts.

Far from kicking myself as I would have done later in my career, I tucked the experience in among my gathering store of golfing knowledge. Most players make a hash of things at some point in their careers and the sooner you go through this the better. Rory McIlroy had his blow-up at the 2011 Masters and was obviously a faster learner than most in that he won the next Major on offer, the US Open.

My second memory from '89 came seven months later, at Quinta de Lago. This time, I was ready. I won the Portuguese Open by eleven shots from Rodger Davis, the Australian famous for his plus-fours. Over the four rounds I scored 67, 65, 69, 63 for a total of 24 under par, pocketing a very significant £41,000 in the process. I treated myself to a BMW 3-series.

My third memory is the most significant of them all and came about thanks to my failure to qualify for the Troon Open.

I am staying at the family home along the road and sitting in the stands by the 18th green. I have a jotter on my lap to keep track of what is happening, a packed lunch at my feet and my mum is sitting next to me. We are laughing and chatting as we wait for each group of players to come through. It is a very happy memory.

Mum died of cancer at home on 10 January 1991. I have missed her every day since; her laugh, her smile, her advice.

Sport played such a big part in our family. Not just golf, all sports. In the early seventies it was common for the four of us to head off to Elland Road to watch Leeds United. They are still my team. Tennis was another one of her favourites. If you were to ask me for my favourite non-golfing sporting memory, the answer would be the 1981 men's final at Wimbledon in which the five-times champion Björn Borg took on the nemesis of the Establishment, John McEnroe, in what was their second final in a row.

For me, it was Borg above McEnroe every time; for Mum it was the tennis. She was a decent player herself and she loved sitting with the rest of us to watch the classic encounters of the day.

Wimbledon was a major event in our family, with the four of us gathered around the television for the three or four hours of the final, wrapped up in every point.

Mum would have loved to have gone to Wimbledon herself but, sadly, she never made it. A few years ago, after she had passed away, I took my dad to Centre Court and watched as he walked into the stadium. He stopped and took a moment to look around. I knew he was thinking of Mum and how he wished she was standing next to him.

Mum was always totally straight and honest in everything she did. Her moods didn't swing back and forth. She was a constant in my life, the one person on whom I could always rely. Her uncomplicated, clear thinking is one of the things I've missed most over the past twenty years. A mother and son have a special bond – we certainly did – and I knew I could ask her advice on anything and she would give me a straight answer. There was never a spin or edge in what she suggested. It would be in my best interests, certainly, but it would always be honest and fair. I trusted the wisdom of whatever she said absolutely.

Dad was the disciplinarian, but it was Mum who ran the house. She may have been more lenient than my father, but she instilled in Douglas and myself a strict sense of what was right and the importance of manners. Reading that again, I realise it might sound somewhat old-fashioned – and if it does seem that way, well, that's how it was. Traditional, solid and happy. Mum made sure it was all of those things.

She also taught us not to expect things to come our way on a proverbial plate. We got pocket money, but we had to earn it by cutting the lawn, washing the car, shovelling the snow. This, too, was an old-fashioned approach but it was an important lesson to learn.

Keeping our bedrooms tidy was not something which prompted any kind of payment. That was a given. Mum insisted and we complied.

You never fully recover from the death of someone you love and who played such an integral part in your life, but I have been lucky in one respect. I have had the opportunity to keep her name and memory alive in an incredibly positive way, through the Elizabeth Montgomerie Foundation.

Of everything I have achieved or not achieved in my life, of all the good I might have done and the mistakes I have certainly made, if I am to be remembered for anything then I hope with all my heart it is Mum's charity.

I wanted something concrete – bricks and mortar if you like – that would honour Mum's memory and help cancer sufferers for a long, long time. I found that in the incredible people who run the Maggie's Centres where frightened, worried or confused cancer patients can seek advice and help. That's what Mum would have done: given sound and honest advice to those who were looking for answers and that is what the experts at the Maggie's Centres offer. It is an invaluable resource, and I am proud to be involved with these amazing people.

The first centres are scheduled for Glasgow and Aberdeen, but in time I hope there will be very many more. It is a long road but one well worth the journey.

Mum might no longer be able to give me the advice I have needed – and will doubtless always need – but I have this reassuring feeling that she approves the path of the Elizabeth Montgomerie Foundation.

No less do I sense that she is still keeping half an eye on Dad, Douglas and myself.

7 | FROM A TO B

You want to do all the right things when you find yourself playing alongside one of the greats and, though I struggled to say anything when I met Seve Ballesteros on the first tee on the Saturday of the 1989 Swiss Masters, I did get some sort of a message across. That was when I made an opening albatross and also notched an eagle during the course of a 67.

I had watched Seve play many times on television, but this was the first time I had come across the Spaniard in person. It wasn't something which was likely to happen on a Thursday or a Friday because players of his calibre tend to be drawn with each other on the first two days in the marquee groups. The reason I was playing above my station, if you like, was because I had started with rounds of 68 and 66 to Seve's 65 and 68.

As we stood on the tee, waiting for the Starter's call, I was almost pinching myself. I was way out of my depth and was still stumbling over a 'Pleased to meet you' when Seve walked across and shook me firmly by the hand.

That, in fact, was what tipped me over the edge. Suddenly I was more nervous than I had ever been on a golf course. I became uncomfortably aware of my grip, my stance, my swing, my walk and everything else.

We teed off and, a few minutes later, Seve was proffering his hand once again after I had knocked my second into the hole for that albatross. I eventually finished the tournament in seventh place, six shots behind who else but Seve.

My Rookie of the Year season had ended with an Order of Merit ranking of fifty-two, which I upped to twenty-fifth in 1989, by virtue of my near-miss in Pals, my victory at Quinta de Lago and my showing in Switzerland. I was on track and continued in this encouraging vein through 1990, a year which included six top-ten finishes and a first appearance at the Open – at St Andrews, as it happens. (I tied for forty-eighth place, sixteen shots behind Nick Faldo.)

From twenty-fifth I moved up to fourteenth in the Order. That was okay by me; better than okay.

That year, 1990, also saw my marriage to Eimear Wilson. We had first met in Nairn, three years previously, when I won the Scottish Amateur championship. The fact that Eimear and I are now divorced is well documented and a matter of record. The circumstances are private and shall remain so. Eimear deserves her privacy and I respect that. What I will say, however, is that for all our relationship did not work out, we are the ultra-proud parents of three wonderful children, Olivia Rose, Venetia Grace and Cameron Stuart. For that I am eternally grateful. I love them dearly.

In golf terms, 1991 was a big year. I had set myself the target of securing my second Tour victory and giving myself a chance of making Bernard Gallacher's Ryder Cup team. But Mum's death in January overshadowed everything.

The pain of her passing scarred me deeply, but somehow I had to get back to golf. It was my job. It may sound trite, but I knew it to be true. Mum was never one to shirk anything. I was married, I had responsibilities and, as she would have seen it, I had a life to live. But from February through to mid-May, I played in twelve tournaments with my mind seldom far away from the family's terrible loss.

Over that period I missed five cuts and had just the one top-ten finish, at the Lancia Martini Italian Open. Fulfilling my golfing ambitions was simply not at the forefront of my mind.

The turnaround occurred at the Volvo PGA at Wentworth. Before the tournament, Dad had a word with me, explaining in no uncertain terms that to let my career slip backwards now would not have appealed to Mum at all. He told me to be strong, to play as she would have wanted me to play.

I responded with rounds of 69, 66, 69, 67, with the 67 including a birdie, birdie finish. I was on the verge of that elusive second victory until a certain Spaniard came along with an eight-foot putt on the last to force a play-off, which Seve won with a spectacular three. Was I disappointed? Oddly, not. Yes, I wanted to win but, more importantly, I saw the tournament as a prominent stepping stone. Mum remained – and will always remain – in my thoughts but my focus was now on honouring her by being the best I could be.

I didn't do too bad a job in that regard. In June, I was second behind Faldo in the Carroll's Irish Open, and in August I fulfilled both of the goals I had set myself at the beginning of the year. At the Scandinavian Masters at Drottningholm, near Stockholm, I hunted down Seve's clubhouse score of 271 with a five under par round of 67. The victory came with an extra bonus, a big one. It confirmed my seat on the plane – Concorde, no less – to Kiawah Island in September with the Ryder Cup team. I know Mum would have been proud of that.

My two appearances in the Walker Cup had given me the taste for international team golf but, back then, the Ryder Cup had seemed a million miles away. Seve Ballesteros, Bernhard Langer, Nick Faldo, Sandy Lyle, Ian Woosnam, Ken Brown, Mark James,

Howard Clark, Sam Torrance, Gordon Brand Jnr, José Maria Olazábal ... The list went on and on. I could never have envisaged the name Montgomerie might one day be among them.

But here I was.

The R&A had taken the Walker Cup very seriously. We had classy uniforms, travel and accommodation were sorted out for us and we were well looked after. I'd been impressed, but it did not prepare me for the reality of the Ryder Cup. My week with that team – Ballesteros, Paul Broadhurst (rookie), Faldo, David Feherty (rookie), David Gilford (rookie), James, Langer, Olazábal, Steven Richardson (rookie), Torrance, Woosnam, and me (rookie) – has had a massive impact on my life. It was the start of a love affair that has grown ever more compelling.

It was incredible before we even got there. Concorde for goodness' sake! I'd never booked that through A. T. Mays. From the flight over, I remember the moment the pilot tipped the wings so we could get a look at the course before we landed.

There are a number of things which have stayed with me about that Ryder Cup. One was the way the two teams conducted themselves. Dave Stockton, the American captain, took on a hard, verging-on-the-aggressive, style. Don't get me wrong, I had no problem with that. There is no right or wrong way to act as Ryder Cup captain, as I found out, and he was never impolite or unpleasant. However, his attitude seemed to be translated by some members of his team into a win-at-all-costs mentality that was perhaps best exemplified when a couple of the US players wore what can only be described as military caps, resplendent with the official Ryder Cup logo.

The First Gulf War was little over six months old and, while this show of patriotism may have gone down well with a sector of the American spectators, to me it stepped over a line. It almost felt as if we were the enemy, when our troops had been fighting side by side with the Americans in Iraq. In my view, such sentiments had no place at the Ryder Cup. It was a long way from the calm, measured and courteous tone set by Bernard Gallacher.

Almost unbelievably, the destiny of the trophy came down to the last green on the last day. It had looked all over for Europe half-way through Saturday when we trailed by three points with only the afternoon fourballs and the singles to come. Having lost heavily with David Gilford in the Friday foursomes, I did not have another outing until the Saturday afternoon when Bernard partnered me with Langer. Me? With Bernhard Langer? I knew they must have discussed this because, although ultimately it is the captain's decision, Bernhard was a senior player and he would have been consulted. Which meant he was happy to have me alongside him. That gave me a great lift and we gelled beautifully, beating Corey Pavin and Steve Pate 2 & 1 to contribute to a superb European fight back. From 7½–4½ down we were suddenly all square at 8–8.

Mark Calcavecchia and I were the third match out in the Sunday singles. With the Americans traditionally stronger in this format, it was vital that we built some European momentum as quickly as possible. To that end, Bernard Gallacher had put Faldo out first and Nick led from the front magnificently, dispatching Raymond Floyd at the 17th. Next was David Feherty, who was at times every bit as fabulous as his 13 under par win at the Cannes Open in May had suggested. At Kiawah Island, on the Sunday, David was in cracking form, defeating Payne Stewart 2 & 1.

As for my contribution to the European cause, most people would have written me off well before I arrived at the turn as many as five down against Mark Calcavecchia. Bernard Gallacher's parting shot before I teed off had been that I should not let Mark get ahead; he was a tough competitor who would not give up an advantage easily.

Try as I might, I could not contain the 1989 Open champion. He was playing brilliantly and I was sinking fast.

The Ocean Course at Kiawah Island was relatively new and, from the start, it had struck me as an unusual design in so many ways. It juts out into the Atlantic and has massive plains of sand to trap a wayward shot rather than regular bunkers. There are also two very distinct halves, one to the right of the clubhouse and the other to the left.

The walk between the 9th green and the 10th tee was over a mile – or at least that is how it felt – and, that Sunday, I took advantage of it to have a more measured look at what was happening to me. I had no real expectation of being able to turn things round, but I was determined not to embarrass myself. It was a case of damage limitation at best.

A stroke of luck at the 10th helped my cause. Having hopped from sand to more sand with my drive and my second, I launched my third towards the pin from 40 yards and watched incredulously as it hit the stick and disappeared into the cup. From there, I pulled another hole back at the 11th only to give it up at the 14th.

So much for damage limitation. Four down with four to play.

Then, though, the wind came in to bat on my behalf, gusting menacingly from left to right. Exactly what Mark's natural slice did not need. His game began to disintegrate.

I won the 15th with a double bogey after Mark's drive disappeared in the rough and the 16th with a par. But, at the next, it seemed that my extra time had come to an end. Calcavecchia had a three-footer to hole for the half and the double bogey – yes, double bogey – which would have been good enough to give him hole and match.

It was a putt I was on the point of conceding until I thought of Faldo and Seve and how they would take a dim view of that kind of gesture. Awkward though I felt, I left him to it – and he missed. Now I was just one down with one to play.

Tony Jacklin was one of Bernhard's support team in 1991 and, as I surveyed the drive ahead, I could hear him telling someone on the tee. 'All Colin has to do now is to keep standing and he'll win the hole.'

He was making the point that I shouldn't panic, that I should stay focused and concentrate on my game, leaving Mark to inflict any damage on himself. Fortunately for me, and unfortunately for Mark, that is exactly what happened. My 40-foot putt narrowly missed for a birdie, leaving him with a nine-footer to snatch his point. He missed, we halved the match and I was on my way to an undefeated run in eight singles starts.

That half-point in 1991 has influenced my views on the Ryder Cup ever since. As the tournament built to its incredible climax, I was very aware that, had I not scrambled those last four holes to walk away with something, there would have been nothing for Langer and Hale Irwin to fight for as they came up the last. The Americans would already have arrived at that all-important figure of 14½ points from the twenty-eight on offer. As it was, with the score 14–13 in favour of the US, we still had a chance to tie the match and take the trophy home.

When my team gathered for the first time at Celtic Manor in 2010 I told the story of my duel with Calcavecchia to emphasise that it doesn't matter who scores the points or when they come: they all count.

'Lads,' I said, 'whatever stage we are at, never give up a position as a lost cause until it is a mathematical certainty. You are not playing for yourselves out there, you are playing for your team, for the eleven men standing beside you. Never forget that. Fight to the end, it may be the half-point that wins Europe the Ryder Cup.' (How it helps to have first-hand experience when you want to get something like that across.)

Unfortunately, my fightback in 1991 turned out to be in vain when Bernhard Langer missed the six-footer he needed to beat Irwin.

As the boisterous American fans erupted in joy at their 14½–13½ triumph, Bernhard, with incredible dignity and class, embraced Irwin and congratulated him on the US victory. That moment encapsulated for me what the Ryder Cup stands for – honour and sportsmanship. That's how a team should conduct itself and Bernhard's actions spoke for all of us.

In our locker room afterwards, there was an astonishing feeling of togetherness. We were a team still more closely bonded by what had been a difficult week. Not just in terms of the result, but accompanying events. There had been telephone calls in the middle of the night to wake us up; a 'History of the Ryder Cup' presentation at the gala dinner that somehow forgot to mention Europe's victories in 1985, 1987 and the retention in 1989; and, of course, there were the military caps I mentioned earlier.

Despite it all, or perhaps because of it, we were as one in that locker room. We'd lost, fair enough, but we were going to do our damnedest to regain the trophy in two years' time. There was a collective European will, the desire to win for each other, and it had a profound impact on me. I wanted to be part of this for a very long time.

The television in the room was showing the American celebrations, on the beach and in the ocean. We'd been gracious in defeat, but we didn't need it to be rubbed in. It was switched off, only for Bernhard Langer's wife, Vicki, an American, to come into the room moments later and – not unreasonably – turn it back on. Mistake. Unwitting no doubt, but a mistake none the less, which Sam Torrance rectified in his own inimitable style. He opted to kick the telly as opposed to pressing the off switch and that was the end of it.

The flight home on Concorde was a quiet, sombre affair, but at least the landing gear lowered automatically over Heathrow, unlike on the flight over when I had witnessed the captain lifting the carpet to reveal an access hatchway to the wheels, which he then released manually. It was an incident – admittedly a minor one – which did nothing to reassure me that air travel was in any way a natural state.

Mind you, there had been rather worse in 1959 when the then British Ryder Cup side were on the final leg of their journey to California. They had sailed across the Atlantic by way of fostering team spirit, though whether or not the fact that they were all seasick helped them to bond I know not. They then took a plane from New York to Los Angeles before embarking on the forty-minute flight from LA to Palm Springs. The match was to be played at the Eldorado Country Club.

That short hop turned into a horrendous ordeal as the plane ran into the tail end of a hurricane which had devastated much of Mexico. According to reports of the day, the plane was tossed like a cork before falling from a height of 13,000 to 9,000 feet. As Ron Heager, then the *Daily Express* Golf Correspondent, wrote, 'it was like the Big Dipper without the laughs. Anything not strapped down took off and floated to the roof of the plane.'

They returned to LA where Dai Rees, the captain, turned down the offer of another flight in favour of a Greyhound bus ...

For myself, I hate flying. I am frightened of it. Which is not ideal, given the career I have followed for the past twenty-five years. In fact, I doubt if I would have flown too many more miles had I been a pilot.

It is not the taking off or landing that bothers me. It is the thought of being suspended 35,000 feet in the air that freaks me out. I simply cannot get my head round it, especially when I am flying over a ridge of mountains. I sit there on the edge of my seat, half expecting the plane to get caught in a pocket of turbulence.

I can trace this fear back to a specific incident in 1969. Mum, Dad, Douglas and I were flying to Ibiza for our summer holiday and were on the first flight out in the morning from Luton airport. The plane was a Boeing 707 – it was probably pretty new – and, as we flew over the Pyrenees, the skies went wild.

The plane not only took a dive but it shook and twisted as the pilots fought to regain control. Bags, books, coats, everything went flying around the cabin. In those days, the overhead lockers were not closed bins but shelves covered by nothing more than flimsy netting which was worse than useless. At one point, we banked at an angle of more than seventy degrees, which resulted in passengers being flung from their seats across the aisles. I later learned that, had it banked too much further, that would have been it. We would have plummeted to the ground like a stone.

As it was, people were screaming as they were smashed against the window and the ceiling. I believe one passenger died of a broken neck.

My lasting memory of the incident, apart from the sheer terror, is of holding tight to one of my mother's hands, while Douglas held the other one, with both her and Dad constantly reassuring us that we would be okay, which we were. The pilots did an amazing job in regaining control, but the fear has never left me. I don't think that particular plane ever flew again, such was the stress damage inflicted that morning.

There is one word in the previous paragraph that I think goes to the root of my problem. 'Control', or, in my case, the lack of it.

This fear of not being in control has become more acute as I get older. Early on, I had few responsibilities. I was young, I had no dependants and my parents were in good health. If anything were to happen to me, it would have hit the family hard but there would not have been too many repercussions. For the past eighteen years or so, I have felt very differently. I have responsibilities – to my children, to Gaynor and her children, and to my father, and I take them very seriously. It all adds to the pressure and anxiety I feel when I step on to the next plane. If something were to happen to me, what would I leave behind ...?

Prior to the 9/11 atrocities, I would often sit in the cockpit watching the pilots at work. While not being a cure-all, it certainly helped. At least I could see someone was in control, even if it wasn't me. As for fear of flying courses, I've given them a go but, as they tend to concentrate on the taking off and landing, the most common root of a flying phobia, they have been of little benefit.

I've also tried a variety of medications, but whatever I take tends to make me feel sluggish for a couple of days afterwards. Not much good if I am on my way to a tournament. Since I have never felt inclined to knock myself out with alcohol, I end up watching DVDs on my computer in an attempt take my mind off the sea of sky below.

Oddly enough, the flight I made to Afghanistan at the end of 2011 to visit the troops helped rather than hindered. After all, I was in the hands of the RAF and one of the pilots had flown Prince Charles on a regular basis.

We took off from Dubai in this windowless C-17 with its seats down the sides and, as we neared the Afghan border, we had to put on bullet-proof vests and helmets.

The plane stays high, then, when it is coming in to land, it takes a dive. The lights had all been turned off because we were over Afghanistan and all I could see on our descent was the luminous watch belonging to the general sitting to my side. 'Hang on,' I was saying to myself, 'we're in a war zone here.'

Where there are windows, you know when to expect the meeting of plane and ground. In the C-17, someone as inexperienced as I was had no idea what was going on. I just had to wait till it happened, at which point my pounding heart must have had my bullet-proof vest feeling that it was being attacked from the inside.

If I can avoid flying, I will. I live in Perthshire and, though it would be the easiest thing in the world to jump on a plane from Edinburgh down to London to attend meetings at my agent's offices in Chiswick, or to play in one of the many tournaments in the vicinity of Heathrow, I prefer to drive. I enjoy it. When you consider how often I am out of the country, the fact that I clock up in excess of 45,000 miles per year gives some indication of how often you will find me chasing up and down the motorways.

I have always been interested in cars. With my dad's job as MD of Fox's Biscuits there was a company car which was changed at regular intervals and I enjoyed being involved in the decision of what the next model was going to be. More than that, I loved tinkering under the bonnet, working out what actually happens when you put your foot on the accelerator. (Apart, that is, from amassing the odd fine!)

I've always had a fascination with how things work. As I child, I would spend my hard-earned pocket money on car magazines and Top Trump cards featuring tanks and aircraft and supercars. How fast something went, the horsepower, the number of people who could be transported, all that stuff fascinated me. Still does.

You can't drive as much as I do without a few hairy moments on the roads. It is inevitable and my experiences are hardly out of the ordinary. The worst incident came only a month after the high of the Ryder Cup win in 2010. I was driving down to meet my father at Glasgow's Princes Square to help him with some early Christmas shopping for the kids. I wasn't convinced I'd be a great help – I had as little understanding as he did of what teenagers were into – but I was happy to spend time together giving it a go.

There were road works on the A80 and I was in the right-hand lane of a two-lane contraflow. I was minding my own business with Michael Bublée belting out 'Hollywood' from the CD player. We were moving steadily, around 40 mph, as I approached Moodiesburn on the outskirts of Glasgow. It must have been around 11.30 in the morning. Suddenly, two cars ahead of me, I saw a white van swerving out of control and crossing the bollards into our line of traffic. The cars in front of me managed to avoid the van by cutting into the inside lane but, as I glanced to my left to make the same manoeuvre, there was this socking great lorry blocking my route to safety.

Though the whole scene was unfolding rapidly, I still had time to think and to react. I slammed my foot down and attempted to cut in front of the lorry. A fraction of a second sooner and I think I'd have made it. Instead, the van smashed into my door, sending me crashing towards the barrier on my left and directly into the path of the lorry, which had no chance of braking in time.

I am trying to think of a word to describe the noise. A massive crack, perhaps, like a thick metallic pole being snapped in half. The lorry shunted into my rear and spun me around before dispatching me through the bollards and side-on to the fast-approaching cars on the other side of the road.

I couldn't see a thing. I had a rough idea what had happened but, with the airbags inflated, I was blinded. I was disorientated but sufficiently on the ball to be aware that a third, far more serious impact, was imminent. Since my driver's door had crumpled and was unlikely to withstand another collision, I honestly felt as if I was about to die. I remember wondering how Dad would find out. Who would go and fetch him from Princes Square in Buchanan Street where we had arranged to meet?

It took a moment or two to realise there was silence all around. Somehow the cars rushing in my direction had all managed to take evasive action. The next thing I remember was a man grabbing my left arm as he reached across to release my seatbelt. I found out later that it was the driver of the lorry. There was smoke billowing from my car and, having found the driver's door wedged shut, he'd sped round to the passenger side – it was badly damaged, too – and managed to yank it open. He pulled me out of the car and helped me to the side of the road. He wasn't to know that the smoke was from the airbags. He'd been prepared to risk his life to save me. Quite incredible.

I was coughing, spluttering, not knowing where I was or what was happening. As I was being dragged clear across the front seats I remember hearing a voice saying, 'Fire? Police? We know where you are. Which service do you require?' One of the safety features in the car automatically connected me to a central unit whenever the airbags detonated. I managed to reply 'Police, ambulance' before I was clear of the passenger door.

From there, my memory is hazy. I was walking but I was wounded, dazed and confused. I know a helicopter turned up from the Glasgow Royal Infirmary, followed by the police and ambulances.

As I was led into the back of one of them for a check-up, I suddenly panicked about Dad. I gave a description of him to the police and explained exactly where he would be.

A Glasgow squad car was dispatched to fetch him and I can only imagine his shock when he saw the blue flashing light speed down the pedestrian precinct and screech to a halt in front of him. It was while they were there that the police got a further message to say that my injuries were not serious and that I was in an ambulance and being driven home as opposed to hospital.

Dad being Dad – he'd forgotten his mobile phone and had no way to contact me – he got the police to give him a lift to Glasgow Central station so that he could make use of the return ticket he had purchased for the day. A practical man, my father.

Knowing Dad was sorted out was a big relief and, when Gaynor arrived on the scene, having been alerted by the police, I began to calm down. So much so that, by the time I arrived home, the adrenalin had given way to considerable pain, especially in my right hip. It turned out to have been knocked out of position as a result of the first impact and took almost two months of regular visits to an excellent physiotherapist – Stuart Barton in

Pittenweem – to come right. Considering I'd been waiting to hear the last noises of my life, the squeal and crunch of a car ploughing into my door at considerable speed, I was happy to be feeling anything at all.

That said, I might have complained just a bit, to Gaynor, the kids, Dad, Douglas, friends, neighbours, anyone who would listen or couldn't escape ...

As I said earlier, hairy moments on the road are part and parcel of regular driving and it is fair to say this was not my first accident. Just one of the first which wasn't my fault. I had three incidents when I was working with my father at Fox's Biscuits during my two-year golfing 'apprenticeship', two of which resulted in the cars being written off.

During those winter months when I was earning my keep with Dad, I'd be rushing around North Yorkshire trying desperately to be on time at Morrisons or Sainsbury's or wherever I was due to stock shelves with biscuits. That's my excuse anyway. The problem was, I hated being late. I still do. I wear a watch everywhere I can. In bed, in the shower, on the golf course, I've always got to know what time it is.

I lost control of one car on black ice in York and ended up spinning upside down; on another occasion I drove into what had previously been a fine example of a drystone wall in Huddersfield; and, finally, I managed to inflict a car-length scrape along the passenger side of a third car as I tried to squeeze through a space that wasn't there. Even Seve, that master of finding the seemingly non-existent gap, wouldn't have been able to pull it off.

That one cost a fortune to fix.

For each incident the police report ended with the hugely embarrassing line, 'No other car involved'.

8 | ORDER OF MERITS

You don't win seven of anything very easily, which is why my winning of seven Order of Merits in as many years has to be the highlight of my career away from captaining the Ryder Cup side to victory. I did win an eighth, but that came afterwards and merely served to make me pinch myself rather more about what I had achieved between 1993 and 1999.

In 1993, Nick Faldo, who had been the No. 1 in 1992, was handily placed to finish in the top spot again. He had finished first, second and third in that order over the Carroll's Irish Open, the Open and the Scandinavian Masters and, when it came to the last tournament of the year, the Volvo Masters at Valderrama, he was £104,000 ahead of the next person, Bernhard Langer. Ian Woosnam was lying third, Sam Torrance fourth and me fifth.

I did not think for a moment that I could overhaul that little lot, especially since Faldo was at that time the No. 1 on the Sony World Rankings and would stay there throughout 1993. He was in a different league. I mean, just look at his European Tour season in 2002 alone – three regular wins and an Open championship to boot.

I had finished fourth on the Order of Merit in 1991, third in 1992 and I was eyeing up the second spot as my next stop on the ladder. I was desperate to make that much happen.

At the start of the season, I had notched a ninth career second place at the Johnnie Walker Classic at Singapore Island. That was the event where Nick, after making the eight-footer he needed to beat me on the home green, prompted a few quizzical looks when he noted, 'Ninety-nine per cent of putts that are short don't go in the hole but this one did.'

There was another second place in store at the Volvo PGA championship of '93, with Bernhard Langer that week's winner.

Following on from there, I grabbed a couple of wins for myself, the first of them at the Heineken Dutch Open at Noordwijkse. This was an event I hadn't planned to enter but, after I had finished as low as fiftieth in the Scottish Open and missed the cut at the Open at Royal St George's, I felt the need to escape that dark place as quickly as possible.

There was a different leader for each of the first three rounds – D. A. Russell, Ronan Rafferty and José Cóceres in that order. Come the last round, though, and everything changed, including the weather. Three glorious summer days gave way to a boisterous links wind which had the 140 yards' 16th calling for a three-iron. Lightning struck when I was on the 18th green but, where I would usually be off in a flash myself, I was so focused on winning what would be my first tournament in two years that I did not even notice. I wound up winning by one from Cóceres and Jean van de Velde.

The prize money was very welcome but the result itself meant more in the way it drove me forward. I finished seventh the following week, fourth a couple of weeks later and then eighth.

In the previous year's Volvo Masters at Valderrama, I had lost in a play-off to Sandy Lyle and sat on the podium and listened not just to Lyle's victory speech but to the one Faldo made for winning the Order of Merit. His was the first Order of Merit speech I had heard and, as he was delivering it, my thoughts were focused on how much I wanted to have that task.

Twelve months on and, after rounds of 69, 70 and 67, I was well placed to win both the tournament and the Order of Merit in one fell swoop. I was one ahead of Darren Clarke at that stage, with none of the other contenders for the Order of Merit in striking distance.

When Darren dropped a shot at each of the first two holes of the fourth round, I was even more confident but, typically, he sprang back with three birdies in a row from the fourth and the pressure started to mount – and mount.

Ultimately, I was round in 68 to beat Darren by a shot. Considering everything that was hanging on the day, and considering how well he had given chase, it was probably the best round of my life.

It didn't surprise me one bit when Darren won the 2011 Open at Royal St George's. Obviously, it gave me heart that he should win it at his twentieth attempt but, as much as anything, I admired the way he weathered the storms with that low flight of his. They talk about horses for courses and Darren had everything it takes to play those wind-tossed links.

Mark McCormack's World of Professional Golf spoke of how I had withstood all the pressure in that closing event of 1993 'without so much as a twitch'. I can promise you that there were plenty of twitches along the way, especially when it came to the last hole. After Darren holed from 25 feet for a birdie, I had to get down in two from the same distance if I was to win.

I was horribly tense and can remember thanking my lucky stars when I hit my first putt to nine inches – so close as not to be scary.

My father was impressed when I rang home with the news that my 274 aggregate was six shots better than anyone else's in the five years the event had been played at Valderrama. Where he was less impressed was in what he had seen of me on TV.

Why, he wanted to know, had I not shaved before the last round?

The answer was that it had completely slipped my mind. I was amazed that I could have forgotten – and still more startled when I looked at my unshaven face on the front cover of the following week's *Golf Weekly*.

*

There were so many repercussions to winning my first Order of Merit, these including a ten-year exemption on the European Tour, along with a trip to the Masters, the US Open and the US PGA championship.

I was still in awe of Nick Faldo at this stage and did not really think of myself as the No. 1. Yet now that I had got to that position, I had no intention of relinquishing it. 'I've made progress every year since turning professional and I aim to keep doing it in 1994' was my parting remark in 1993.

I have suggested elsewhere that I was the reverse of a daredevil golfer. I was content to leave the heroics to others and I must say I smiled when I heard Richard Boxall's answer to a question he was asked on Eurosport as I was playing the last hole in the 1994 Peugeot Open de España at Club de Campo.

Boxall, like Mark Roe and Mark McNulty, had finished at 10 under par and I was 10 under with one to play when someone thrust a microphone in front of him and asked for his opinion on what I would do down the 18th.

'Well,' said Boxall, who has turned into an excellent commentator, 'he'll hit the fairway because he hasn't missed one since 1987. Then he'll hit his sand wedge to three feet and then he'll hole the putt.' The only thing he got wrong was that I hit to two feet rather than three.

In the 1994 Open at Turnberry, I had my best Open finish – fifth – until 2005 when I would land a share of second place behind none other than Tiger Woods.

At Turnberry, I had a third-round 65 in which I played with Tommy Nakajima, a fine player who has been unlucky in that most people have never associated him with anything other than the Road Hole Bunker at St Andrews. For a while, the hazard was known as the Sands of Nakajima after Tommy had putted into the trap and taken four to escape on his way to a nine.

Tommy had been a lovely playing companion and, though he did not say much on the way round, he had a sentence he wanted to deliver at the end. 'Monty,' he began, 'you best putter.' Then, after further consideration, he added the word 'ever' in front of a bemused cluster of R&A officials. It was a great moment, even if I knew in my heart of hearts that he was some way out. He had coincided with one of my better putting days when, for the most part, my putting was not on a par with the rest of my game. I would probably have won a whole lot more had I had the golden touch of a Ben Crenshaw in his prime.

In August, I defeated Barry Lane to win the Murphy's English Open at the Forest of Arden – my first victory on UK soil. I felt bad for Barry at the time but, my goodness, he has enjoyed a wonderful career. He had five victories in the European Tour and played in the 1993 Ryder Cup before switching to the Senior Tour where he finished second in the 2011 Order of Merit.

At the Forest of Arden, I was two shots off the pace after three rounds and was neck and neck with Barry on 12 under par after he had reached the turn in 33 to my 35. Barry then made a couple of huge putts, a 20-footer at the 13th and a 15-footer at the 15th, before finishing on 13 under.

I replied with birdies at the 15th and 17th to arrive at the same tally, which meant that I needed one more down the 18th to win. Even now, I can still picture the four-iron I knocked over the ravine to eight feet. It was one which deserves a place among the twenty best shots of my career.

I was aware of Barry standing at the back of the green as I stood over my right-lip eight-footer. I've always liked Barry but, keen competitor that I am, I made my two, pocketed the £100,000 winner's cheque and went to the top of that year's Order of Merit. That done, I consolidated my position by winning again the following week in Germany in Düsseldorf.

To beat Bernhard Langer on his home patch – I played alongside him in the last round – was good news. He is a particularly tough customer in his native land. Though not an obviously emotional man, he feeds off the German support and, time after time, others have folded against this backcloth. I dropped a couple of shots coming down the stretch but beat this great champion by a shot – and stopped him from packing a sixth German Open under his belt in the process.

This was the first time I had won back-to-back titles in Europe. It was startling how competitive I felt.

The Order of Merit was a done deal when we arrived at that year's Volvo Masters at Valderrama but I was nonetheless desperate to add the title to that year's CV. After three rounds, Ballesteros was two clear of Langer, who had returned an unbelievable second-round 62, and myself.

I was playing with Seve and, though you always expected the odd drama when you played with him, the first commotion was all to do with me as I hit some unsuspecting spectator on the head at the 7th and my ball ricocheted out of bounds. Not least because the tee shot had been pretty appalling, I was blaming myself rather than the spectator who, thank heavens, was not badly hurt.

The hole cost me a double bogey but I collected birdies at the 15th and 17th to be on the same seven-under mark as Seve. If we were going to force a play-off with Bernhard, we needed a birdie apiece.

Neither of us got what we wanted, for that last hole was the scene of a much-publicised rules incident involving Seve, who was tight up against a tree and in some sort of hollow. Guy Hunt, a rules official who had been a good enough player to have won the old Dunlop Masters tournament, came to give a ruling and was not prepared to go along with Seve's suggestion that the cavity was the work of a burrowing animal.

Seve called for John Paramor, the head referee and, though this imposing character arrived on the scene as quickly as he could, it was clear nothing was going to be resolved in a hurry.

John went to work like the most cunning of barristers, asking Seve if he thought the hole could have been made by a dog.

'You're right,' returned Seve. 'That's what it was – a dog.'

At that, Paramor pointed out that a dog did not count as a burrowing animal and he could not therefore permit a free drop.

Seve and I both made a hash of the hole. After what had been a twenty-minute wait, I had ended up tugging my second into the rough en route to a share of fourth place. There is no question that I was thrown by the delay – no less so than would apply when I had to wait for Vijay Singh to be given a lengthy ruling at the last hole of the US Open at Winged Foot in 2006.

It would have been a tall order for me to make a birdie from where I was at Valderrama but I did have a sliver of a chance and that chance was taken away.

Because of the way I am, I was more down about losing the tournament than I was up about winning the Order of Merit. I have been irritated with myself since for seeing things like that though, in my favour, I had had no trouble in congratulating Bernhard.

'Anyone,' I said, 'who can shoot sixty-two round this course deserves to win any tournament.'

*

In Order of Merit terms, 1995 was probably the toughest year of the seven as I did not scrape past my old friend Sam Torrance until the eleventh hour.

Though Sam may never have been aware of this, it was a broadcast he did with Julian Tutt after winning the British Masters at Collingtree, four tournaments from the end of the season, which aroused my competitive instincts as never before. I was listening on the car radio as I drove from Collingtree to see my father, who had been ill. What got me in the interview was Sam's semi-jocular reference to how he had pinched my spot at the top of the Order of Merit. 'Game on' is what I said to myself that day.

I won the Volvo German Open and the Lancôme, with Sam in second place each time, and generally crept up on him to the point where, when it came to the Volvo Masters, I was only £3,000 behind.

As I teed up on Valderrama's homeward half on the Sunday, I thought I was home and dry, only to see Sam's name going up on the leader board behind the 10th green. He had been among the earlier starters that morning but, without my having a clue up until now as to what was going on, he had stolen round in 68 to be the leader in the clubhouse on 285. At that point, he must have felt quietly confident that he would top the Order.

I began to think so too when I dropped a shot at the 11th but I came back with a two at the short 12th as my then caddie, Alastair McLean, and I, had one of those days when player and caddie are in perfect unison. We made sensible assessments and we carried them through. I am not saying I played sensational golf but I did what I had to do in the knowledge that Sam was watching every shot in the clubhouse.

When it came to the 18th, the pressure was really on as I failed to give my second enough and was miserably short with my first putt. My whole year hung on a four-footer which, I am sure, paved the way for the first of my grey hairs. The ball did not go in the middle; instead, it fell in the left-hand side of the hole and made my stomach lurch in the process. I had finished second in the tournament to Alex Čejka but I won the Order of Merit which, on this occasion, was the thing that mattered most.

Sam was one of the first people to appear on the green. 'Unbelievable!' he said. Later, when he, Čejka and I were sitting on the podium waiting for the start of the prize-giving, he turned to me and said, 'I can't believe I'm sitting up here and that I haven't won the Order of Merit.'

Those words made me value what I had achieved all the more. At the same time, it was good for European golf and good for Scotland that Scots had dominated the year.

Still more than in 1995, I spent 1996 playing catch-up in the Order of Merit. The pressure had been gathering all the time as I won my first three and I have to thank my daughter, Venetia, for making me take the break I so badly needed at the start of the season.

Venetia was born in the January and I took a three-month sabbatical in which to spend time with her and to get myself fit.

I am not into fitness and fitness trainers but I knew it was necessary and I buckled down to follow my tormentor's instructions. Boy, did I hate it. Weight training, sit-ups, rowing machines, jogging, sprinting ... the Spanish Inquisition could have learned a thing or two from this bloke. But over the period I lost 30lbs and I must admit I felt better for it – at least until I started putting those pounds on again. If only my weight could be as consistent as my scoring used to be.

I reappeared on the 1996 circuit at the Dubai Desert Classic in mid-March having missed seven ranking tournaments, two of which had been won by Ian Woosnam, giving him a significant head start in the race to be No. 1.

The lay-off and boot camp had obviously done more than help me to shed a few pounds because I returned with a bang. Rounds of 67, 68 and 67 had me locking horns with Miguel Ángel Jiménez going up the last.

Over the years there is one question I have been asked on numerous occasions: what is your most memorable shot in golf? The answer has been consistent since the afternoon of 17 March 1996: hitting my driver off the 18th fairway in Dubai and watching the ball soar over the lake and on to the green. Not only did that shot enable me to win the tournament by a stroke but it also landed the Canon Shot of the Year award.

It would feature at the top of my twenty best but, proud though I still am of that particular strike, I must confess that I would love to have bettered it in 2006 with the seven-iron I had to the 72nd in the US Open at Winged Foot. Which, of course, I didn't.

Taking my driver off that 18th fairway in Dubai was a high-risk strategy, particularly because I had to clear the water. I was never going to get a lot of height, so I had to hit it right on the button. Standing on the fairway, up against Jiménez, who was in one of his spectacularly good playing moods, I knew I had to do something special if I was to win and make a statement after my prolonged absence from the Tour.

Around this time in my career I think it is fair to say that I was one of the top iron-players in the world, perhaps even the best for a while. So deciding to swap my trusty six-iron for the driver and go for the green instead of playing safe went against my natural game. I wasn't nervous as I addressed the ball but I was aware that I was taking myself outside my comfort zone, which is why it meant so much when I pulled it off in such style.

Over the years my way of golf has tended to be one of playing chess with a course, looking at the percentages and taking the less risky option. I plot my way up a hole rather than attack it full on. To no small extent, this approach goes back to my days with Bill Ferguson at Ilkley when he taught me how to read a course, but in the main it is because it suits my playing style.

I swing the golf club, as opposed to hitting the ball. I have a slow, natural tempo that will never generate great distances and, though this does limit my ability to play extravagant shots, I have mostly been entirely accepting of that fact.

Keeping it straight off the tee, making sure I hit the fairways and then letting my irons do the talking has stood me in very good stead over the years. If I had tried to do what Nick Faldo did and tear my original swing to pieces before building it up again, heaven knows what might have happened. I certainly don't think I'd have succeeded to the extent that I have.

My natural shape of swing is from the outside to the inside; I cut across the ball. Golf is a game of opposites, so if you swing outside to in, the ball is going to go the other way, left to right. A fade.

If you go the other way, from inside to out – almost like a cricket cover drive, if you like – that will draw or hook the ball. Neither style is better than the other. Ian Woosnam was a great hooker of the ball and he did all right. What matters is knowing what your ball is going to do and aiming accordingly.

I have been lucky with the coaches I have had. Bill Ferguson was a teacher in a million and so, too, was Denis Pugh, to whom I was introduced in 1996. We have stayed friends ever since.

Whenever Denis made any recommendations about my technique I always listened, because he was not interested in radical surgery. He recognised my natural action and left it well alone. Because of that I trusted him, and over the years I began to seek his opinion on rather more than simply the path of my swing.

If you are lucky, you may find two or three people in your life you can trust implicitly, especially when things are not going your way.

Through my divorce and other negative press headlines, Denis has been one of the people to whom I have always turned. He is one of life's great listeners and, though he can tell you a whole lot more about the ins and outs of the golf swing than I can, we're on the same wavelength.

I was certainly grateful to Denis in 1996. I don't know if it was anything to do with the tweaks he suggested to me just before I flew out to Sun City to play the Million Dollar Challenge, but I won that tournament following a play-off with Ernie Els. I'd be lying if I suggested the money wasn't wonderful, but truly the best part of that tournament was the fact that my dad was there watching, less than three months after undergoing heart bypass surgery.

If only Mum could have been with him.

Winning in Dubai set me on course to overtake Woosie and claim my fourth Order of Merit with Tour victories eleven and twelve at the Murphy's Irish Open and the Canon European Masters.

Having equalled the Oosterhuis record (Peter Oosterhuis won four Order of Merits in a row from 1971 to 1974), my goal was to keep on the conveyor belt and go one better, a feat I achieved the following year as a result of the most consistent golf of my career. Of the twenty-two European Tour events I entered, I did not miss a single cut and notched two more wins, the European Grand Prix at Slaley and the Murphy's Irish Open. All told, there were nine top-ten finishes. There was a touch of Luke Donald in the consistency I showed that summer, though Luke rather outshone my efforts in 2011 when he had twenty top tens in twenty-six starts. Incredible.

Yet 1997 will hardly be associated with Colin Montgomerie's 'consistent' march to a fifth Order of Merit. It will always be the year of the Spanish Ryder Cup.

And of Seve.

9 | THE UBIQUITOUS SEVE

I didn't make the best of starts to that 1997 Ryder Cup campaign in that I fell foul of Fred Funk. That was down to some inadvertent comments I had made shortly before the contest.

I was giving a routine pre-tournament interview to a couple of well-respected journalists. They covered a variety of topics and when, towards the end, they explained that they had to do a two-line pen portrait of each member of the US team, I had no hesitation in lending a hand.

I was trying to do nothing more than give a fair assessment of the relative strengths and weaknesses of the American players. I had nothing but respect for them all and I might have got away with my thoughts on how the tight fairways and awkward greens of Valderrama might not play into the hands of some of the US team, but for something I said about Brad Faxon. When his name came up, I mentioned that he might struggle to focus at a time when he was going through his divorce.

CBS picked up my comments and, to my horror, I was portrayed as someone who revelled in the private problems of fellow professionals. Nothing could be further from the truth but the damage was done.

It is a simple fact of golf that off-course distractions can affect your game but I wince when I look back on what I said – and not least because I was faced with similar questions over my own game following the announcement of the break-up of my first marriage. My marriage break-up was no one else's business then, and, back in 1997, Faxon's problems were very clearly nothing to do with me.

I wrote to apologise to Brad, whom I count as a friend, and I also apologised to the captain and everyone else in the US side.

Out of context, the words looked far worse than they actually were, and I think the Americans understood that. Certainly, they did not take advantage of the situation by purporting to be desperately offended – something which would, of course, have made me feel ten times worse.

I don't suppose for a minute that Brad felt the need to get his own back but, if he did harbour any such feelings, he found the answer a month or so after the Ryder Cup. That was when he defeated me 2 & 1 in the quarter-final of the Toyota World Match Play.

So at least from my point of view, the 1997 Ryder Cup had a pretty distracting start which would get worse when the event got under way.

Torrential rain, the like of which I have seldom seen before, and certainly not in Spain, had delayed the Friday fourballs, the traditional order of foursomes followed by the fourballs having been reversed at Seve's request, though don't ask me why.

Jamie Patino, the owner of Valderrama, may have been in his seventies at that time but, typically, he orchestrated a massive salvage operation and it was that, thanks to the astonishingly efficient drainage on the course, which enabled the 1977 Ryder Cup to begin. By the time we teed up, the puddles had disappeared and the only evidence of all that rain was in the green bin bags dotted around the course. They were weighed down with six inches or so of rainwater.

I don't know whether Seve was too bothered with my pre-match problems with Faxon. In the knowledge that Bernard Gallacher had captained the 1995 side to victory, he was focused on nothing other than winning the match on Spanish soil.

Seve had played on the winning side of '95, winning one fourball with David Gilford and losing the other. It was an okay finish to a colourful Ryder Cup record in which he had annexed twenty points from thirty-seven matches and finished on three winning sides.

He was still a good bet for fourballs in '95, but way too wild for foursomes, which is why Gallacher had not used him for that format. Yet, as Gallacher recognised, he remained a deliciously disconcerting opponent, what with his ability to get down in a chip and a putt from anywhere.

In a move which must have startled the Americans, Gallacher placed him at the top of the line-up for the singles and I have always felt that, if he had been up against anyone other than the endlessly stoic Tom Lehman, he would probably have won. (Having lost twice to Ballesteros in his Seve Trophy match, I can speak with a certain authority on the subject.)

Everyone was intrigued as to what would happen in the Seve–Lehman match and it was the perfect sub-plot to encourage relaxation as we embarked on the other games. I know that when I was walking down to the practice ground with Nick Faldo, we stopped to look at the giant screen which was showing the early holes and could not, for the life of us, recognise where Seve was. He was playing from parts of the course we had never seen previously.

Lovely to take my children to Buckingham Palace. At the time Olivia was aged 13, Venetia aged 10 and Cameron aged 8 (Charles Green)

Above: With my father James at Loch Lomond – three hours before I got married

Left: I was really dreading this: Guy Kinnings's best man's speech (Lloyd Dobbie)

Right: This book is dedicated to Gaynor – and this photograph was taken on our wedding day (Lloyd Dobbie)

Gaynor with her children (from left to right): Lynsey, Aimee, George and Christy

Perthshire is special, particularly walking our dogs Max and Cody in the Glendevon Hills

Above: In Dubai. One of the delights of being named Captain (Getty Images)

Right: A life-size portrait by Iain Faulkner that Gaynor had commissioned for my birthday, the house and pond in the background (© Iain Faulkner, 2010, oil on canvas, 84" × 60")

If I didn't look nervous, I was (Getty Images)

Wishing Corey Pavin and his team all the best – hoping they didn't get as close as they did! (Getty Images)

The Opening Ceremony of the Ryder Cup. Part of the Captain's job that is probably the most daunting (Getty Images)

Leaving the Opening Ceremony, Thursday evening (Getty Images)

Ryder Cup wives: the real bosses (Getty Images)

About to call Seve on the Tuesday evening before the Ryder Cup – the most passionate Ryder Cup player of all… (Getty Images)

As I remember it, he chipped in at the 2nd and had no more than six putts in his first seven holes on his way to extending the match to the 15th green. A gloriously gallant effort.

It was our numbers two and three who paved the way for the winning of that year's match. Though some had feared that they were being sacrificed in those lofty positions, Gallacher knew that they had it in them to get the job done, which they did. Howard defeated Peter Jacobsen on the home green and Mark had the better of Jeff Maggert by 4 & 3.

At a time when Ian Woosnam was heading for a halved game with Couples and Gilford was shaping to beat Brad Faxon, I was walking off the 13th green all square against Ben Crenshaw. I then reeled off four successive threes, only one of which was not a birdie. My win was rather tucked away as others bagged more timely points but the score when Ben and I shook hands was 11½–11½. There was then a win from Sam Torrance and another from Nick Faldo who had been one down against Curtis Strange after fifteen holes.

After that, Europe needed to win one of the last two matches for victory. Since Per-Ulrik Johansson was on the point of losing to Phil Mickelson, all eyes were on the shy Philip Walton as he played Jay Haas. Though three up with three to play, nerves had started to kick in. He lost the 16th and the 17th and the worry was that the 18th would go the same way and America would get the half they needed to retain the Cup. Instead, Haas drove into the trees and our ashen-faced Irishman was able to finish things off. The pride we all felt in him superseded all else.

Moving on to the 1997 match, I was delighted when Seve decided to restore my 1991 partnership with Bernhard Langer. However, if I had assumed we would start up where we left off, I was sorely mistaken. On the first morning, we were up against Mark O'Meara and the sensation that was and still is Tiger Woods.

I knew the danger Tiger posed all too well. I'd played alongside him in the third round of the Masters only months previously, when he shot a 65 to my 74. It was one of those occasions when my reaction was not what I had grown to expect. Instead of being angry at myself, I was lost in admiration at what Tiger had achieved. I remember being asked in the press room afterwards whether I thought he could sustain that sort of form. I replied in the affirmative and added that he would win by more than the nine-shot lead he had then. Which he did. He won by twelve.

The Tiger magic was evident from that first Ryder Cup and not too much has changed. His is the first name you look for when the draws are announced. If you are up against him in the fourballs (probably your best shot as he doesn't manage the alternate shot format quite as well), or the singles, it is exciting. There is nothing to lose. There is almost an air of freedom because you are not expected to win.

On that Friday morning, Bernhard and I were not expected to win and we didn't. I played poorly; Bernhard and Tiger were okay; and O'Meara was sensational as they whipped us 3 & 2. Especially when I had played so indifferently, it really felt like a whipping.

When the draw revealed the same match-up for the afternoon session, Tiger was reportedly pleased.

But we were pleased, too. To be given the chance to have our revenge bucked me up to an astonishing degree.

By the time we teed off I had spent an hour in the company of my old mentor Bill Ferguson and had ironed out the wrinkles in my game. Bernhard and I were back to our old selves and we walked off the 15th green with a 5 & 3 scoreline in our favour. Things were looking up.

The following morning saw me paired with Darren Clarke, second in the qualifying table and a touch miffed at not having seen any action the previous day. He was out to prove a point – and he played some super golf on the way to our one-hole victory over Freddie Couples and Davis Love.

The match was shaping well from a European perspective and Seve, our captain and inspiration that week, was determined that we should keep the momentum going, so much so that he was in perpetual motion, urging his players on, giving advice and making sure we all knew the significance of every shot. It was as though someone had given a hyperactive kid a crate of Coca-Cola and asked them to drink it in one sitting. He was buzzing.

For the first time in my Ryder Cup career, I felt the 'senior' partner playing with Darren and I did my best to help and advise him. As I said, he was keen to make a point and I remember cautioning him, successfully, to play the percentage game when he was contemplating a Seve-style escape from the trees with what was only his second shot in a Ryder Cup context.

But I had no such luck at the 17th when Seve got to him first and talked him into going for what I saw as a suicidal bid for the green from the rough. The shot wasn't there and, inevitably, he found water. Fortunately I was able to carve out a half through playing the percentages and we won the match.

Seve was up to more tricks in the afternoon when I was back with Bernhard for the foursomes, with our opponents Lee Janzen and Jim Furyk. I had just completed the morning session when Bernhard caught up with me to explain that we were first out. 'When?' I asked. 'Ten minutes ago' came his response.

I grabbed a sandwich, had a quick wash and change and tore to the tee to avoid keeping our opponents waiting any longer than necessary.

Though I wasn't best pleased with the turn of events, I can see now that Seve was paying Bernhard and myself a huge compliment.

With all the matches running late because of the necessity of completing the Friday matches that morning, there was every chance that the first group out in the afternoon would be alone in getting finished. Seve wanted points on the board before Sunday and he had clearly deemed the Langer–Montgomerie combination as the most likely source.

We were one up with one to play and, as I drove into the trees, so Seve roared to the scene in a bid to conjure up one more great escape. Never mind that it was beginning to get dark, he said that there was a clear path to the green if Bernhard were to hit over one branch and fade it under another.

As Seve went through his far-fetched plans again and turned to me for support, so Bernhard did a bit of jiggery-pokery of his own. He seized the moment when Seve was looking in my direction to play the ball safely back on to the fairway. From there, I chipped on to within around six feet and we won the match.

This might sound as though I am being less than positive about Seve's contributions as captain. Not at all. Seve was Seve. He saw shots that no one else could see. Of course he was going to suggest them – he wouldn't have been the man we all knew and loved if he hadn't – but he struggled to comprehend that what had been the right call for him was not necessarily the right call for more ordinary mortals.

To be honest, there was a positive side to his constant darting-around-and-popping-up-everywhere approach. His passion and determination spread like the proverbial wildfire. He wanted to win so badly and we wanted to win for him.

By the time we were ready to embark on the singles, Europe had a lead of five points. Unassailable, surely?

You would have thought so, especially after we bounced back from the disappointment of Woosie's loss to Couples in the top match with brilliant victories from Per-Ulrik Johansson over Davis Love and Costantino Rocca over Woods. What a win for Rocca that was, incidentally; what a story to tell his grandchildren. I remember hearing how he celebrated by carrying his wife round and round the green. Great stuff.

All of a sudden, however, the scoreboard began to turn USA-red. Clarke, Parnevik, Olazábal, Westwood, Faldo and Ignacio Garrido were beaten one after the other, with the only break in the sequence Thomas Björn's half with Justin Leonard. Faldo in particular had a rough time of it, having to watch helplessly as Jim Furyk chipped in twice, at the 14th and 15th, on his way to a 3 & 2 American win.

Langer steadied the ship with his victory over Faxon, which gave Europe the fourteen points necessary to retain the trophy. But given the lead with which we had started the day, a tie would have been a moral victory for the US. I would certainly have thought so had I been in the Americans' position and I have no doubt whatsoever that Seve would have thought the same.

In the end, it all came down to my match with Scott Hoch. We were all square with one to play. I needed a half-point for European victory: Scott required a point for American bragging rights.

There are moments on a golf course when everything just seems to click into place. My drive down the 18th was one of them. There was nothing different as I completed my back swing, but when the club head connected with the ball the sound was perfect, just perfect.

As I walked down the fairway, Seve was next to me, encouraging me with this passion and intensity of his to hold it together. There was absolutely no way I could let him down. I had left myself a routine nine-iron to the green and, when Scott failed to make the putting surface in two, I knew victory was ours.

Scott's pitch landed about 15 feet from the pin, giving me two for a half at least. As I said before, when you have got them, take them. I rolled up the first putt to within inches and Scott nodded at me to pick it up. Europe had won the Ryder Cup. Seve had won the Ryder Cup. It was a glorious feeling.

But, needless to say, Seve had the last word. He had one more trick up his sleeve, which was to pick up Scott's ball and officially award him a halved match.

Would I have preferred for Scott to have putted out, thereby giving me a chance to claim my point? Yes, of course I would. I am a competitor and my Ryder Cup record matters to me, especially my unbeaten singles run.

But was I cross with Seve?

Had this been anything other than the Ryder Cup, I might have been furious. But not in this context. We had our 14½ points and the match – one of the most memorable of them all – was won.

*

Writing here about these moments with Seve at Valderrama, I still find it hard to believe he has gone. His laugh, his smile and that wagging finger of his were so much a part of the game in my era. How unfair that someone who had done so much to give the game its more youthful image could have died at fifty-four.

Every golfer of a certain generation has a 'Seve moment', one when his golf took your breath away. Mine came twenty years ago, during the play-off for the 1991 Volvo PGA championship at Wentworth. To start with, he made a birdie on the last to match my clubhouse lead of 271 and force a play-off.

He then seemed on the point of undoing all his good work with a drive down the first that veered off line and hit a buggy. No one, I thought, could recover from that. After all, I was sitting pretty on the fairway with a straightforward approach and probably two putts for victory. Wrong. I would have said that the shot which Seve pulled off was impossible but for the fact that I saw it with my own eyes, not to mention a sinking heart. From 200 yards or more, he launched a five-iron that settled to within three feet of the hole. His victory was a formality from there.

Fast-forward two decades to the second round of the BMW PGA at Wentworth and I am surrounded by players in navy sweaters and white shirts in what was a tribute to Seve. It was a very poignant moment for me, thinking back to that play-off and that very special glimpse I had had of golfing genius.

Was I close to Seve? I'm not sure any of the players, other than José Maria Olazábal, can claim that, but we all respected him immensely and loved him for the character he was on and off the course and for what he had done for the Tour. During his playing days and beyond, he was vital to the success of European golf, like nobody else before or since.

There is no question in my mind that Seve Ballesteros was the most talented and skilful golfer the world has ever seen. He is the reason that the European Tour is in the strong position it is today, envied worldwide.

Tony Jacklin was the catalyst for European success in the seventies, but it was Seve who catapulted the game over here into the global mainstream by going to the US and consistently winning in his own unique style – with a swashbuckling swagger. It was thanks to Seve that the European Tour developed the kind of marketing clout without which we could not have survived. Which is why I, for one, am sorry that the decision was taken at the end of the 2011 season not to change the figure on the European logo from Harry Vardon to Seve.

To me, the iconic silhouette of Seve's clenched-fisted celebration captures the drive and excitement of today's European Tour.

As a man, Seve was very intense. I rarely saw him relax. He wasn't interested in having a beer with the boys after a round; his golf was all about unrelenting passion. It is fair to say that at times I found his constant focus and drive a bit over the top, but it was never anything less than inspiring.

Did he fulfil his potential? Yes, in golfing terms he did. He was born with a natural talent and had the good fortune to be brought up near the golf course in Pedrena where, like so many of the Spaniards of his generation, he learned the game through caddying. He acquired a single four-iron and there was not a shot he couldn't play with that club. Which makes you wonder if we do today's youngsters a disservice by starting them off with a shiny new set of implements.

Seve absorbed everything he could from those early days and then launched himself on to the world stage with a brand of golf no one had ever seen before.

Could he have made more of the gifts he had been given in financial terms?

I think so. With everything he brought to the game, he should have enjoyed the lifestyle of someone like Greg Norman, who has transformed his image and success into big business. Seve could have done something similar, maybe even more, but perhaps he wasn't interested. Marketing wasn't his life, golf was. I certainly hope this was not a regret as he came to the end. I doubt it. He had too much soul to have entertained that sort of regret. I believe he would have looked back on his career and smiled that dazzling smile one last time.

I find it hard to put into words the admiration I had for Seve. I was not in his league and yet he treated me as an equal. He was very kind. The fact that he asked me to captain the British and Ireland team for the first ever Seve Trophy in 2000, and then again for the following three events, is in itself a treasured memory.

The tournament, Great Britain and & Ireland versus Europe, was very important to Seve, not just because it carried his name (it is now known as the Vivendi Trophy with Seve Ballesteros) but because he had created it in order to provide European golfers with match-play experience; in other words, to give Europe the best possible chance of winning the Ryder Cup.

That's what the Seve Trophy was all about and it is the mark of the man that he established it with that single goal in mind.

Seve captained the continental side in the early years and, though I didn't enjoy it at the time, he beat me at the top of the line-up in 2000 and 2002. I was winning tournaments at that time and he was barely making cuts but Seve the match-player was still vintage Seve.

I found an old cutting about the match of 2002 not too long

ago and this little passage appealed: 'No one setting out to follow Ballesteros would have spent too much time wishing he had an official arm-band. The place to get close to this wily old champion was in the crowd. Though his first drive hit the fairway, the rest of his tee-shots landed variously on a chair in the woods, in the midst of spectators clutching their heads, and behind every species of bush and tree that Druids Glen has to offer.

'At the third, he shattered the peace in the walled garden area by cannoning into an ancient oak. At the 14th, he achieved that rare double of hitting not just from the men's tee but, after hacking out of undergrowth, from the ladies'.

'Yet wherever he was, he mostly succeeded in getting down in a chip and a putt. It was the Ballesteros of twenty years ago.'

Suffice to say that I was one down after seventeen holes and missed the 12-footer I needed on the home green to draw level. I remember saying, then, that if Seve could only hit his tee-shots 'somewhere in the vicinity of the fairway' he would still be a contender in the Majors.

Mind you, with my captain's hat on, I had done well enough. Thanks to the performance of others, we won that match 14½–11½.

Seve's funeral was held in his home village of Pedrena on 11 May 2011. The procession was led by a bagpiper playing 'A Scottish Soldier' in recognition of his wonderful win at St Andrews in the 1984 Open. I attended alongside Nick Faldo, Ian Woosnam and Sam Torrance, all previous Ryder Cup captains and colleagues, plus his friend José Maria Olazábal who will hold the reins in 2012.

As we made our way towards the church, the local residents lined the streets and applauded. At the service itself, very little golf was mentioned, which I found extremely moving. This was a celebration of Seve the man, not Seve the golfer. It made me think that, whenever I go, if I had that form of tribute, local people from my hometown coming out because of who I was rather than what I did for a living, then I would certainly have achieved something in life. To the people that mattered most to him, Seve could have been the postman as much as an international sporting superstar.

Another extremely compelling moment for me came when we arrived at his house and his ashes were being carried in an urn by one of his cousins. Seve had been cremated a few hours before the service. I don't know what I was expecting, but it wasn't that. Was this what everything finally amounted to? This enormous personality, a man who had had such influence on my life, was now a heartrending mix of ashes and memories.

The fragility of life can be hard to take but it does force you to reassess your own priorities. Past worries and concerns, perceived slights and annoyances, are forced into perspective. This attitude may not last for ever, I know, but it is yet another thing that Seve taught me.

The last thing.

*

After what we will always call 'Seve's Ryder Cup', I completed my run of seven Order of Merits by winning the 1998 and 1999 instalments.

Not for the first time, I made a late entrance in 1998. By the time the Volvo PGA championship came around at Wentworth, I had played in only three of the fourteen tournaments I could have entered. I was living dangerously but, in a way, that helped to fuel my determination.

I was determined to win at Wentworth but looked like missing the cut on the Friday. In fact, the journalists would have been planning their 'Monty misses cut' stories.

As it transpired, Andy Prodger, who had stepped in to carry my bag when Alastair McLean was injured, played his part in the birdie, birdie, birdie finish which had me surviving to the weekend. That done, we proceeded to have scores of 65 and 69 over the weekend to win.

On the Sunday, I was playing with Dean Robertson, a fellow Scot, who was all set to take the trophy until he hooked out of bounds at the 16th. How I felt for him because to win at Wentworth would have been a great result at that early stage in his career.

At the 18th, I needed a birdie to avoid a play-off with Ernie Els, Gary Orr and Patrik Sjöland. With my record in play-offs – played three, lost three on the European Tour – I could not afford to let things go that far.

As was noted at the time, the orthodox way to achieve a birdie at the 18th in those days was to hit a long, fading drive round the dog-leg and find the green with a medium-to-long iron. The way I did it that day was to overdo the fade from the tee and hack out from a thick clump of rough before hitting a lob wedge to nine feet. The putt was downhill and somehow – I can feel the relief even now – I had willed it into the cup. 'Willed' was the operative word because I didn't have too much of a putting stroke going for me at that point.

People go on about my not having won a Major but that Volvo PGA championship felt like a Major to me. It was my fifteenth European Tour title and the £200,000 first prize was the biggest of my career. As I said in my speech, it was a nice change to have

Ernie sitting in the runner-up's seat for a change as he had had the better of me in two US Opens.

I played seventeen tournaments in 1998 and of those I won three and had ten top-ten finishes, while my stroke average came down again and my winnings increased.

Of my three wins, the Linde German Masters was arguably the most important because Darren Clarke and Lee Westwood were catching me fast on the Order of Merit and I was keen to widen the gap. Doubly keen because of something I had heard in the bar.

It was all about Darren and Lee and how, if they finished first and second on the money list, they would have the power to change a few things on the Tour, with specific reference to the 'perks for top players' situation.

Appearance money is not called appearance money as such but, if a sponsor wants you at his tournament, he arranges a shoot-out, or some such thing, to make extra money available by way of encouraging the relevant players to come. Like my management company, I was happy with things the way they were but Darren, Lee and their manager, Chubby Chandler, were seeing things a little differently.

I was perhaps being super-sensitive but I had the feeling that they were planning ahead as if I were out of the picture. That, above all, was why I won the Linde German Masters, though I have to admit it was a close-run thing.

Shades of what had happened that day at Valderrama when I had to wait while Seve Ballesteros tried, unsuccessfully, to get a free drop on the 18th, I had a long wait at the last while Padraig Harrington needed a referee to ascertain whether his ball had crossed the hazard. It took for ever and, at the end of it, I had to get down in two from 45 feet to win the tournament from Robert Karlsson and Vijay Singh. You would not need to have been too good a lip-reader to get the gist of the relieved expletive that escaped my lips as my second putt – it was all of six feet – fell into the hole.

That result left me so far ahead of Lee that I took the Belgacom Open off. I thought I would enjoy the rest before the Volvo Masters, this time at Montecastillo. Instead, I had a perfectly wretched week and the family would have wished I was anywhere but home. I was riveted to the TV as Lee, who really is a magnificent player at his best, holed his second at the 10th on the Saturday and went on from there to win the tournament in extra holes. Why, oh why, had I taken that week off? It almost killed me.

Lee was now well placed to catch me at Montecastillo. If he won the tournament the OM was his. Meanwhile, if Darren won, I could not afford to finish outside the top eight. There were all sorts of complicated permutations ...

The press were writing of how, if Lee or Darren were to win the OM, it would spell 'the end of an era', or 'the end of the Monty years'.

That script did it. I had to demonstrate that I was not finished. Darren won the tournament but I played safe, secure golf to finish in third place and to win my sixth Order of Merit.

In terms of the way I was striking the ball, I was probably at my peak. In collecting my seventh I won five regular tournaments in 1999 along with the Cisco World Match Play, where I defeated Mark O'Meara, who had won the Masters and the Open the previous year, in the 36-hole final.

The Scottish Open was among my wins of 1999 but I played so well at Loch Lomond that week that I had nothing left to give for the Open at Carnoustie. Mind you, there was one thing I could not have got more right. I predicted very early on the Sunday that ~~Paul~~ Peter Lawrie would win the Claret Jug.

After the Open, Lee Westwood surfaced in the battle for the Order of Merit when he won the Dutch Open and the Smurfit European Open before I re-established myself with victories in the Scandinavian Masters and the BMW International Open. Thanks to those two wins, my quest to win my seventh OM was virtually complete, though, because of the wealth of prize money available at that year's end-of-season event at Valderrama, any one of Lee, Sergio García or Retief Goosen could have overtaken me had they picked up the winner's cheque.

As it turned out, Tiger took care of things for me by making off with the event.

After Tiger had given his winner's press conference, I was summoned to talk about my seven-in-a-row feat. Much was made of my official earnings for the season being in excess of £1.8 million but, delighted though I was to be making that kind of money, the fact that our earnings are so public has often had the effect of making me cringe.

In fact, if you were to ask me to name the thing I like least about my profession it would be this eternal emphasis on how much everyone is making. I was brought up in a house where my father would never have dreamed of disclosing how much he earned. He would have thought it the height of vulgarity to put such figures about. Why on earth, you have to wonder, could the Tour not have opted for a more discreet points-based Order of Merit?

In the media tent, Gordon Simpson, the then press officer, made mention of the number of times over the year I had used the word 'stress'. Would I confirm that the pressure was more than it had been in the six previous seasons?

The answer was in the affirmative, the reason being that I had turned the Order of Merit into something I *had* to do.

Crazy but true.

I finished sixth in 2000 as Lee Westwood did what he had threatened to do for a long time in overtaking me. I won the Novotel Perrier Open and the Volvo PGA but where, in 1999, I had five second-place finishes to set alongside my wins, there were none of those in 2000. It was hardly a bad year but it felt like one to me.

When it came to the end of the 2001 season, on 6 November to be precise, the PGA European Tour held a dinner party for me at Wentworth to celebrate my seven Order of Merits.

Strangely enough, it was perfect timing. By then, I had backed off and been able to take a realistic look at what I had achieved.

Had the Wentworth affair been any earlier, I would still have been pondering on where I had gone wrong.

10 | HAVE A NICE DAY

I have a tremendous admiration for the United States. Ever since my days at Houston Baptist I have held Americans in very high regard. I admire their patriotism, their never-say-die attitude, their zest for life. If they could only make bacon rolls as well as we do in the UK, it would be nigh on the ideal country. But for a period of time in the middle of my career, it seemed America did not like me. More accurately, a small but vociferous element of American golf 'fans' did not like me.

It is the spectators who make golf what it is. Without people coming to watch us battle it out on courses around the world there would be no atmosphere, no excitement and no point.

I remember watching on television the scenes at The Belfry in 1985, the year Europe finally defeated the US in the Ryder Cup, and feeling very emotional as the players and crowd sang together 'For he's a jolly good fellow' to captain Tony Jacklin. That image comes from a different world from the one we live in today.

The inane and usually drink-laced cries of 'Get in the hole' when you have just hit your drive on a 500-yard par five can be decidedly irksome, as can the 'You're-up (Europe)' chants that mark modern Ryder Cups and Solheim Cups. I don't mind the latter quite so much but I think there are a lot of people who would like to go back to 'the good old days' when the clapping and cheering was altogether more discerning.

Having been on the receiving end of some frankly appalling

behaviour from the galleries over the years, I was very aware at Celtic Manor in 2010 that I wanted the very best of European support to be on show. Fair play and respect for your opponent lie at the heart of golf, especially in the Ryder Cup, and I was determined that the boundary that marks fun from the unacceptable would not be overstepped – especially at the first tee and, still more especially, when an American was about to play. The last thing I wanted was any suggestion that I had let the crowd get out of control or tried to wrest an advantage from encouraging them to be more vociferous on Europe's behalf.

To that end, the rain delays didn't help. The supporters were taking shelter in the bars where inhibitions tend to get left behind after a few hours/pints. Private thoughts can turn into public exclamations, often at precisely the wrong moment. Whatever is said might not have been intended as a nasty jibe but beer and wine can make anyone think they are a whole lot funnier than they actually are and the results can play their part in damaging reputations along with the spirit of the game.

I have to be honest here and say that at Celtic Manor I felt we came within a hair's breadth of crossing the line. The chanting five minutes before the matches started didn't worry me in the least because you want to see people revelling in the emotion and excitement of it all. I loved 'There's only two Molinaris', but I was happy the chant did not ring out on the backswing of any American. Everyone managed to stay on the right side of that line – just.

The American team take a lot of credit for this thanks to the way they joined in with the fun. If they had adopted a different attitude, who knows what might have happened? Stewart Cink's interaction with the spectators as he prepared to tee off against Rory McIlroy in the singles is a good example. A veil of mist had descended over the course and the players were being held back for a few minutes to wait for it to lift. Taking advantage of the momentary lull in proceedings, some wag in the crowd shouted out what was, to be fair, a very funny line.

'You've got Big Mac, we've got Little Mac', at which Stewart laughed out loud, turned and smiled up at the stands. This was then followed by a rousing chorus of 'He's got more hair than you'. Once again Stewart reacted with considerable class and style. He smiled broadly and removed his cap to show his bald head. This received a great cheer of approval and things settled down as Stewart prepared to address the ball.

You really have to admire that man. When he won the Open at Turnberry, the entire crowd was willing the then fifty-nine-year-old Tom Watson to come out on top. In that instance, too, he did not begin to remonstrate. He said he understood how everyone was feeling.

Tiger was on the receiving end of a few throwaway lines about his private life at Celtic Manor and he, too, took them in his stride, laughing off the comments.

The policing and marshalling throughout the week was absolutely terrific but, like it or not, things were within a whisker of going badly wrong at the match's end. I am talking about the crazed goings-on that occurred on the 17th green after Graeme McDowell had secured the winning point. I think we have to learn from this and perhaps adopt more of a football-style approach whereby stewards circle the green as the end approaches to ensure that things do not spill over.

I am not trying to be a killjoy in saying that. The crowd all week had been incredible and those final moments were wonderful. The raw emotion and happiness that erupted will stay with me for ever but, as bedlam ensued, it became impossible for me to seek out Graeme and shake his hand before going straight from him to Hunter Mahan and from Hunter to Corey Pavin. In the spirit of the game, I think I should have been able to do that and should have been seen to be doing that.

In fact, as more and more people poured forth, the situation bordered on dangerous. Gaynor and her daughter had to grab hold of the belt of a policeman to help them through the crowds. If someone had tripped, all sorts of injuries could have ensued and the day would have finished on a grim note.

Yet those moments apart, the spectators came out of the Celtic Manor match with great distinction.

The same, unfortunately, could not always be said for some of the galleries I have had to face in America over the course of my career.

It started during the second round of the US Open in 1997 at Congressional.

Why then? Why me? I believe there are a number of answers to both questions.

At the time, I was Europe's No. 1 player and the greatest threat to US ambitions, both in their home-grown Majors and, perhaps more importantly, in the Ryder Cup, which they had narrowly lost in 1995 at Oak Hill, Rochester, NY. In addition, I was not a particularly familiar face on that side of the Atlantic. Since I was predominantly a European Tour player, all I ever did was to go over to the US, do okay and leave, so I had not really developed any kind of rapport with the crowds.

Which is why I suspect I was already a target even before I shot a 65 in the first round at Congressional. Mine was not a name they cared to have at the top of the leader board. They wanted one of their own.

The following day there was a rain delay, which drove the spectators to the hospitality tents. When they re-emerged, the gloves were off.

I am afraid I have to accept a degree of responsibility. I am a perfectionist on the golf course. Like every other sportsman and woman, I want to win, and become frustrated when I fail to perform at the level I know I am perfectly capable of attaining. This frustration then seems to work its way very quickly to my face. I can't help it. When I am playing well, I am all smiles. When I am off my game, it shows. My shoulders slump, my head goes down and there have been times when I have caught sight of myself in this unhappy state on TV and struggled to believe that character I am watching is me.

Finally, when I am concentrating, planning my shot and preparing my mind for what I am about to attempt, I can become hyper-sensitive. An innocent cough in the distance can put me off, as can the crunch of a sweet wrapper or the click of a camera.

I realise that I should be able to block such things out and have tried various techniques, most of which have been pretty unsuccessful. I hear things and they put me off. I think I can safely say that I am at the opposite end of the spectrum to the legendary Joyce Wethered. When Lady Amory, as she became, was asked if she had been disturbed by the train which steamed past her back at Sheringham as she was winning her fifth successive English championship, she asked 'What train?' Me, I would have heard it when it was still a mile away.

Following the two-hour rain delay at Congressional, wolf whistles were the least of it. Shouts of 'Get lost', 'Go home' and worse followed me around the course, until I snapped and answered back. 'Save that for the Ryder Cup' came my unwise retort. It was an error of judgement on my part; I should have known better and kept my mouth shut.

The genie was now out of the lamp and it would take me years to reverse that situation. Overnight I was fair game, and once again I accept that I did not exactly help my cause.

The pen portraits of the US team prior to Valderrama? Hardly my finest hour and unlikely to put the brakes on the 'Let's bait Monty' bandwagon.

My relationship with the media has also played its part in stoking the fires. On the whole, I have enjoyed a good relationship with the press. I understand their job and I like the challenge of coming up with something from the day's events which might be of interest.

That said, there have been occasions when I have been snappy after a poor round, or given short shrift to what I regarded as a daft question.

Perhaps worst of all, I have pulled out of pre-arranged interviews at the last minute when I have just not felt up to it. None of this is helpful and of course such incidents get their mentions and contribute to a picture of me as a moody so-and-so who will always rise to the bait if people prod in the right places. There is a degree of truth in that, I know.

In my defence I also believe that the press can go looking for a story that isn't there, blowing the smallest of incidents out of proportion. Yet you only had to listen to the Leveson Inquiry at the end of 2011 to realise how the media are under pressure to get stories and are competing with one another to deliver the best of them. In plenty of instances, it can't be any more fun for them than it is for the people they are writing about.

I have already mentioned the odd clash with my friend Ian Poulter that made the papers, while another incident that comes to mind occurred at the 2002 Open at Muirfield.

On day one, I shot a poor round of 74 but followed it up with a 64 which I believe is still the course record. I was well placed for the final two days and in good form, only for the weather to throw tantrums all its own on the third day. It may have been the middle of summer but conditions were desperate, with the weather so cold that I lost all feeling in my hands. They were like blocks of ice.

I know it was the same for everyone but I couldn't have coped worse than I did. There were a handful of 68s, including one from Steve Elkington and another from Justin Leonard, but the fact that there were ten scores in the 80s gives some indication of the level of difficulty out there.

I returned an 84, which was only three worse than Tiger Woods who came out with a classic when we met up the next day. We were both a million miles away from being in contention but he at least saw the funny side of the situation. 'Hey there, Monty,' he began, 'I sure kicked your butt yesterday.'

The Sunday morning papers were full of reports of how I had supposedly 'stormed off' after my round, refusing to talk to anyone. I had been given the ultimate test and I had failed. Looking back, I should have proffered an amusing account of just how bad it was.

Not too many days afterwards, I asked one of the journalists – that's one of the ones who had had a go at me – how he would have felt had he shot an 84. He answered with an entertaining, 'Delighted!'

Freddie Couples deserved rather more marks than I did that week at Muirfield. He missed the cut on the Friday after taking eight up the last and when, as he came out of the scorer's tent, an American journalist thrust a microphone under his nose and said, 'Freddie, how did you make eight at the last?' Freddie kept his cool brilliantly. 'Because I missed my putt for a seven,' he returned, not in a smart way but humorously.

So for all these reasons, some of them of my own making and some not, I was the target of abuse and jibes in the US for many years. One of the worst occasions was at the Accenture Match Play at Carlsbad, California, when I lost in the first round to Scott McCarron. Once again the beer had been flowing and a few of the so-called fans decided it would be clever to applaud when I missed a putt and offer me some advice about my weight.

This was not what golf was all about but, foolishly, I let it get to me once again. On my way to the clubhouse I was taunted by sarcastic inquiries into how I was doing. They knew I had lost and their comments were unnecessary and, frankly, impolite, I felt. But that does not excuse my comment that the only thing worse than losing would be to spend another day in their country. I didn't mean it and I shouldn't have said it. It was a heat-of-the-moment thing for which I quickly apologised. But it was one more black mark against me in the eyes of the American golfing public.

As upsetting as I found Carlsbad, the nadir of my experiences with unruly American spectators came three years prior to that incident. Namely, at the 1999 Ryder Cup staged at The Country Club, Brookline, Massachusetts.

There were a number of factors going against me that week. My comments prior to Valderrama were given a fresh airing, while I was Europe's No. 1 and the US team and supporters were desperate to avoid a third defeat in a row. Too desperate, I would say. The overpowering desire to win clouded their judgement.

It was a combustible mix that would ignite. At Congressional in 1997, I had told the hecklers to 'Save that for the Ryder Cup'. They had waited two years, but, boy, did they deliver.

The treatment I received that week was appalling. And it wasn't just me. Darren Clarke and José Maria Olazábal were also targeted, though I was on the receiving end of the bulk of the abuse. And that is what it was. Not heckling but abuse. Throughout the week I was being called all sorts of names beginning with 'c's, 'b's and 'f's.

I found the whole experience thoroughly distressing. At times, I was shaking with frustration and anger and was truly grateful for the support I received from the whole European team and especially from our captain, Mark James, and his vice-captains, Sam Torrance and Ken Brown. They helped to keep me focused on my game, counselling me to turn the abuse on its head by playing the best golf of my life. I took that on board. A haul of 3½ points out of a possible five was the right response.

Everything came to a head during the Sunday singles. A drunken abuser was ejected by the stewards, at which point I turned to the crowd and said, 'He's the first to go. And if anyone says anything more, he won't be the last.' Again, I should have kept quiet, but I found it impossible. The language being aimed in my direction was so offensive that my father had to walk out halfway through my round. He couldn't bear it any longer.

As horrible as the events were, the wonderful side of the US was also on display that day in the shape of my opponent, Payne

Stewart. He was a gentleman throughout and clearly upset by what he was hearing. At one stage in the match he even pointed out a group of culprits to the marshals and requested they be removed.

I could not have asked for better support from Payne. I suspect that, as the reigning US Open champion, he felt a responsibility to try to preserve the dignity of the game in his country and he succeeded.

What of the golf? Europe was up against it that year. The Americans had a fabulous team, featuring the World No. 1 and 2 in Tiger and David Duval and other Major champions, whereas we were without Faldo and Langer and had a side featuring seven rookies.

It was Faldo's failure to make the team that resulted in the infamous 'letter in the bin' controversy, revealed by Mark James in his book *Into the Bear Pit*, published after the tournament. I was not in the room when Nick's good luck message arrived so I cannot comment on what actually happened. All I know is that the note definitely found its way into the rubbish among the Styrofoam coffee cups.

In my view it was an unfortunate thing to happen. That Faldo and James did not see eye to eye was presumably fuelled by some of Nick's comments prior to Brookline, when he appeared to take a swipe at the lack of in-depth quality on the European Tour. Personally, I still regard it as entirely appropriate that Nick sent his letter to the team to wish everyone well. He had been the mainstay of Europe's resurgence over the years and suddenly he was no longer in the team after a run of eleven consecutive appearances. That must have hurt but he still had the good grace to put pen to paper. I thought he was in the right.

It may sound strange, given the fact that the note was binned, but its arrival was of great benefit to the team. Perhaps because everyone was so eager to get behind the captain, it pulled us all together. Sometimes you need an incident – it doesn't necessarily matter what the incident is – to create a bond and Nick's letter served that purpose.

During the match, there was no shortage of criticism of James and the way he left out three of the rookies, Jean van de Velde, Jarmo Sandelin and Andrew Coltart, from all of the Friday and Saturday matches.

In my view, if Mark had stood up on the flight over on Concorde and said, 'We are going to be ten–six up going into the singles', no one would have cared who had played or not. Personally, I think he got it dead right. In hindsight, the only error Mark may have made was in the final day line-up. Clarke and Westwood were not as fit as they are now and both were physically and mentally tired. To put them out first and second was a big ask. As it turned out, too big.

They both lost. He also placed out the three untried rookies together, at third, fourth and fifth. This probably put too much pressure on them. As I have said before, momentum is everything in the singles; you feed off the matches around you. It was always likely that the US captain, Ben Crenshaw, would load the top of his order with his best players as he needed points quickly. For us to have played Sandelin, Van de Velde and Coltart in a row was a risk.

When the draw was released and the trio were up against Mickelson, Love and Woods, you could sense a shift in the balance of power already – and never mind that we had a four-point advantage at that stage.

With only two matches left alive, the Americans were already at fourteen points and only needed half a point more to win. Stewart and I were contesting one of those two matches, with Olazábal and Justin Leonard in front. Both matches were all square.

Watching from 100 yards down the fairway as Ollie and Justin prepared to putt, Payne and I were very much aware of the score and tightness of the contest.

What happened next will never be forgotten. As Leonard, who was miles, simply miles, away from the hole, sank the putt of his life across the evening shadows, the American team and their wives exploded on to the green as if the match was won. It wasn't. Ollie still had his putt for the half to take the match up the last. (To be fair, as a result of some confused radio commentary, I think some of the Americans may genuinely have thought that Olazábal's putt was irrelevant.)

Ollie took it incredibly well, like the gentleman he is. He stood and watched it all happen in front of him, knowing he still had a very difficult putt himself to keep the Ryder Cup alive. Did the incident put him off his putt? It must have done. He made a gallant effort which missed. That was when the match was over.

I have always wondered what would have happened if Seve had been in Olazábal's shoes. I think I can guess. Seve would have summoned both referees and both captains and he would have made a heated case for the hole either to be replayed or forfeited.

In my view, what should have happened – and I am certain I would have done this had I been in their shoes – is that Crenshaw should have walked over and picked up Olazábal's ball and given him the putt. That way, they could have slogged it out down the last.

I accept that is easy to say now, but something should have happened because the scenes on that green were not acceptable and, in my view, they were bad for golf.

From the American perspective it was a shame because their brilliant play that day has been overshadowed by those events and by the small minority of trouble-makers in the crowd. To have come back from 10–6 down was a stunning achievement and, taking a step back, they deserve great credit for the quality of their play.

Not that we saw it like that at the time. In the European locker room afterwards there was very much a siege mentality – it was them and us. None of the Americans came in to offer any form of apology or explanation. And, to be honest, we didn't want them to. We had our own thoughts and they must have had theirs. We were worlds apart. From my perspective, I think we did extremely well in the 1999 Ryder Cup and I am very proud to have been a member of that team even though we lost. It was a tremendous effort to have come so close.

Leonard's putt and Ollie's miss guaranteed the US their 14½ points.

Ollie won the 18th to square his match rather than lose it and now the only game left on the course was mine.

All day Stewart and I had been engaged in a battle royal and it was one of those matches which deserved a good finish, even though the Ryder Cup was already won. I had been three up at one stage and Payne clawed me back to all square going up the last. He hit his second at the 18th into a greenside bunker and played his third to about 25 feet. I, meantime, was also on the green in two, about 10 feet outside him.

Walking up the fairway to the green was quite an experience, and not a particularly pleasant one. I would almost go as far as to say it was bordering on dangerous, with the fans swarming everywhere, waving flags, cheering and at times grabbing at us. Both caddies did extremely well to keep our bags on their shoulders.

'I think enough's enough, Colin' was what I heard Payne saying through the din. He picked up my ball, shook my hand and conceded the hole. It was a very generous act and one befitting the man. Yes, I was favourite to win the hole, but you never know in golf. I could easily have three-putted and he could have knocked his in. But it was the right thing to do and I appreciated his gesture.

Looking back now, it seems almost unbelievable that I never saw Payne Stewart again after Brookline. Two months later he was dead. I was in Spain at the Volvo Masters when I heard on the television that he was a passenger in a plane that was in trouble. At that stage, the plane had not yet crashed, but, listening to the constant reports and updates, it was clear the end was inevitable and we now know all the people on board were unconscious because of a loss of cabin pressure.

It was very sad news. Tragic news. To lose one of our most talented players was truly shocking for everyone in the game. It might sound a little simplistic, but I mean this as the greatest of compliments. Payne Stewart was a fierce competitor, a huge credit to his country, a proud American and one of the good guys. His was a life taken far too soon.

*

In many ways the 1999 Ryder Cup was one to forget, but in another respect it is one to remember: for the reasons I have tried to set out above, we – and I mean we, because both teams have responsibilities – let standards slip very badly.

After Brookline, the responsibility fell on Sam Torrance and Curtis Strange to repair the damage. Their task began as soon as they were appointed and should have been completed in 2001, until the dreadful events of 9/11 quite correctly delayed the tournament for twelve months and added a sense of perspective.

A year later, and still tasked with rekindling the spirit and heart of the Ryder Cup, both Sam and Curtis did brilliantly. All credit to them. They brought the two teams together and reminded everyone what the competition was all about – pride, passion, sportsmanship and respect.

Returning to my treatment at the hands of the American golf fans, it is entirely different today. Nowadays, I get nothing but good humour and encouragement.

Perhaps it is because I have changed, relaxed more and have a better outlook on life, or perhaps it is just because I am no longer the threat I once was; it doesn't really matter which. I still receive comments, but they have taken a definite turn for the better.

There was a bloke at the WGC-CA championship in Doral, Florida, in 2008 who tested our new relationship.

I had returned a 75 followed by a 74 in the first two days of the three-round competition and, as I was walking off the 18th green, with head down and shoulders slumped, a voice rang out from the gallery.

'Good job there's no cut,' he cried.

Five years earlier I might have felt like punching him. Now, I was enjoying his comment as much as the next person.

11 | MIND GAMES

As an on-top-of-his game Lee Westwood won the 2000 Order of Merit, so I was entering what was the start of a pretty difficult period in my life. As I have said, details of my divorce hardly need another airing but, for the purposes of this autobiography, I think it is entirely relevant to explore the impact of the event on my golf.

There is no question that off-course worries and distractions have had a negative impact on my game. They affect every golfer and I am no different. It happened when my mother was ill and then died, and it happened over the years from 2000 to 2004.

A huge proportion of the game of golf is about how you react to errors. Following a birdie, you walk off the green relaxed and smiling; with a par there is a degree of satisfaction that you have not messed up; but when it comes to a bogey, that's another matter altogether.

In normal circumstances, you cannot help going over and over the mistake which led to the dropped shot but, by the time you are standing over your ball on the next tee, those thoughts will more often than not have been banished. You will have reasoned with yourself that it doesn't really matter, that you have what it takes to pick up the stroke on the next hole: in the greater scheme of things, a bogey does not need to be any more than a very minor setback.

It is a very different story if outside concerns are crashing around your brain, disturbing your normal mental process. They are not so easily shrugged off. Everything negative in your life forces its way to the front and, suddenly, one wayward drive or putt assumes a ridiculous degree of importance. If I was playing okay, it was fine. I could separate my personal life from my golfing life. But one screw-up on the course and that was it.

'How could I do that? How could I be so stupid? Nothing is right in my life! Nothing! I'm useless, a failure! Why am I even bothering? I don't want to be here. I don't want to play this crazy game. Who cares about the next hole? It is all so pointless.'

It's irrational, I know, but that is how it was for me.

The walk to the tee should be an opportunity to clear your head, but once you are down and upset that becomes impossible. And from there, it is very difficult to find a way back. You begin to expect errors, an attitude which only serves to bring a fresh supply galloping into your game. One bogey leads to another and another and, before you have had time to get a hold of yourself, you are spiralling out of control and the round is over. And the journalists – at least the braver ones – are asking what happened.

I used to find a certain gallows humour in some of the press reports on my golf at that time. 'Monty shoots error-strewn 76.' If they only knew, I used to think. Seventy-six? That was actually pretty darned good in the circumstances.

At the 2000 Open at St Andrews, my caddie Alastair McLean came into his own. Over the years, the press tend to make a big thing about bagmen and players splitting up. I have never understood that. From my point of view, caddies move on to work with other players on a reasonably regular basis. It can turn into something of a merry-go-round and that is as it should be. Alastair and I were together for a long time, all through the seven Order of Merits, and then we parted company. Later, we came together again, and parted again. The same applies for almost every other player.

There is very rarely a story. Either side of the equation can decide it is time for a change, a new perspective. That is all there is to it. In the case of Alastair and me, we did not fall out and I have to say I was mighty glad that he was the man walking next to me in 2000 during that final round.

I could barely putt on the 12th green because I was so upset at the way things were at home. The fact that the 12th is away at the far end of the course, a distant outpost if you like, may have had something to do with it but, whatever the reason, that was the point I found myself fighting tears. I turned to Alastair and said, 'Put the yardage book away. I just need you to talk to me, to keep me going. Is that okay?'

Alastair had been in the dark about my problems but he cottoned on to what was required over those final holes. He listened as I poured my heart out, while simultaneously pointing me in the right direction, handing me my clubs and guiding me through a round I had thought I could not complete. Quite how I managed to shoot a 70 to finish in a tie for twenty-sixth, I do not know. It was more Alastair's round than mine.

For a long time, I refused to accept the obvious reason as to why my game was falling apart. My agent, Guy Kinnings, and my dad did their best to help, explaining that anyone going through a traumatic experience such as a divorce is bound to find it spilling into other aspects of their life. 'It's human nature, Colin,' they would tell me. 'Be patient, focus on what matters and don't worry about your golf. That will fix itself in time.'

My reaction to their advice was not very helpful. 'Okay, when? Tell me a date and I will be fine. I will work towards that, but I need to know when it will get better.' My impatience and need for control was evident but, no matter how hard I pushed, there was only one answer they could give me. 'You will get better when you are ready to get better.'

I wasn't to be reasoned with at this juncture and I was still more impossible when a new level of stress came in the guise of the aforementioned back problems.

I have told the story of how Dale Richardson, at that point a regular physiotherapist on Tour, helped me from the point where I could scarcely crawl from my bed to get through the weekend of the 2001 Volvo Masters at Montecastillo, Jerez. And of the wonderful woman doctor I saw at the Mayo Clinic who advised that there wasn't a whole lot anyone could do until my stress levels dropped.

Exercises helped but there were various times in 2002 and 2003 when my back would suddenly go into spasm and force me out of tournaments. In January 2002, I flew to Perth, Australia, for the Johnnie Walker Classic, only to have to abandon play after one round; the same thing happened again at the WGC-NEC Invitational at the Sahalee Country Club, Washington, in August. In other words, I was doing a lot of flying for very little golf.

With the unpredictability of my back merely adding to the pressures, I grew more and more discouraged. One moment I'd be hitting the ball well and feeling no side effects – I suddenly had a run of four top-ten finishes – and the next I'd be in agony again, unable to play, or withdrawing after a round.

Foremost in my mind over that summer was the Ryder Cup. The decision had been taken that those players who qualified for 2001, before the event was postponed in the wake of the Twin Towers disaster, would constitute the teams in 2002, so I had no concerns on that front, especially given that run of top-ten finishes mentioned above. I finished the season in fourth place in the Order of Merit but I was worried that I would not be fit enough to participate.

With less than a month to go, I attended a meeting at the IMG offices with Guy Kinnings, Hugh Mantle (the sports psychologist, who was providing me with a lot of assistance) and my coach, Denis Pugh.

We were agreed that I should not join Sam Torrance and his team at The Belfry unless I was certain I could give them my all. It was decided to give my back one final try-out at the WGC-American Express championship in County Kilkenny, Ireland. If it held up, fine. If not, I would pull out.

With rounds of 72, 70, 69 and 68 and a thirty-first place providing the necessary encouragement, I was on my way to the match with a secret weapon in the person of a physiotherapist called Clive Lathey.

Clive was a godsend that week. He worked on me every morning and evening in my room and even walked the course in case there was a problem. Whenever it was necessary, he applied heat packs and back rubs.

Clive's assistance, coupled with the all-consuming nature of the Ryder Cup, freed me up to play in all five of the matches and to provide Sam with a return of 4½ points.

There was a downside, however. Because of all the physiotherapy, I missed a number of team meetings and get-togethers. While the others would be breakfasting or dining together, I'd be lying flat out in my room, being pummelled and manipulated by Clive. In conjunction with the fact that I had missed out on so many of that year's tournaments, I felt one step removed from the team.

Given that this was my fifth Ryder Cup, I should have been one of the leaders on and off the course, but circumstances demanded that I was not and I found that difficult to take. Bernhard Langer took on that role and, to an extent, I withdrew into myself. Sam, a wonderfully astute captain, spotted the danger signals early on.

For the first three matches, he paired me with Langer, which was perfect. We knew each other so well that I did not need to start explaining things. Langer is a thoroughly good man and a very steadying influence on the golf course. I felt comfortable alongside Bernhard and did not feel I was being called on to provide any additional assistance other than to play my shots to the best of my ability.

The matches were all tight, but we came out on top by one hole in two of them and halved the other. The half was a bit of a disappointment in that we had been three up with four to play but I refused to dwell on it. After all, we had been playing the formidable pairing of Mickelson and Toms, and to have held on as they fought back was an achievement in itself.

For the Saturday afternoon fourball, I knew I would have a new partner as Bernhard had requested a rest. My initial thought had been to suggest Paul McGinley, as I felt he was playing as well as anyone that week. Sam, though, had other ideas.

Langer had played his part in preventing me retreating into my shell, but, without Bernhard's support this time round, Sam feared I might go downhill. The match situation was very tight – we were one up going into that final session before the singles – and he needed to get another result out of me. His solution was Padraig Harrington and it was inspired.

Apparently Sam's instruction to Padraig had been to do whatever he could to 'keep Monty going'. I had never played with

Harrington before then and I really had no idea what to expect. Certainly, comics did not feature.

The last comic I bought was probably the *Beano*, but Padraig is a fanatic and, from the moment we strode off down the first fairway, he started on about various cartoon characters and he didn't stop. He was brilliant. It was exactly what the doctor ordered. He was funny and enthusiastic and left me no time whatsoever to become moody or withdrawn.

It was all a little surreal but so entertaining that I soon got swept away. Padraig played some outstanding golf as we defeated Mickelson and Toms 2 & 1, which was one hell of a result given that this particular US partnership had gone into the match having secured 2½ points out of a possible three. (The half had come from the match with Langer and myself.)

At the close of play on that second day the teams were tied at 8–8 and it was then that Sam came up with yet another master stroke – a top-heavy line-up which caught Curtis Strange, his counterpart, on the hop.

Sam had not spoken to me in advance about his plans for the singles but had indicated that he had something up his sleeve. 'Listen, Monty, I've got an idea for tomorrow that involves you. Do you want to discuss it?'

Not least because of the special treatment I had needed for my back, I did not want to put myself out by asking Sam to spell out to me individually what he had in mind. 'Sam,' I said, 'you can put me anywhere you want. Don't worry about me. You're in charge.'

I wasn't there when the announcement of the draw was made. Instead I was in my room, probably bent over double or flat on my back while the Deep Heat treatment penetrated my muscles.

But I remember the charged atmosphere when I did eventually appear downstairs for a bite to eat.

'Have a look, Monty,' one of the boys said to me, handing me the sheet. Between mouthfuls I scanned the list of names. Had Sam's fiendish plan been to withdraw me? I couldn't see my name anywhere. I looked again, concentrating on the middle of the order, where I suspected I might be, but no. As one of the longer names, Montgomerie is usually easy to spot but I couldn't see it. Then there it was: 'Monty', at the top of the order.

I looked across at Sam and raised my eyebrows, as if to say, 'What have you done here?'

'Take a closer look, Colin.'

I did as instructed and that is when it began to dawn on me what he had done. Montgomerie, García, Clarke, Langer, Harrington, Björn ... He was looking to close it out as quickly as possible, and with the US big guns lurking at the foot of the list, there was every chance he was going to succeed. 'Good heavens, Sam,' I said, 'you've got the better of him here!'

Sam had put his faith in me by sending me out top. He wanted points on the board right from the off and he felt I was still good enough to deliver. He knew what he was doing and, sure enough, that decision gave me enough of a lift to stop any of my problems getting in the way.

On the Sunday morning a rather odd thing happened. My tee-off time was 11.15 and, about an hour beforehand, I headed down to the practice range to hit a few balls. On arrival I was greeted with the sight of two stands packed with spectators. The gates had opened at around 8.15 and people had made their way to the range because this would be their first chance to see some golf.

Denis Pugh and I were there, alone. Since my opponent, Scott Hoch, apparently restricts his pre-round practice to half an hour, it was just me and Denis, and seven thousand onlookers, all of whom were seeking a spot of entertainment.

My embarrassment was there for all to see as I began my stretching exercises to the accompaniment of bemused 'Ooohs' and 'Aaahs'.

I explained to Denis that I was not prepared to go on making a fool of myself and cut short the stretches to hit a few shots with my sand wedge. When I was feeling a bit looser, I decided to have a go at hitting the 100-yard marker and, after a couple of narrow misses, I succeeded in hitting the target.

'Well done, Monty,' began some bright spark in the stand. 'Pity it took three goes!'

Turning and smiling at the vast crowd behind I called out, 'Who said that?' The culprit's mates started pointing at him as he squirmed awkwardly in his seat. 'Come on, then,' I said, to the delight of his mates, 'why don't you have a go?'

'What are you doing?' whispered Denis. 'This could be a disaster.'

I looked at him and shrugged. 'It just came out.' It was too late to worry about it because the bloke was already down from the stands and approaching us. He was getting quite a reception in the process and fairly lapping it all up, bowing and waving to his audience. It was all very light-hearted and fun, except for the fact that he was about to be using my clubs. Goodness knows what he could have had on his hand – sun cream, hand lotion, grease from his bacon roll. If my grips became slippery, it was going to be bad news.

'Hello there, what's your name?'

'Eric.'

'Pleased to meet you, Eric. What's your handicap?'

'Seventeen.'

My heart sank. My beloved sand wedge was going to be in the almost certainly slippery hands of a seventeen-handicap man and I was now in a position where I had to play along with it.

'Come on, then, let's see how much better you can do.'

He thinned his first attempt, hitting so much ground before the ball that he delivered what we call 'apple turnover', a state of affairs in which the divot actually lands on top of the still stationary ball.

At this point Denis tried to intervene. 'Thanks very much, mate. I think that's probably enough for now.' Our hero was having way too much fun to stop. 'No, no,' he cried, 'you had three shots, I'm having three.' Fair enough – and fortunately, on his third go, he managed to get the ball into the air to prompt the rapturous applause he craved. Thanking us both, he handed me my club and wandered back to his seat to further cheering and clapping.

There had been no harm done to the club and it had all been a good laugh, but what we hadn't realised was that the whole incident had been broadcast by Sky Sports, live. This meant it had been beamed into the players' lounges, where they were having breakfast. The European team had apparently been glued to the screen throughout and thought it was hysterical. I gather that the sight of me acting the clown with a complete stranger had helped to release the building tension.

The Americans are generally less inclined to have a laugh at any kind of goings-on in a Ryder Cup context than we are, so I have no idea what they were thinking. But I can promise you that not a second of what happened had been planned in advance. It was entirely spontaneous and, if it gave us a slight edge, that was good fortune and nothing more.

What probably helped rather more was that I birdied the first with a 30-plus-foot putt to set the tone for the whole day. Europe were ahead. Not too many minutes earlier, I had been unusually nervous because expectations were so high and Sam had gone out on a limb to have me leading the way. Again, on a personal level, I was anxious to maintain my unbeaten run in the singles.

That first 30-footer was the first of a series of putts to drop and the momentum which came with them was something which Hoch could not begin to match.

After closing out the match on the 14th, I was able to watch the drama of the day unfold.

It was classic Ryder Cup. Sam's gamble of going out heavy seemed to pay off with 4½ points from the top half of the draw. That, though, was when the US began to fight back.

Niclas Fasth seemed to have the destiny of the trophy in the bag in the eighth game when he was one up with one to play against Paul Azinger, only for Azinger to chip in from a bunker for a half. Suddenly, Strange's decision to have Davis Love and Woods playing at ten and twelve respectively did not look so foolish after all.

Phillip Price had already won a famous battle with Mickelson in the eleventh match but we needed a half-point from Paul McGinley. He had to hole a 10-footer to make that happen and, not so many minutes after his ball disappeared into the hole, he disappeared into the lake, courtesy of his grateful team-mates. I was careful not to get involved. Bad back and all that. Plus, with the likes of Clarke and Harrington in the team you just never knew who might have been next ...

It was the Dunhill Links championship the following week and, when Paul was asked if he would able to come down to earth in time for the first round, he said that that was the last thing he wanted to do. He would be enjoying that putt for as long as he could.

He said that the moment he would never forget came when he looked up to see the ball a foot from the hole and heading, at a perfect pace, for the middle of the cup. It could not miss.

During that same week at St Andrews, the press renewed questions along the lines of when I might captain the Ryder Cup. I can remember saying that I would love to get the job one day – 'and if that should happen, I would try to do as good a job as Sam did last week'.

I had putted well at The Belfry, especially on the Sunday. Given that the flat blade is the weakest part of my game, why should that have been the case?

I wish I knew, but in part I think it had something to do with match play. Throughout my career I have always been a little negative when it comes to stroke play, concentrating more on protecting my score than landing a killer blow. My putts always die into the hole rather than charge into the cup.

In match play I feel less restricted. The worst thing that can happen is you lose one hole, whereas, in stroke play, a four-putt green can throw you from a leader board and out of that championship.

My match-play putts are firmer. In fact, I would go as far as to say that I hit the ball a foot harder in a normal 10-foot putt. When you do that, more of them drop. I am convinced that if I had been able to transfer that match-play putting mentality into my overall game, I would have won at least one Major by now. It doesn't sound that difficult but, though I could make it work at the start of a round, my stroke-play persona would soon take over.

Another problem with putting is that you have too much time to think. After you have marked your ball, given it a wipe, replaced it, surveyed the shot from every angle, perhaps removed a stray leaf from the grass or flattened down a bump that could knock your ball off line, there can be an awful lot going on in your head.

To counter this, I used to recite the thirty-seven-times table in my head. By the time I was struggling with four times thirty-seven, my subconscious self was on auto-pilot and the putt would be on its way. It all sounds pretty ludicrous but there are plenty of players who have hit on some far-fetched solution which works for them. For me, at least, that thirty-seven-times table worked quite well.

Perhaps the most obvious manifestation of my relative timidity on the greens can be seen in my record at the Masters. My highest place finish at Augusta came in 1998 when I tied for eighth. A year later I finished in a share of eleventh place and, thereafter, my next best performance, perhaps surprisingly, came in 2002 when, after withdrawing from the Johnnie Walker in January, I played in the Tournament Players' championship at Ponte Verda Beach, Sawgrass, Florida, followed by the Shell Houston Open at Woodland, Texas, and the BellSouth Classic at Duluth, Georgia, before moving on to Augusta. Surprisingly, my back obviously survived the heavy schedule and I managed a tie for fourteenth.

Other than on those three occasions and a share of nineteenth place in 2000, I have not troubled the top twenty. Indeed, I have missed the cut six times in fifteen starts.

The reason is straightforward. If, on those Augusta greens, you want to keep the ball on line, you have got to hit it firmly which is something I cannot bring myself to do on these highly polished surfaces. I just don't have that mindset.

I love the tournament, the location, the traditions and the mannerly spectators (or 'patrons' as they are known). Unfortunately, however, the course does not work for me. Tee to green, I do not have a problem. In fact, in 2000 I believe I actually led the field in terms of greens in regulation – and only just squeezed into the top twenty.

No, whatever people might say about me hitting the wrong shape of shot for the course, it was the greens which found me out.

12 | ACT OF FAITH

For me, 2003 was a bad year rendered all the worse because I started out with such high hopes.

Following our success at The Belfry, I had finished the 2002 season with three top-five finishes, including a joint first place with Bernhard Langer in the Volvo Masters at Valderrama after we had shaken hands on the second green of the play-off when we could barely see each other through the half-light.

It was the second time this had happened to Bernhard. Back in 1986, he had shared the Lancôme Trophy with Seve in much the same circumstances. However, despite these good omens and my fourth-place finish in the Order of Merit, my back problems seemed to intensify after Christmas. My swing departed its habitual groove and I failed to win a tournament throughout the entire twelve-month period.

But it was not my back which forced me out of the Open of 2003 at Sandwich ... I was staying in a reconstructed barn that had been turned into a bed-and-breakfast and, as I sauntered down the front steps to my car on the Thursday morning, determined to kick-start my season, I tripped and fell. Maybe I was picturing where I would hit my opening tee shot. Whatever the reason, I pitched headfirst down the last few steps and on to the shale driveway, ripping open my hands as I tried to break the fall.

After a quick rinse to wash away the blood, I wrapped hand-kerchiefs round the cuts and headed for the course. 'It's not too bad,' I thought. 'I'll get some plasters when I reach the locker room and I'll be fine.'

Not so. By the time I arrived at Royal St George's and removed my makeshift bandages, it was clear that all was not well. The bleeding had stopped, but my hands were red and raw.

I was six over par by the time I reached the seventh, while the swelling on my hands was similarly out of control. So much so that I was virtually unable to grip the club.

At that point, I turned to one of my playing partners, Brad Faxon, a man for whom I have the greatest admiration, and showed him what was going on. 'Sorry, Brad,' I said, 'I'm going to have to pack it in.' He took one look and shook his head. 'What were you doing out here in the first place?' he asked. 'You have got to get them sorted.' Then he smiled, 'That is the reason you've been so useless today, right?'

I went straight to the R&A doctor, who gave me something to clean the cuts and cleared me to withdraw from the tournament. I felt a real sense of disappointment as I drove back to London that afternoon. I had started the week with my back feeling in decent shape and had ended it after a stupid accident that meant another Open had slipped away from me. I was conscious of the fact that I had just turned forty and did not exactly have time on my side when it came to trying to pin down a Major.

Colin Montgomerie, the forty-first best golfer in the world: that's how I ended the 2003 season. Not exactly where I wanted to be, but, on the plus side – and I was struggling to find one – my back was beginning to feel better.

I knew I had no option but to buckle down and get on with it. Being so low in the world rankings meant that, barring a meteoric rise in the first half of 2004, I was going to have to go through qualification for the next Open. I accepted that but I was determined that the same would not happen again in 2005.

By the start of 2004, it was clear my marriage was over and it was with a heavy heart that I flew off to the Laguna National Golf and Country Club in Singapore for the Caltex Masters in mid-March. I wasn't expecting very much of myself, but at least on a personal level I knew where I stood. The separation was shortly to be announced and, with everything in place, the pressure that had been building for a couple of years began to retreat.

I was on the other side of the world, with a new caddie, Andy Forsyth, and nothing to think about other than golf for a week. 'Give it a go, Colin, but don't worry too much about how you get on' was my attitude. After three days, I was four shots off the lead and happy with how I was playing. By the end of the final round I had carded a 65 which included seven birdies and no bogeys, to win by three. The victory was as unexpected as it was welcome.

Winning in Singapore was a boost and my hope was that it would serve as the perfect platform to accomplish the three targets I had set myself at the start of the year: to propel myself inside the World Top 50 (something which would secure me a starting slot in all the key tournaments of the following season); to qualify for the Open; and to make the Ryder Cup team. Unfortunately my Singapore success proved to be something of a false dawn ...

From March until the end of the season, I managed only two further top-five finishes – at the Scandinavian Masters at the end of July and, crucially as it turned out, at the BMW International in Munich at the end of August. The rest of the season was peppered with too many missed cuts. By the close of the year, I was a limp eighty-first in the world.

That I was not an automatic qualifier for the Open was an even bigger disaster than it might otherwise have been in that the venue was Troon, my family hometown since 1987, when Dad accepted the job as secretary of the Royal Troon Golf Club. Whatever it took, I had to be there.

I did not enjoy the qualification process. I recognised that the reason I was at Sunningdale in June battling it out with a horde of other hopefuls was because I had not been playing well enough to be anywhere else, but I found it hard to shake the 'What on earth are you doing here, Colin?' mentality.

I should have just got on with the job in hand, but I let the situation get to me. Bogeys were coming thick and fast and I was struggling. My caddie, Andy, was a great help and helped pull me out of my semi-strop in time to make a play-off where ten of us were vying for five slots.

I felt as if I was taking on the player I had been twenty years previously with so many young guys in the play-off party and I found it tough to handle. If the Open destination had been anywhere else other than Troon, I'm not sure I would have found the reserves necessary to make it through, but the lure of playing down those familiar fairways brought out the best in me. When I made it, the relief was immense.

The 2004 Open was among the more emotional I have ever known. The support I received from the home fans was extraordinary. They knew I'd been going through a tough time and they responded with such positive energy that at times I felt swept along by it, buoyed in a way I had never previously experienced.

Standing on the first tee on the Thursday morning, collecting my thoughts as I waited to be announced, I looked back over my shoulder towards South Beach and could see my family home. Even though my mother had died more than ten years earlier, I swear I saw her standing at the window, watching me about to play. She was smiling.

I don't know if Dad knew what I was thinking, but, as I glanced across at him, I could see that he, too, was smiling. I loved the fact he was going to be there walking the first few holes with me before leaving the growing bustle to return to old friends in the clubhouse.

As I stepped up to hit my drive, a thought skipped across my mind. 'It will be many years before the championship returns here: this is most likely my last Open adventure on these links.' I was determined to marry my best golf to the links and to make Mum and Dad proud.

I believe I did so. Three rounds of 69, 69 and 72 kept me among the leaders, which was important to me – and to Dad. I was making a statement that I was not a spent force and that was really all I could have hoped for.

I could have done without the 76 on the Sunday, but you can't have it all. Coming down the last with the crowds cheering and applauding on both sides of the fairway was incredible, dramatic even, and a shaft of light in my golfing and everyday life.

It was around this time that I bought a little flat in Albion Riverside, Hester Road, overlooking the Thames on the Battersea side, facing Chelsea. I also bought myself a new car, a navy blue Bentley Continental. I know, I know, not exactly necessary or practical around London – my manager Guy and my accountant were dead against it – but to me both the flat and the car represented a new beginning.

I was missing the children terribly, not seeing them as regularly as had been the case before when I wasn't out of the country, but I also knew I had to start rebuilding. As daft as it sounds, the car was part of that, and when I was left some money by my mum's mother when she died at the grand old age of ninety-seven, I spent it on a personalised number plate: CSM1. Every time I saw it I thought of Granny and smiled. It was comforting, which is what I needed just then.

I furnished the flat well but, to be honest, I was out socialising so much I never made much use of the various mod cons I'd had installed. So much so that, when I sold it a couple of years later, the new owner discovered the instruction booklets for the microwave, the oven and dishwasher inside the appliances, still in their plastic bags.

It wasn't a bad life but there is no getting away from the fact that it was at times sad and lonely. There were occasions when I shut that front door and felt imprisoned. I would go out on to the balcony and look over the river, wondering what I had come to, being on my own, away from my children. Scanning the city skyline in those moments made me think of all the families who were laughing and joking with each other. Yes, I had a lovely flat and a fancy car, but they didn't begin to fill the gap.

Walking helped me to make sense of things. I would walk and walk and walk. I'd take off across Albert Bridge to the King's Road, then up to Sloane Square and from there into Knightsbridge, towards Harrods. Mainly I wanted to be around people, but if it was the middle of the night, that was fine too. The streets might have been deserted but I knew there were people living in the flats and houses I passed.

I undertook these solitary expeditions for a number of months, until on one occasion I found myself in Oxford Street in the very early hours. It was cold, bitterly cold, and yet in almost every alley or shop doorway I passed I could see a homeless person trying to bed down for the night. I shouldn't have needed something like that to put my life into perspective; it sounds selfish to say that I did when I had so much and was so lucky, but sometimes it is impossible to see reason and open your eyes properly until the other side of life is staring you in the face.

It is a very thin line that we all tread. Some people are terribly unlucky and unfortunate, and I knew I was not one of them. What on earth was I complaining about? Why was I allowing myself to wallow in self-pity?

There came an evening when I arrived home to my warm flat and promised myself that I would put an end to all this self-indulgent nonsense.

*

Despite my tie for third at the Scandinavian Masters and my tie for fourth at the BMW International, I failed to qualify for the 2004 Ryder Cup. Actually, I was a mile off, but that didn't make it hurt any less. Since that flight back on Concorde from Kiawah Island in 1991 I had set my sights on making every Ryder Cup. It had become a part of me, and now I had come up short. If I was going to be on the plane this time, I would need help.

'Colin, you are my number one pick.' It was early Sunday evening after the BMW and Bernhard Langer, the Ryder Cup captain, had pulled me aside. 'And listen, this didn't just come from me. The rest of the guys on the team want you there.' How much was that the right thing for a captain to say? If he hadn't added the last bit I would have been left wondering what on earth the others thought about me getting a place.

Would I have picked myself? In America, yes, I would have done. There were perhaps others who, purely in a playing sense, deserved their place ahead of me but, with my experience of America, I think I would have come to the conclusion that I would be an asset to the team. Luke Donald, a rookie, was Langer's other pick and I think he wanted to balance out his two selections. So, yes, I would have picked me, not on golf alone, but for everything else that I brought with me. It is the best team you want, not necessarily just the best players.

Crucially, I had also done well enough in the preceding months to show I was competing at much the same level as the rest of the team.

I like to think I justified the belief they held in me. I holed the first putt of the 2004 Ryder Cup at the Oakland Hills Country Club in Michigan and I holed the last.

Being there on my own was a strange experience. I sat alone on the flight out and there was only one rail of clothes in my room. Yet, I never once felt isolated or separate from the team. I was surrounded by friends – Harrington, Clarke, Westwood, Jiménez, Björn, Langer – all of whom supported me, as did their wives. I had also been reunited with my caddie Alastair McLean for the all-important BMW International and I was delighted that he was going to continue to be by my side as we took on the Americans.

Alastair is a strong character and a good friend, and having seen me through those dark final holes at St Andrews in 2000 I knew he would be a hugely positive presence in the days ahead. There was a very strong bond across every element of that team and it helped me enormously, on and off the course.

At that time, I needed help on the course no less than anywhere else.

I must have given Bernhard Langer one hell of a scare when I told him, just before we set off for the States, that I was struggling badly with my swing. Not exactly what the Ryder Cup captain wants to hear from one of his two picks.

Why had my natural, smooth-tempo swing suddenly deserted me? I think it was probably because I felt under pressure to perform, to justify Langer's decision, to show it wasn't just because we were mates.

I suspect most picks feel something similar. Harrington did in 2010, I am certain. It is almost as if you have to be better than everybody else. That is definitely how it was for me. In the run-up to the event I began pressing too much and, before long, I was hitting the ball like a beginner.

Bernhard looked at me when we were out practising and called me across. 'It's your backswing, Colin. Let me see if I can help.' It was astonishing. A day before the competition was due to start and the Ryder Cup captain was giving me lessons. He followed me round for a while and then drew me to a halt. 'Okay, I think I've got it. Let's stop here and I'll show you.' And he was off, demonstrating how my take-away was causing the problem and offering technical advice on how to fix it. The leadership and patience he demonstrated that day were second to none.

Bernhard's diagnosis was accurate and his remedy effective. The only problem was that I didn't really have enough time to incorporate the change so that it became second nature. I had to think about it over every shot, rather than rely on it having soaked into the muscle memory.

You never want to be in the position of trying to correct a flaw mid-competition. Out of sight on the range is where that work should be conducted but, in my case, there was no choice. I had to keep Bernhard's advice to the forefront of my mind and hope for the best.

A key moment for me in that Ryder Cup, in fact a key moment for me in my career, came when Langer put me out with Padraig Harrington as the first pairing on the first morning – and that although he knew we would almost certainly face Tiger Woods and Phil Mickelson.

In many ways that single act of faith by Langer set me up for what happened in 2005. I respect Langer in everything he does and for him to have the confidence to put me up against the world's greatest golfer had a profound impact.

We all played well in that morning fourball. I had a spring in my step from the moment we walked out on to the first tee. I was relishing the challenge, relishing being back at the heart of European golf after too long an absence. This was where I wanted to be more than anywhere else on the planet and I wasn't going to blow it. My birdie at the first put us one up and, as I like to tell anyone who will listen, we were never level again. Padraig and I eventually beat the No. 1 and No. 2 players in the world 2 & 1.

That Ryder Cup can be summed up in that one word: confidence. In this case, it was a confidence which had its beginnings in the support I had received at Troon. It somehow reassured me that, whatever was going on in my personal life, people still liked me. I am not going to pretend otherwise: that mattered. It made me feel better about myself.

From there, it picked up all the time ... Langer made me one of his picks; he paired me with a partner with whom I was comfortable; and he set us up for an opening match against the game's dominant figures. After our morning results, our opponents in the afternoon foursomes, Fred Funk and Davis Love, didn't stand a chance.

A good demonstration of how I was feeling was apparent in the shot I played from the rough at the 8th. Three months previously, I'd have thought it was madness even to contemplate, but when Padraig's second rolled on a touch too far and left me with an impossibly awkward little chip, I didn't hesitate.

I realised there was no way I could go directly towards the hole – the slope on the green was too severe for that – so I played it backwards into the bank, hoping to kill it and let gravity take control. It seemed a simple decision at the time, but I would have felt a right idiot if I had made a hash of it. People would have thought I'd lost the plot completely. Fortunately, my plan worked.

The critical thing was to be positive – confidence again – and ensure that I hit the shot hard enough to allow it to gather enough momentum on the way down to the hole. It came to a rest inches from the cup.

Back in my room that night, after our 4 & 2 victory, I lay in bed reviewing the day's events. I can do this, I told myself. I might be on my own, but I can do this.

On the Saturday I think the emotion that had swept me along all summer, and which had carried me through two wins out of two the day before, took its toll. I was drained and could not produce the golf necessary to support Padraig in our fourball against Cink and Love. We lost 3 & 2 and, that afternoon, my record run of thirty consecutive individual Ryder Cup matches came to an end. I was rested and happily so.

Langer made the right call and I backed him completely. As I have said often throughout my career, the Ryder Cup is about the team, not about individuals, and it was right for the team that I sit out the afternoon foursomes. Frankly, I was knackered.

By the end of day two, Europe held a commanding lead, 11–5 and, while you can never rule out the US when it comes to the singles, we all knew that it was going to take a disaster of biblical proportions to mess up our defence of the trophy.

Much of the discussion in the locker room on the Sunday morning centred on where the hammer would fall. With Langer sending me out sixth, it wasn't impossible that I would be there or thereabouts when it came to the denouement, but such a scenario was far from my main focus as I headed off to face David Toms. First and foremost, I wanted to win a point for my team; second, I wanted to maintain my unbeaten singles run.

I knew Toms was going to be a tough opponent. He was a Major winner following his US PGA victory in 2001 and he had arrived at Oakland Hills on the back of an impressive display at the FedEx St Jude Classic in May, where he tore the field apart, taking the title by six shots.

Early on I fought my way to a two-hole lead, thanks in the main to my putting, but David came back at me and, by the 11th, we were all square. The ding-dong nature of the match continued through to the 16th, where I managed to sink a 15-footer to take the lead once again. I was one up with two to play and, when we halved the 17th, my relief was palpable. I could not be beaten: my record was intact. But the job in hand had still to be completed. Europe needed a point and I was determined to deliver.

It wasn't until I was standing over my third on the 18th, a long and tricky putt from off the back of the green, that I sensed this could be the moment. Teeing off on that final hole I had known Europe must be close to winning: I did not know the exact state of play but the atmosphere around the green left me in no doubt. A point was required to complete our second victory in a row and I was in a strong position to secure it.

David was still 15 feet away after his chip and, when my putt stopped four feet away it looked for all the world as if I would have two for the match. My opponent, however, had not read the script. He drilled home his putt with considerable courage, leaving me in a position where I had to hole.

As I stood over the ball, my mind was suddenly flooded with unwanted thoughts.

This was not the moment to be contemplating what this would mean for Bernhard Langer, how it would justify his decision to pick me. This was not the moment to be questioning whether it was left to right or straight. This was not the moment to begin worrying about my tendency to glance up too soon.

Concentrate, Colin. You have been putting well all week. One more, that's all you need.

As with so many putts, if the first foot is on line and at the right pace, you know it is going to be good. With my head locked in position, I pulled the club head away and stroked it through the ball. The first foot was on line. The pace was good.

The ball in the hole, I became aware of a wave of European cheers. I turned towards the noise and clenched both fists in celebration and relief. A moment such as this had seemed impossible to imagine throughout the barren year of 2003 when I could barely string two shots together. Now, here I was, the lucky so-and-so who happened to be in the right place at the right time to seal the Ryder Cup victory. It was a team effort, no question, but I did enjoy my moment in the sun.

I have one regret, however. I should have shaken the hand of my opponent first. David and I had been engaged in a fantastic battle which was played in a wonderful spirit and I should have turned to him before anyone else. Amid the emotion of it all, I made the mistake of going straight to Bernhard. There is more to golf than merely hitting a ball in a straight line and occasionally winning. I forgot that at Oakland Hills. I hope David understands.

I said afterwards that it didn't matter who holed the winning putt and I meant it. It was a team effort, everyone playing his part. To emphasise as much, it is not even 100 per cent certain the moment was mine. Back on the 15th, almost simultaneously, Ian Poulter had guaranteed a half-point against Chris Riley. With the half I already had in the bag, that would have secured the European victory.

I happened to be the focus of attention, but it could just as well have been Ian. With considerable grace, Ian insisted that the winning stroke was mine as his game was not yet over. I appreciated that gesture very much, but I will say it one more time: it was a team effort.

When the dust had settled, Bernhard Langer gave me a memento that I will cherish for years to come. The flag from the 18th green, signed by all the players, plus Langer himself. It had been rescued from the green by Lee Westwood's caddie and passed around for everyone to write a message. To quote a few: 'No. 1!!!' (Darren Clarke); 'You're the bollocks!' (Ian Poulter); 'This team would be nothing without you' (Sergio García); 'To Monty – my great partner in crime' (Bernhard Langer); 'We all owe you,

Monty. Thanks!' (Paul McGinley); 'You're my hero' (Paul Casey). It is something very special.

*

There were no further highs in 2004 but, despite that, my confidence remained intact as I prepared for 2005.

I set my sights once again on breaking into the Top 50 and was prepared to travel the world to that end. My attitude was very much to view 2004 as a springboard. I'd proved to myself I could compete with the best of them at the Caltex, the Scandinavian and the BMW International, as well as at the Ryder Cup.

At Oakland Hills, others had believed in me; now it was my turn to believe in myself. 'Come on, Colin. You can do this. Eighty-first in the world is ridiculous. Your back is fine, you have no ties to speak of. It is time to get on with your golf.'

13 | MAJORS?

Lots of other people who have finished second behind Tiger Woods will have had the feeling that they were winners. I know that that is how it was for me when I was a runner-up to him at St Andrews in the Open of 2005.

Why did I do so well? It was down to a variety of things. My game was there, the support was amazing and my desire was as keen as it had ever been following my second place in the European Open a fortnight previously. In fact, I was not only thinking that I was about to break back into Europe's top ten; I had my eye on the Order of Merit which I had not won since 1999.

Hitting my opening drive into the Swilken was hardly the start I had in mind. I had never done that before and I left the green with a watery and horribly public bogey. 'You idiot,' I said to myself. 'You absolute idiot.' A few years earlier and that same phrase might have been ringing in my ears for the first five or six holes. On this occasion, I somehow shrugged off my anger straight away and concentrated on the holes ahead. I opened with a 71 and followed it up with a 66 to find myself playing alongside Tiger in the third round.

As had applied back on the Saturday of the 1997 Masters, I could not stop watching him, only this time I kept my own game together rather better than I had done at Augusta, when I handed in a 74 to his 65. This time, I was round in 70 to his 71.

I was only three behind going into Sunday and was even better placed after nine holes. But that was when Tiger moved up a gear and returned a 70 against my 72 to finish five ahead. The better player had won and rightly so.

The support I received throughout the week at St Andrews was out of this world. I was cheered and applauded at every corner.

My other near-misses in Majors were not such cheerful affairs ...

The first of them came in the US Open of 1992 at Pebble Beach. That was when I was the clubhouse leader after completing a third-round 70 for a 288, level par aggregate.

'Congratulations on being our national champion,' said Jack Nicklaus in the on-course CBS broadcasting studio.

Unfortunately for me, Jack was a little ahead of himself with his congratulations in that Tom Kite and Jeff Slumen were still doing battle with the dreadful conditions.

Jack reiterated what he had said when I was taken to the studio for an interview and, the interview over, I retired to the Pebble Beach Lodge to watch the final few holes on TV. As I made my way to my room, almost everyone I met echoed Jack's words, assuring me that I was a certainty for a play-off at the very least.

Kite and Slumen were magnificent that day. True, they benefited from the wind slacking off a little, but the main reason they overtook me was because they played great golf in what were still thoroughly trying conditions. When they finished, Tom was three ahead of me and Jeff one.

My overriding feelings as I watched them were of mingled admiration and resignation. But because of what Jack had said, there was this terrible sense of let-down that would not go away. All I could do was to try and convince myself that my time would come, that it was early in my career and that it was purely a matter of staying patient.

Two years on from Pebble Beach, again in the US Open, I went one better, tying for second with Lauren Roberts behind Ernie Els after a three-way, eighteen-hole play-off. My golf had been a little erratic that week in that I followed a second-round 65 with a 74 but, overall, I had been happy with how I performed over the four days. It's just that when I came to the Monday play-off, I had nothing left in the tank. Try as I might, I couldn't raise my game and came in four shots adrift.

Ernie was my nemesis again at the Congressional Country Club in 1997. After winning at Slaley Hall the previous week, I had an endless drive back to London and no sleep at all on the Sunday night. Again, thanks to my fear of flying, I had no prospect of getting any rest on the transatlantic crossing.

The high of Slaley Hall helped me to an opening round 65 but the next day I was a weary eleven shots more.

In the final round, where I was playing alongside Ernie, I had a putt on the 17th green to stay tied for the lead but delayed taking it in what was a futile attempt to wait for the spectators to keep quiet. Doubt crept in, as it always does. I missed the putt and I lost by one.

As Ernie would say later, the American crowd were not too concerned as to whether we had any peace or not. Indeed, we had learned at one point in the round that Bill Clinton had turned up at Congressional in anticipation of presenting an American with the trophy, only to depart when he learned that the winner might be Ernie or myself.

How that loss hurt.

In the US PGA championship, I had my best chance of winning the famous Wannamaker Trophy at Riviera in 1997. There, I birdied the final three holes, sinking a 25-foot putt on the last to force a sudden-death play-off with Steve Elkington.

Heading back to that 18th tee, I was the heavy, heavy favourite because of the way I had just finished my fourth round. I, too, believed I was going to win and duly set about playing the hole as I had done twenty minutes earlier.

My drive almost ended up in the divot I had left at the 72nd and my eight-iron was dead on line, though it stopped a little sooner than I had anticipated, about 20 feet short of the pin.

Steve's ball was outside mine but he had the easier route to the hole. He made his putt, I missed – and all I could do was congratulate him.

That's the game, but I'd be lying if I didn't admit that that was one more Major shock as far as I was concerned.

I truly believed the title would be mine but, looking back, I wonder if that birdie, birdie, birdie finish was my undoing. The adrenalin had stopped pumping and maybe that is why that eight-iron stopped short.

*

Going back to my second place at St Andrews ten years later, I felt hugely heartened in the wake of that week and, by the time it came to the Dunhill Links championship of that year, my Order of Merit plans were entirely realistic – and that applied still more after I had handed in a 65 at St Andrews, my course for the second day. (The Dunhill is played over all three of Kingsbarns, Carnoustie and St Andrews, with the last-mentioned in use for a second time on the final day.)

Autumn on the east coast of Scotland can be unpredictable, to put it mildly, even if mildly is hardly the right word. It was cold and blustery, which normally goes against me but not that day. I followed birdies on the first, second and third with an eagle three on the fifth, where I holed a 40-footer. Six under after six on the most famous course of them all was the stuff of dreams.

Over the years, as I have noted elsewhere, it has been my putting which has let me down and, all too often, the Old Course had exaggerated that weakness. What helped in that 65 was that my iron-play was gloriously on song over those first six holes.

I only managed one more birdie that day, but if I tell you that the average score for the second round at St Andrews was 73.5, you will understand why I was so elated with my performance.

I went into the third round – this one at Carnoustie – leading Kenneth Ferrie by one, and walked off the 18th green five shots adrift. To many, Kenneth's 67 compared to my 73 seemed to have scuppered my chances, only I did not see it like that.

For the final round, we were back to the Old Course, which felt like an old friend. The weather was pretty wretched but the fairways were lined with warm support and I knew anything could happen.

I got off to a good start with a birdie at the 2nd to reduce the deficit to four but, in a see-sawing first twelve holes, first Kenneth dropped three shots before I followed suit.

The key moment came on the 15th where I snatched a birdie to Kenneth's bogey to put us on an equal footing with three to play. That was still the case as we teed up at the 18th. That's when the confidence which had been flowing through my veins since the Ryder Cup made its presence felt as I tackled one of the more notorious accident black spots in golf, the Valley of Sin.

My approach finished three feet from the hole and I made the putt for a birdie. When Kenneth failed to improve on his par, I had won what was my twenty-ninth Tour victory.

There is a pro-am format at the Dunhill and my playing partner for the week had been Michael Douglas. He was super company and definitely helped me to stay relaxed, especially during the last round. I think he was as thrilled as I was when my three-footer went to ground, because he rushed over and gave me a hug.

It was a lovely moment but his win over cancer tops anything I have ever achieved on the golf course.

If there is one thing I learned that day it is that there can be few things better in life than to be a Scotsman sinking the winning putt on the 18th green of the Old Course. The crowd went wild.

As I drove back to London that night, I realised that the positives in my life were gathering force.

*

Following my Dunhill victory, New Zealander Michael Campbell came very much into my sights. He was leading the Order of Merit, having won the US Open and the World Match Play, and I was on a mission to overtake him and stay ahead of him.

The overtaking was something I would achieve a week later when I tied for third place behind Tiger at the WGC-American Express championship at Harding Park, San Francisco.

When it came to the Volvo Masters at Valderrama, which was still the last tournament of the season at that point, all I had to do was to stay ahead of Michael.

I left nothing to chance, arriving in Spain with my full complement of helpers – Alastair McLean, Denis Pugh, Hugh Mantle and Guy Kinnings. Throughout the week, I was constantly being informed of Michael's progress. As a team, that was our focus, more so even than winning the tournament, which I think goes a long way to explain how I blew a two-shot halfway lead to finish in a tie for third. Third was not good in those circumstances but I was four ahead of Michael and the Order of Merit was mine.

Winning that eighth Order of Merit meant more to me than the seven in a row. Throughout those years from 1993 to 1999, I had expected to win and I did. I didn't really contemplate any other outcome.

When that period came to an end and my ranking, along with my personal life, began to nose-dive, people were starting to write me off for good. Thankfully, they were wrong. I had many darker moments, that's for sure, but I never really lost faith in my ability. Somewhere inside was the golfer I had been.

I had worried lest I couldn't unearth it again but, when I succeeded, the sense of achievement was like nothing else I had ever known as an individual.

That the 2005 OM Trophy stands on a shelf above the rest tells its own story.

*

The 2005 season may have been over but not the year. In December, I travelled to Hong Kong for the UBS Open and came away with an early Christmas present, my thirtieth Tour title. It had been an amazing year and I looked forward to 2006 with considerable enthusiasm. World No. 8, European No. 1: I was in good shape.

On to the US Open at Winged Foot and the Major near-miss which can still wake me up in the middle of the night.

To this day, if there was one shot in my career I could take again – and have taken again a million times in my mind's eye – it would be my seven-iron from the 18th fairway in the fourth round. It will probably go down in the golfing annals as my fifth and last chance of Major glory.

I travelled to Mamaroneck, NY, in June with my confidence still high. The first half of the year may not have matched the dizzy heights of 2005 but four top-ten finishes were enough in themselves to prove that the previous year had not been a flash in the pan. I also knew that the US Open, as per usual, was the best place to capture that elusive Major. Wherever it was staged, the course was always set up to favour straight hitting, something I regarded as the backbone of my game, both off the tee and from the fairway.

Winged Foot was particularly good news. It suited my eye in much the same way as most of those other old-established courses in America's North-East, courses like Oak Hill, Pine Valley, Brookline and Shinnecock Hills.

Apart from the above, the details of my divorce had by then been finalised – and that was a massive relief.

The first event of note in that US Open of 2006 was that Tiger, who had lost his father shortly before, missed the cut. It was the first time since he had turned professional that he had not been involved in the last two days of a Major. He had been so dominant for so long that I think we all sat up and said, 'Hang on, we've got a chance here.' I know my belief soared, while I was also conscious that the lack of wind was no bad thing from my point of view.

Three shots off the lead going into the final round, I pushed on and found myself coming through the field as all sorts of quality players fell by the wayside, a common occurrence in a US Open. I managed to sink a fantastic birdie putt on the 17th from something like 45 feet and then, would you believe, there was my name at the top of the leader board alongside that of Phil Mickelson, who was a hole behind.

It was a short walk to the 18th tee and I had to settle myself down. Alastair McLean, my trusty caddie, was there with me. Alastair had been a great help all week, keeping me focused and relaxed and, as I prepared to take one of the most important holes in my career, I felt good.

I hit a sweet tee shot down the right-hand side, which was vital as the trees on the left close down your approach if you stray in that direction. Position A. So much so, it won the European Tour's Canon Shot of the Month award.

I put my driver away. I had done the hard bit. I knew the pin was positioned to the right-hand side of the green, which would favour my fade. I couldn't have asked for anything better. The strength of my game has always been my iron-play. Surely, all that was required now was a simple seven-iron.

Then my playing companion, Vijay Singh, hit his drive.

Position Z. It ended up in the woods on the left, somewhere among the hospitality tents and required a ruling. The referee was called out and it must have been a good quarter of an hour later that Vijay finally played his second.

Throughout this delay, I had been standing over my ball and thinking. Thinking too much.

In hindsight, I shouldn't have waited. I should just have played my shot. It would have been perfectly justified and well within the rules of the game, but protocol suggests you wait for your playing partner if his ball is behind yours.

By the time it was my turn, I was beginning to second-guess myself. Was it a seven-iron? Was it not a six? Was it a big seven-iron or a little one? Did I detect a touch of wind?

They say that he who hesitates is lost and the phrase could not have been more apposite. I settled on the seven-iron but the swing was hesitant, one in which I never got the club fully back. Damn, damn and damn again. I knew it was bad from the moment I made contact. The shot was heavy and finished in rough to the side of the putting surface.

It was playable, but I had to come out sideways across the green. In my mind, I was still in the hunt. I could get up and down from there. I hacked out and left myself with a monster of a downhill putt. I thought I hit it well and, to this day, I don't know how it rolled 12 feet past. The return for a five would have put me in a play-off. Instead, I walked off with a double bogey six.

In the four other Majors in which I was runner-up, I had been beaten. In such circumstances, you shake hands with the opposition and say, 'Well played.' This time around, I beat myself. I was good enough to win and I blew it. It was my fault and it was almost certainly my last chance. Yes, Winged Foot hurts badly and always will.

I know it is illogical to put it down to that one shot, the seven-iron, when there were 285 others, a couple of which I could surely have done without. The double bogey at the third in round three? But that is not how I can see it. It is that seven-iron that robbed me of my Major. Fair enough, if it had been a three-iron to an island green and it had been windy, hard and bouncy. Anyone could mess that up. But this was bread and butter to me. Everything was playing to my strengths.

Why did I hesitate on that backswing? I don't exactly know anything more beyond the fact that my mind certainly wasn't clear. I knew at the time that I had hesitated. It would have been possible to pull out of the swing since it wasn't complete and that's what I should have done. Stopped, regrouped and started all over again.

Easy to say but almost impossible to do. If I had, I would have won the US Open. There you go.

Phil Mickelson did exactly the same as me in double-bogeying the last, all of which meant that Ogilvie's par, par finish was good enough.

I had a very bad flight home that night. I remember sitting there in a daze, not knowing what to say or do. I wasn't crying. I had gone beyond that. I was incapable of any analysis. The same three words, 'What just happened?', kept going through my head.

A number of the people on the flight had been watching the final few holes on the television in the airport lounge. None of them said anything to me and, if a little belatedly, I would like to thank them for that.

Even the press were looking at rather more than the presumably very readable golfing disaster story they had on their hands. My life was beginning to come right, I was on the point of getting the result I craved and, at the eleventh hour, my hopes had been dashed.

Putting aside the Ryder Cup and my eight Order of Merits, I will always be Colin Montgomerie who failed to win a Major.

I can live with that.

There are, of course, different ways of saying these things, and for myself I have always found the media's kind take on the situation altogether more palatable. 'Colin Montgomerie, the best player never to have won a Major.'

14 | THE PERFECT EIGHTEEN

I may never win a Major but how I would warm to the task of designing a course built with a Major in mind. That would be quite something. You strive for perfection every time you start out on a new project but, when you think about it, the perfect golf course does not exist.

Mother Nature is not that kind and her work should not be unduly tampered with in an attempt to force golfing perfection on to natural beauty. In all the courses that I have designed over the years – eleven currently in play, in locations as diverse as Wales, Turkey, Scotland, Malaysia, Vietnam and Dubai, and two more under construction, in the Netherlands and China – I have always been very aware of working with the existing contours rather than fighting them. If I had to identify one guiding principle that I hope is evident in all my courses, that would be it. However, there are additional elements which I also believe should be very much at the forefront of all course design. Unfortunately, I am not sure they always are.

A golf course should be able to satisfy the needs of the amateur and the professional in equal measure. For amateurs it has to deliver on two levels. First, it has to be a good experience: it is people's leisure time we are talking about and that should never be forgotten. Secondly, the course should be enough of a challenge to lure the amateur back, sometimes to meet and overcome the challenge, sometimes to be defeated by it.

For the professional, I don't believe the course should be set up in such a way that low scoring is more or less out of the question. In my view, the golfing public want to see the occasional record being slashed, always provided – and this is key – that every aspect of the professional's game has come under scrutiny.

Every club in the bag should be brought into play over eighteen holes. To win, you should be required to prove you can overcome the shortcomings in your game rather than hide them from view.

The biggest mistake in modern course design – and I have been guilty of it myself in the past – is making courses too long. Because the modern golfer can hit the ball so far, thanks to his own superior fitness and to the equipment he has at his disposal, designers are often under the impression that the best antidote is to make the holes longer. For myself, I do not believe that that has to be the case. Once again, look to nature first. Think of how much can change on a course overnight, let alone from spring to summer, from autumn to winter.

From one morning to the next, the wind can pick up or drop, the sun can bake the bunkers, the rain can prevent the ball from running on; the rough can grow, the trees can shed their leaves, the greens can dry out and the fairways can get heavy.

With careful thought and attention, it is perfectly possible to work with the elements to help create a course that is both short and tricky, forcing players not merely to hit the ball as far as they can, but to think about where they are hitting it, what the next shot will be and how they will avoid the hazards around the green. When they do arrive on the putting surfaces, the surfaces should be both hard and fast. That's the way to force the best out of the modern golfer, instead of merely making him walk further. At which point, I should mention the extent to which

I dislike those courses where you have to walk miles between a green and the next tee. Golf was never meant to be like that.

As I indicated at the beginning of this chapter, Mother Nature has not blessed any single course with topography suitably diverse to allow the construction of eighteen holes, each of which represents the best of its kind in the world – the perfect course. However, if such a tract of land did exist, I believe it would look something like this ...

Tenth at Sunningdale Old Course, Surrey

You hit your drive downhill and your second uphill. It is a very strong par four which, though it measures in the region of 475 yards, mostly plays at about 420 because of the slope which can send your tee shot bounding down the slope. If I were to be restricted to one British course for the rest of my time, it would have to be Sunningdale Old.

I'd take my golden retriever – some kind of dog seems to be a prerequisite at Sunningdale – and I'd carry my clubs in a small bag. Simply put, this course is a glorious place to be. There's beauty, solitude and space – and that despite the fact that it is only twenty minutes or so from Heathrow.

Eighth at the Emirates, Dubai

I won the Dubai Desert Classic at the Emirates in 1996 but, as much as anything, I have loved studying the way the venue has developed over the last ten to fifteen years. At one point, there was desert all around – sand to the left, the right and straight ahead. Before too long, there were a couple of skyscrapers at which you could aim your ball and then, a couple of years later, there seemed to be dozens of them. It was all very confusing.

The world around the Emirates may be changing fast, but the 8th hole remains constant – an excellent, 434-yard dog-leg, with the drive playing downhill and the second uphill. Any time you make a four here, as opposed to making a bogey or, worse, via the desert, you walk off happy.

Second at Castle Stuart, the Scottish Highlands

I suspect I am influenced by the fact that I eagled this 550-yard par five twice during the course of the 2011 Scottish Open. But it is a genuinely great hole, one asking a lot of excellent questions.

You have to fade your drive into the right-hand side of the fairway and, when it comes to your second, you need pinpoint accuracy to hit to what is a dramatic 60-yard-long green.

The opportunities to make an eagle come with significant perils. If you are off by a whisker, you will find yourself either in the Moray Firth on the right, down the slopes on the left, or in the bunker at the back. It is a real risk/reward hole and that's why it appeals so much: you have to weigh up the conditions, your form and how you are striking the ball before you decide to go for it or not.

Eighth at Royal Troon: 'The Postage Stamp'

No wonder they call this 'The Postage Stamp'. The hole is very tiny, very perfect. If you hit a good shot and it sticks, you wonder what all the fuss is about. The legendary Gene Sarazen obviously didn't find it particularly tough. At the age of seventy-one, this winner of seven Majors played in the 1973 Open at Troon and had an ace at the 8th on the Thursday and a two on the Friday when he holed out from sand.

You only have to be fractionally off-line to watch your ball being gathered up in one of the yawning bunkers and, unless your bunker play is as hot as Sarazen's, you can end up hitting from one trap to another.

'The Postage Stamp' is the shortest hole in championship golf in Britain, 123 yards of pure hell and a potential card wrecker. It is the best illustration I know of that old saying that par threes don't have to be long to be good.

Twelfth at the Montgomerie Links, Da Nang, Vietnam

Having overcome any reservations I felt about including a hole from Carton House in my Perfect Eighteen, I am now opting for a second Montgomerie-designed hole, the 527-yard par-five 12th at Da Nang. It's a signature hole which works particularly well. Though it is reachable in two for a professional and three or four for an amateur, it has a well-protected green which can be maddeningly difficult to hit and hold.

Da Nang won awards as the best new course in a region comprising Cambodia, Laos, Vietnam, Thailand and Burma, and I am extremely proud of that recognition.

With all the distressing history and images that the name 'Vietnam' can conjure up, I have found it hugely inspiring to be involved in a bit of this wonderful country's progress. It is an honour to have a course bearing my name in Vietnam and one where we have created an academy for local youngsters. We are providing opportunities and experiences they might never otherwise have had and you can guarantee that there will be plenty of children who will make the most of them.

Thirteenth at Pine Valley, New Jersey

Pine Valley is the No. 1 ranked course in the world and has been for the past twenty years. I was lucky enough to play the Walker Cup here in 1985 and, to me, the 13th hole – it was Bobby Jones's favourite par four in the world – epitomises what the course is all about.

It currently measures 448 yards and calls for a drive down the right-hand side of the fairway. From there, you take aim on a green which is entirely large enough to accept your four- or five-iron. However, if you go left or big, you are dead.

To me, this is America's Sunningdale Old, similar in style and built around the same time. If I were still at the top of my game, which unfortunately I am not, this would be my No. 1 choice of course.

Seventeenth at Carton House, County Kildare

This is a course I designed back in 2004 and we have held two Nissan Irish Opens there, in 2005 and 2006 – something I saw as a great honour. I am perhaps a bit biased because of my input but the 17th worked out better than I would have dreamed possible.

It is a par three bordering the River Liffey with a pretty boathouse on the far side. The hole is stunning to look at but tricky to play. For me, it's a seven-iron to catch a green which is well protected by bunker and slopes off to the left at the front.

I always like a false front to a green to ensure that the player cannot get away with less than a good shot. Finding that good shot is the big ask. I am obviously a bit nervous about including a hole in my top eighteen from a course I have designed, but I genuinely believe it is worth its place.

Eighteenth at Valderrama, Spain: 'Casa Club'

This is a 454-yard hole on a course which brings back a lot of happy memories and will for ever hold a special place in my heart.

Not only was it the scene of our Ryder Cup victory of 1997 but I've twice won the Volvo Masters here. To me, the 18th captures the course as a whole. It is very tight off the tee and you have got to hit the fairway with your driver or three-wood, but not just anywhere.

If you go right, even if you remain on the fairway, your second will be blocked by the trees. You have to stay left, which gives you a line into the green but still leaves you with a lot of work to do. From the fairway, you need a seven- or an eight-iron to the elevated green and, here again, your shot needs to be 100 per cent.

That is what the whole course is about: precision. It is quite simply a great hole to finish a course which was deservedly ranked No. 1 in Europe for many years.

Eighteenth at Pebble Beach, California

This isn't necessarily one of the greatest holes in golf, but it is worthy of its place in my dream course because of its situation. In my opinion there is none better, with the Pacific Ocean crashing against the sea wall. It was here, incidentally, that competitors in the US Open of 2000 drove into the water at an eve-of-championship ceremony to mark the passing of Payne Stewart, the winner of the 1999 US Open. Payne, as I have already written, was the victim of an air crash at the end of that summer.

The views on this 543-yard par five are awesome and never fail to put me in mind of Turnberry in particular and Scotland's west coast in general.

Tenth at Turnberry, Ayrshire: 'Dinna Fouter'

You can't talk about golf in Britain without mentioning the No. 1 ranked course in the country: the Ailsa Course at Turnberry. The new back tee at the 457-yard 10th – it was put in for the 2009 Open – is a real success. It takes you even closer to the roar of the Atlantic, while simultaneously offering more dramatic views of both Ailsa Craig and the Heads of Ayr.

Perhaps it is best described as being a 'Beauty and the Beast' hole – stunning to look at but fully capable of murdering a scorecard.

Fifteenth at Golf National, Versailles

Now we go back to the Ryder Cup, but fast-forward in time to 2018 and this wonderful course in France where the event will be held. This is one of the players' favourites on the European Tour: everyone wants to play and win here.

The 497-yard 15th kicks off what is arguably the best finishing run we have on the circuit and I suspect that this stretch of French countryside will prove to be the highlight of the clash in seven years' time. I see the 15th as a 'sleeper' hole, initially benign but with lethal capabilities. It is a three-wood off the tee to a fairway position that requires no more than an eight-iron into a green which is surrounded by water. Suddenly there is no bail-out: you have to go for it.

Exactly what you want in match play.

Twelfth at Augusta, Georgia: 'Golden Bell'

You can't consider Augusta and not think about this 155-yard par three. If the pin's at the front, it is a wedge, and if it's at the back, it is an eight-iron. The green is set at an angle, which is what makes it so difficult. The further right you go, the more you are likely to be troubled by Rae's Creek, which swings around in front. A dramatically picturesque hole for the patrons and a dramatic hole, full stop, for the players. You are always happy to arrive on the 13th tee unscathed. A par represents a job well done.

Seventh at Loch Lomond, Scotland

On a personal level, Loch Lomond holds incredibly happy memories. As I describe later, Gaynor and I married here in 2008. On the Saturday morning, I played the 8th hole – a pretty par three in front of Lomond House – eighteen times with our guests as each party in turn came past in the early-morning competition we had arranged for them. I could play that little hole for ever without getting fed up with it but I have opted for the 402-yard dog-leg 7th for my Perfect Eighteen. The hole is stunning but relentlessly tough, with the loch flanking the right-hand side of the fairway before curling in behind the back of the green.

After threading your drive through two trees and a bunker, you have to take positive aim with your second. You cannot afford to be too short, too right or too big.

Sixteenth at Celtic Manor, Wales

How could I talk about my favourite eighteen holes of golf and not include Celtic Manor? The 500-yard 16th has to be the hole for me, the one where Graeme McDowell secured the point we needed to win the Ryder Cup. Yet it also happens to be the best hole on the course.

You have to split two bunkers with your drive before tackling a downhill second to the green.

But what am I going on about …? If you want to know how to play it properly, I suggest you turn to your 2010 Ryder Cup DVD, if you have one, and watch how that brave Ulsterman made his birdie.

Fifth at Augusta, Georgia: 'Magnolia'

This 455-yard par four brings back great memories. I have had two eagles here during the Masters and, considering my record in the tournament, they were moments to savour. It is a great driving hole, the best line down the right-hand side to give you a shot into a green that does everything it can to shrug off your ball. The firmness of the putting surface and, more often than not, the pin position, do not embrace a five- or six-iron coming in at speed. That's what makes it so great. You have got to do a lot with the ball to hold it up and give yourself a chance. Anyone who makes a par is doing well.

Seventeenth at the Tournament Players' Club, Sawgrass, Florida: 'Island Green'

This really is an island green, with the nicely rounded putting surface rearing from the lake on a wall of railway sleepers. In fact, it is the first real island green that the architect Pete Dye created.

One of the reasons the hole is so fearsome and dramatic is that, if you mess up here, there is no time to save your round and get back on track. At only 135 yards, it calls for a nine-iron to the back of the green or a wedge to the front.

There is nowhere to lay up; you have got to hit the putting surface or you are sunk, quite literally. Some people don't like this hole, but I think it is great – and that although I have missed the green on several occasions. At the Players' championship, there are spectators who head straight for this hole, complete with lunchboxes, and never budge all day. They love seeing people – especially non-Americans – ending up in the depths. There's a touch of ghoulishness about their love of a good golfing mishap but I have to admit it's fun. The atmosphere around that hole is unique.

Seventeenth at the Old Course, St Andrews: 'Road Hole'

Once again, you can't talk about the very best of golf and not include this course and the now 490-yard 17th. If you designed it today, you would be shot. Playing over a hotel? Navigating an old railway shed? With a road at the back of the green? Come on!

But it works and is probably one of the most loved and talked about holes in world golf. It is really all to do with the second shot. Once you have hopefully negotiated your drive over the hotel wall (as if that is an everyday event on a championship course), it is decision time, and I like that.

Do you go for the pin over the treacherous bunker? Do you go short right? Big left? Play a hit and run? To be honest, I don't know what you are supposed to do, and that is the beauty of it. I won Shot of the Month here when I captured the 2005 Dunhill Links. On that occasion, I hit an eight-iron out of the left-hand rough and I drew it round to about 20 feet from the hole. I won the event because of that shot, which set me on my way to my eighth Order of Merit.

It was a shot to remember on a hole with a gloriously rich history.

The Road Hole Bunker on the green's front left has taken on a life of its own. In 2011, for the first time, HSBC built a replica of this infamous trap in their HSBC Golf Zone at Royal St George's and 6,939 fanatics tried their hand at getting out. Gary Player, the best bunker player of them all, hit to within a couple of inches of the hole at his first attempt. Me? I wasn't that close but I was the proud recipient of one of the certificates they gave to everyone who caught the green. It was fun.

One way and another, this is a hole which makes me very proud to be Scottish. I know the course was designed by Tom Weiskopf, an American, but he could not have done a better job in marrying our Royal and Ancient game to the best of Scottish landscapes.

Eighteenth at Gleneagles King's Course, Perthshire: 'King's Hame'

I haven't picked any holes here from the PGA Centenary course, where the 2014 Ryder Cup will be staged, but I have gone for this wonderful 525-yard par five on the King's Course.

I wish it were possible to somehow transport over to the Centenary, because the amphitheatre as you come over the saddle down towards the clubhouse creates an incredible sense of drama. And one worthy of the closing stages of any Ryder Cup.

In many ways, it encapsulates match-play golf, the one-on-one gladiatorial battle coming down to the final showdown. Every hole on the King's Course and the Queen's is super but, if I were forced to pick just one, it would have to be this 18th. It is one of the best I have ever played and it means a lot to me personally in that it has been the scene of two good, as opposed to disappointing, second-place finishes.

Before moving on, it is worth mentioning that the 18th hole on the Centenary Course could be altogether stronger by the time of the Ryder Cup. Jack Nicklaus, the original course designer, has been involved in its reinvention.

It will be reduced from 533 to 513 yards to make it a more reachable par five and will start from a set of elevated and more uplifting tees. If it is not a contradiction in terms, the green will become a cosier cauldron for the crucial putts you can get on the home hole in a Ryder Cup. It is taking a shift to the right and dipping down 1.6 metres into the surrounding hillocks.

At the time of writing, there is a lot of earth being shifted and the signs are good.

15 | TEARS, HUGS, CIGARS AND A FIRST DANCE

The 2006 Ryder Cup at the K Club, County Kildare, belonged to Darren Clarke.

He had lost his wife, Heather, to breast cancer a month before the tournament. Heather was well known in the world of golf and extremely popular. She was a lovely woman, a great mother and a super wife to Darren. She is greatly missed by everyone on the Tour.

Darren was one of Ian Woosnam's two picks that year (Lee Westwood was the other). It was a big call for Ian because, with Heather's death coming so close to the start of the tournament, it was going to be asking a lot of Darren to be able to cope with the swell of emotion he was bound to face. Yet, without question, it was the correct call. I think Ian's decision was partly based on the fact that Ireland was hosting the event. He could picture the emotion working for Darren rather than the reverse – and he sensed that the team would benefit from having him in their midst.

Woosnam was a brilliant captain. He was very aware of the powerful feelings there were towards Darren from every quarter. Normally the captain is the focal point of the team, but in 2006, Woosie, as we call him, was entirely happy that the spotlight should be firmly fixed on Darren.

We talked about Heather a lot, celebrating her life. Understandably, Darren was very fragile, but he was determined to do his best, not least for Heather, who had wanted him to be there, and for his two wonderful sons. As a team, we went out of our way to protect him at the dinners, during the practice rounds and in the heat of the matches themselves.

But he was no passenger. I played with him a couple of times in practice and he was hitting the ball well. He was in the team on merit.

When his name was announced at the opening ceremony, there was a massive cheer, which I hope he saw as support for what was going on in his life, but also as recognition of him as a golfer. He deserved it.

For the Friday morning fourballs, Darren was partnered with his old friend Lee Westwood. That was another example of Woosie's excellent captaincy. It may have been obvious to match the two of them, but it still had to happen and Ian made sure that it did. Padraig Harrington and I were out first, against Woods and Furyk, and, although it looked as though we were getting off to a grand start when Tiger drove his ball into a lake that I had not even noticed, we never really got going. We missed too many gettable putts and, even if we only lost on the last green, we were never really in the match.

Darren and Lee were out last, facing Phil Mickelson and Chris DiMarco. Although I wasn't there at the time I have watched Darren's drive off that first tee on a number of occasions and I still do not know how he managed it. The tears were streaming down his cheeks. Westwood was in a similar state and he was supposed to be lending support. The fact that the two of them got their act together to go on and win was a truly remarkable achievement.

Woosie's initial plan had been to send Darren and Lee out again in the afternoon. It made sense, especially because they had won, but when I saw Darren sitting in the locker room on his own after completing his victory, it was clear there was no way he could take any further part in the day's proceedings.

He was emotionally drained and needed time on his own to recover. Ian recognised this and asked if I would take Darren's place alongside Westwood for the foursomes, with Padraig hooking up with Paul McGinley. I told Ian I would be more than happy to do as much, but that I wanted to speak to Darren first. It had to be his decision whether to play or not. I had no intention of taking his place without such a discussion.

Darren agreed without hesitation. He knew in himself that he would find it almost impossible to refocus.

In the end, Lee and I bagged a good half-point against Mickelson and DiMarco, but it went to the wire. One down with one to play, I hit the green – just – with my three-wood second on the par-five 18th, the ball coming to rest about three miles from the pin. Well, at least 100 feet away. It was a monster of a putt but not one which, in normal circumstances, would have bothered Lee overmuch.

The problem was that he hadn't hit a putt since the 5th. That can happen in foursomes play and when Lee mentioned it to me as we were walking up the fairway, there wasn't much I could say other than, 'Don't worry, the greens have changed pace in the last couple of hours. Just get it as near as you can.' Not terribly helpful, but it was the best I could do.

Lee's putt ran about eight feet past. The Americans, meantime, were in a bunker on the right. Mickelson chipped out to about 20 feet and DiMarco missed the putt.

So it was down to me to make our eight-footer to tie our match and keep Europe's lead at 4–3 at a time when Luke Donald and Sergio García were still out on the course battling Woods and Furyk.

There's no question that I felt a degree of extra pressure because I knew it should have been Darren standing over that putt. Instead, he was offering support from the side of the green and I was determined that we would come away from the match with something – for him. The stroke was sound, the putt dropped and I can remember feeling nothing but relief as we shook hands with Phil and Chris.

All attention then turned to Donald and García, who made a brilliant fist of winning at the last. Europe had lost only one match all day (Padraig's and mine) and the 5–3 scoreline made for a happy team room that evening.

The next day followed a similar pattern. Darren played in the morning with Westwood and beat Woods and Furyk again, and I played in the afternoon with Lee, halving with Chad Campbell and Vaughn Taylor. I had not played in the morning fourballs and it did not bother me in the least. It wasn't a case of being 'dropped'; it was more to do with our team being the strongest Europe had ever assembled. Woosie had so many options. Four of us had to miss the morning session and I was one of them.

Lee had a 20-footer on the last to win after I produced an almost carbon copy of my three-wood from the day before, only 80 feet closer. To this day I do not know how Lee's putt missed. It was incredibly close and it meant we took a half instead of the full point, which was unfortunate. We should have beaten them, but it had been a great game against two of the soundest of our opponents. They might not have been household names over here but, if you are in the top twelve in America, you can play.

In the run-up to the tournament there had been a slightly dismissive tone from some sectors of the press over the American contingent. Vaughn Taylor, who's he? J. J. Henry, who's he? I never subscribed to that. This was the cream of American golf, each one of whom was a quality player, and it was just unfortunate, from their point of view, that they came up against such strong opposition.

For the singles, the Irish fans were in party mode. Actually, they had been in party mode all week, but with a 10–6 lead going into the Sunday, on a course we all knew well and with a team that never looked like losing, the celebrations were starting early. And what an atmosphere they created. It was a joy to be involved.

On the Saturday night Woosie had asked for a word with me:

'Look, Monty, I know Sam put you out first at The Belfry, how do you feel about doing it again here?'

'That's fine, Ian. I'm happy with that but it's entirely up to you.'

'Colin, just think about this for a second, before you agree. Think about your record in the singles. The US are well down, so what are they likely to do? They need something to happen for them fast tomorrow, so I'm betting it will be Tiger at the top of their list. How do you feel about that?'

I thought that was brilliant of Woosie to be thinking about me and my record when he was trying to capture the Ryder Cup. 'I really appreciate that, Ian, but I promise you that it doesn't mean that much to me, not when there is still work to be done to win this thing. I know what you're saying, but if it's what works best for the team, I am happy to play Woods. I have no issue with that whatsoever.'

Ian submitted our order for the following day. He put Darren at number seven, in the middle with strong protection in front and behind. Good captaincy once again. So we sat listening in the players' room over a dodgy intercom as John Paramor, the head referee, sat between Woosie and the US captain, Tom Lehman, to announce the singles line-up.

'Game one, eleven fifteen,' announced John. 'Colin Montgomerie against ...' Just at that moment the line crackled and I couldn't properly hear the name of my opponent. Tom? Was that it? It didn't make sense. As John continued his run-through I was trying to work out who I was playing. There had to have been a mix-up. I was so convinced about who I'd be facing that I decided John must have misread the list, his eye catching the US captain's name rather than Tiger's.

Then I heard the fourth match being announced: Robert Karlsson versus Tiger Woods. Now I was thoroughly confused. It wasn't until the full list was read out again that I knew I was up against David Toms. I was shocked. So was Woosie.

Once the matches had all been confirmed, the room was opened up to questions. 'Ian, are you surprised that Tiger is going out at number four?' Woosie replied that he was, and that I would be too. Tom Lehman was then asked about Tiger's placement. I was quite taken aback by his response. 'We were almost certain that Monty would be going out first and that is exactly why Tiger is not.'

Tom Lehman is as honest as the day is long and, if he said that was the reason that Tiger did not go out at number one, that was the reason. I looked at one of my team-mates, who just raised his eyebrows. Tiger wasn't afraid of me, that was for sure. He isn't afraid of anyone on a golf course. So if indeed he had indicated he'd prefer to avoid me, it was some compliment.

Where David Toms was concerned, I suspect he may have pushed to have himself at the top of the order in the hope of extracting some revenge for his narrow defeat in 2004. David is a lovely bloke and an excellent player who keeps his mistakes to a minimum. There is every chance he would have wanted another crack at me following his one-hole loss two years earlier. Certainly, it is what I would have wanted had I been in his shoes.

Once again, we were involved in a very close contest. In the pouring rain, I reached the 17th two up and had a putt to halve the hole and maintain my unbeaten run. I'd been truthful the night before when I told Woosie that I had never put my record above what was best for the team but, standing on that green, I cannot deny that the thought of making the putt meant a hell of a lot to me personally.

Being brutally honest, I would even go as far as to say it was one of the most vital putts of my career. When it dropped, the weight of hope and expectation evaporated. I was still desperate to win, but now, thank God, I could not be beaten.

David birdied 17 and suddenly the pressure was back on. A full point would set Europe firmly on our way to victory and I was determined to deliver. Having hit a decent drive I pulled out the three-wood that had already served me rather well at that hole all week. It didn't let me down. In fact, I connected too well, ending up in a tricky bunker on the far right-hand side of the green, while my opponent was safely on the putting surface. My sand wedge came to my rescue, leaving me with a five-footer for a guaranteed half and the match. There is every chance that that five-footer, which I made, was my last putt as a Ryder Cup player.

I was tired. The additional stress of going out first had drained me and I needed a few quiet minutes with my dad, my brother and Gaynor, away from my team-mates, the press and the whole Ryder Cup experience.

The team room was empty and I sat there gathering my thoughts while watching Dad enjoy the odd combination of a whisky and a slice of pudding. Feeling rejuvenated, I then made my way to the 16th green to watch Darren come home. And, boy, did he do it in style. Moments before, Henrik Stenson had wrapped up Europe's victory on the 15th but, when Darren signed off from his 3 & 2 victory over Zach Johnson, all hell broke loose, in the best possible way.

I have this picture in my mind of tears, hugs and the smoke from a Darren cigar. It was fantastic. It was Darren's Ryder Cup and the team had won it for him and for Woosie. On the clubhouse balcony the two of them soaked up the atmosphere as I happily stayed in the background on a day I will never forget.

Afterwards, with the party having moved into the team room, there was a knock on the door. It was the US team who had come to congratulate us on our victory. It was a fabulous thing for them to do and not a common occurrence at a Ryder Cup. In 2010, Corey Pavin and his vice-captains made an appearance and had a drink with us, but I would not have expected the rest of his players to have done so.

But 2006 was different because of what Darren had been going through. That's why the Americans, to a man, all came down to support him.

Throughout the entire match, the Americans had been superb. From Tom Lehman and Tiger Woods down, each of them had rallied around Darren, helping whenever possible to make him feel comfortable. Golf is a close community and for one of its members to lose his wife in the way Darren had lost Heather had a huge impact on everyone.

All credit to each and every one of that visiting side; they were gentlemen. The integrity of the Ryder Cup was fully restored.

*

The remainder of 2006 tailed off in rather unspectacular fashion, perhaps best exemplified by my showing at the Dunhill Links in October. I think I finished a little matter of 113 places below Padraig Harrington, that year's winner.

In 2007, the K Club was once again responsible for one of the highlights of my career: my most recent Tour victory. That is not an easy fact to write. Four years seems a long time ago. It *is* a long time ago.

Gaynor and I arrived in County Kildare for the Smurfit Kappa European Open in good spirits, happy to be back in exactly the same room we had occupied for the Ryder Cup, with memories of Europe's triumph all around us, including the weather. At times it was awful. In between spells of glorious sunshine, it was a common sight that week to see the golfers running for cover as play was once again suspended thanks to lightning or torrential downpours. In fact, the 18th fairway was so sodden that the organisers were forced to shorten the hole from a par five to a par three. If they hadn't, it would have been unplayable.

In many respects my slow-tempo swing lends itself to such conditions. It is human nature to do whatever you can to avoid a soaking and golfers are no different. The sanctuary of the umbrella is a powerful pull as you stand over your ball, rain running down the back of your neck and dripping off your nose.

The tendency is to rush the shot, swinging like a madman to get it out of the way.

When you are slow to begin with, the increase in pace has less impact. But if you are a speed merchant it is different. Technique can fly out of the window faster than your ball flies out of bounds. It is one of the reasons we wear waterproofs – they not only protect but the extra bulk tends to slow you down.

On a storm-ridden fourth day, the title came down to how Niclas Fasth and I would play the shrunken 18th.

I knocked my tee shot dangerously near the water hazard, leaving myself with a very awkward stance – one foot on the sloping bank, the other on the rockery surrounding the lake. Thankfully I knocked it to within around four feet and sank the putt for a score of 269. It was then a case of waiting to see what would happen to Niclas, who was a couple of parties behind.

The result hinged on his 20-foot birdie putt on the last. If it dropped, we'd be in a play-off. I have never willed anyone to miss a putt, but I have to be honest and say that once his ball was rolling I had no desire to see it drop. I had been waiting nineteen months for this victory; I didn't want that to stretch to twenty. It didn't.

It came as a total surprise to me when I was informed that I was now the holder of the British record for European Tour victories – thirty-one, one ahead of Nick Faldo. I honestly had not been aware of the significance of the win. It is a great honour to be the British player at the head of the 'most wins' list, and to have achieved it at the European Open made it all the more significant.

I was thrilled to be back to winning ways again. It wasn't getting any easier out there. When I had first started in 1988 there were maybe twenty guys realistically in contention, but by 2007 that number had swelled to fifty or so – and they were mostly younger than me. At forty-three I was beginning to feel like an old-timer.

The nature of the game had changed as well in those two decades. Over the years I have been able to offset my sometimes iffy putting with strong iron-play, but in the modern game, with the way courses are now set up, that's no longer an option. If you can't putt, you can't win.

At the K Club in 2007, my putter was working well, but over the years since I am afraid it hasn't performed to the level that is now required.

My Order of Merit rankings illustrate my point. From ninth at the end of 2006 I dropped to twelfth a year later, then twenty-seventh in 2008. I don't count 2009 and 2010 (87th and 129th, if you must know), because my commitments as Ryder Cup captain severely curtailed my play. I really only played tournaments in those years in order to get a good picture of how my would-be team members were getting on and, of course, to be a constant figure in the run-up to the match.

That was my prime motivation, rather than the accumulation of ranking points. As to what happened in 2011, I was still not back in the swing of things. The odd good round here and there but nowhere near enough in the way of consistency to stop me from plummeting down the Order of Merit I had so often topped.

*

The second highlight of 2007 came at Mission Hills, China, in the Omega World Cup. In 2006 Marc Warren and I had lost out to Germany in a play-off at the WGC-World Cup (as it was then known) in Barbados and a year later we were faced with another sudden-death challenge.

The format consists of four stroke-play rounds, alternating between fourballs and foursomes. At the end of the seventy-two holes, if two teams are tied, as we were with the US in 2007 on -25, they then compete against each other in what amounts to a series of match-play extra holes. As soon as one team wins a hole, that's it.

We were up against Heath Slocum and Boo Weekley and it was nearly a very short-lived affair. On the first play-off hole I made a bit of a mess of my drive, hitting it into a bunker on the right. From there Marc knocked our second into the bunker beside the green, which was a good shot from where he was, only for me to duff again, leaving my partner with a nasty putt to keep us alive. Brilliantly, he made it. So it was back to the tee to start all over again.

At the second attempt we both parred, but on the third go it was the Americans' turn to struggle and, when Boo missed his putt, Scotland were World Champions. You don't get the opportunity to write that very often.

It was the first time Scotland had won the tournament after having been runners-up six times over the various incarnations. It was super for the country, super for Marc, who had played so well, and super for me. It might not have counted on the European Tour as a victory but it was the perfect way to sign off from 2007 and move into 2008, the year of my marriage to Gaynor.

*

I first met Gaynor in August 2006, after a near-miss in June. I had lost the US Open at Winged Foot shortly before and, though there wasn't a morning when I didn't wake up kicking myself, I was back to playing pretty well. At the halfway stage of the Johnnie

I'm telling the press to pick José Maria Olazábal as the next Captain – we all wish him well
(Getty Images)

Above left: The youngest ever vice captain at 30 years old – hopefully for Sergio never to be repeated (Getty Images)

Above: An iconic shot – my screensave and wallpaper on my computer (Getty Images)

Self-explanatory – 14½ (Getty Images)

Right: With the troops holding the Ryder Cup. All credit to every one of you lads, you do a fantastic job

Below right: 'Monty, aim slightly left of the pin'

Below: The official opening of Camp Bastion crazy golf course

Left: In Sky's TV Studio: a new venture for me with David Livingstone and Butch Harmon, overlooking the practice range at Augusta (Sky)

Below left: Artist's impression of Maggie's Centre at The Elizabeth Montgomerie Foundation Building, Aberdeen

Below: I wouldn't swap any of these eight Orders of Merit or the nine Ryder Cups I've been involved in for a Major! (Alastair Devine, *Hello*)

At home, the one place in the world we can relax (Alastair Devine, *Hello*)

Walker championship at Gleneagles, I was leading the field, but I was knackered.

The Scottish sports commentator Dougie Donnelly was hosting a barbecue on the Friday night and had invited me along. He had it in mind that I might be interested in meeting a friend of his, Gaynor Knowles, who, tragically, had lost her husband, George, in 2003. On my dad's advice I declined at the last minute.

In the state I was in, still dealing with the emotional fallout of Winged Foot, Dad pointed out that there was no way I could go off and socialise and still focus on my game. My tie for fourth is probably testament to the fact that Dad was spot on.

The next day, however, I heard all about Gaynor from a couple of the Sky Sports guys who had been at the barbecue, how gorgeous and funny and bubbly she was. 'You should have been there, Colin,' they told me. I suspected they were right.

A couple of months later, I was in the Netherlands for the KLM Open, with this mysterious Gaynor still very much on my mind. We might not have met but I couldn't stop thinking about her. Dougie was at the tournament and I invited him out for dinner, with an ulterior motive. Dougie and I have known each other for years and are good friends but, on this occasion, it wasn't his companionship I was after. It was information. I wanted to know all about Gaynor, and, once he had told me what he could, I was more intrigued than ever.

'Dougie, I'd love to give her a call. Do you think that would be okay? Could you find out for me.' I felt about ten years old, excited and nervous, waiting for Dougie to ask his wife Linda to speak to Gaynor and check if it would be okay for me to ring. When Dougie came back with her telephone number, my nerves multiplied tenfold. Not even the most slippery of three-footers has ever affected me in quite the same way.

I eventually plucked up the courage to pick up the phone and, though my conversation was more than a little stilted at the start, it became easier and easier. To my great glee, Gaynor agreed to dinner for four with Dougie and Linda.

We chose the Strathearn restaurant at Gleneagles for the following Saturday evening.

At about six o'clock that morning, I set off from London so that I would arrive at the hotel in plenty of time to unpack, shower and double-check as to the whereabouts of Dougie's house where we were due to meet for drinks at 7.30.

I had butterflies, but, the moment I met Gaynor, a new sensation took hold. I was bowled over.

Dinner was a great success and when, at the end, Dougie and Linda said they would call a taxi and Gaynor said she would share it with them, I forced myself to intervene.

'Perhaps I could give you a run home?' I suggested, surprising myself that I had managed to say anything. Initially, Gaynor protested, saying that it was ridiculous that I should go to so much trouble when I was staying at the hotel. Eventually, she relented.

As I escorted her to her front door, it really was as if we were sixteen again. Just as we approached, the door was opened and her dad, Bill, was standing there. He and Gaynor's mum, Marion, were babysitting. It was our first date and I was meeting the parents. Not only that, but after I was invited in for coffee I also met the kids. How strange that none of them had been able to sleep that evening and just had to come downstairs for whatever reason.

It was great fun and in fact much easier for me because I had no time to be nervous. It all felt incredibly natural.

I left after an hour or so and called her the next day to ask if we could meet again. We went out for dinner, just the two of us, and we've been together ever since.

In golfing terms, it was a baptism of fire for Gaynor because a month later I invited her to join me at the Ryder Cup at the K Club – and that though she knew absolutely nothing about the game. In fact, no one among Gaynor's close relations had ever evinced the least bit interest in golf. That is most unusual in Scotland, especially for folk living within a few miles of Gleneagles.

All of a sudden, Gaynor was being exposed to the biggest team event in the sport. Not only that, but she was meeting my dad and brother for the first time. She must have wondered what on earth she was letting herself in for.

Thank heavens, once again, for the Donnellys. Dougie was in Ireland working for RTÉE and Gaynor flew over with Linda on the Friday and the two of them walked round the course together. We owe the Donnellys an awful lot.

Having Gaynor with me over that weekend made me feel like a million dollars. We had clicked in a way I had never imagined possible and I have no doubt at all that her presence helped me enormously out on the course, especially in my tight match with David Toms on the Sunday. Just knowing Gaynor was around calmed my nerves at vital moments. My only worry was that she was going to start thinking all tournaments were like this.

I was going to have to explain, gently, that the sponsors don't usually leave you gifts on your pillow each evening and Ronan Keating doesn't normally turn up and belt out a few hits. But I decided that could wait.

We flew home with Dougie and Linda on the Monday morning and this time it was Gaynor's turn to show her nerves. We'd arranged to drive from Glasgow airport to meet her late husband's parents at the restaurant situated within the family furniture store, Sterling Furniture, in Tillicoutry. Gaynor must have been there thousands of times but we still got lost. I will say no more than that I was just following the directions I was given.

It was important and appropriate for me to meet George Snr and his wife, Isabel. They were a huge part of Gaynor's life, not least in their role of grandparents to her children. While it wasn't a case of seeking approval, I knew it meant a lot to Gaynor that George, Isabel and myself should hit it off. We did.

They were both charming, and George and I chatted all through lunch about the various places we had been lucky enough to travel to – him through business, me through golf.

From there, Gaynor and I spent the next couple of years getting to know each other. In any relationship, there is history for each partner, and it is important to discuss all the various aspects fully. Obviously Gaynor had faced a terrible tragedy in her life, the loss of her husband, and I had been previously married.

We both had children, seven in total, and there was much we had to discuss and understand. We had no intention of rushing into anything and I believe that has made us stronger. We knew we were great together but, in our respective circumstances, it was not just about the two of us; we had other people to consider and we took that responsibility very seriously.

When we decided the time was right to marry, we both agreed we wanted a big celebration. In many ways it was a 'thank you' from both of us for the support we'd received over the years, for different reasons. I wanted to acknowledge the people who had stood by me during my divorce, while for Gaynor it was in recognition of her family and friends, for everything they had done in rallying round so magnificently following George's death.

Everybody who was there had a reason for being there and our ambition was for them to drive off on the Sunday morning having had a party they would remember for a long time.

The location was Loch Lomond Golf Course, a truly stunning setting. On the Friday night we had a get-together at Cameron House, just along from the clubhouse, where I explained how the following day's golf for guests was going to work. We'd be playing on the Loch Lomond course, with an 8 a.m. tee time for everyone. (There were a few groans when I announced as much.)

There were eighteen fourballs, all teeing off in shotgun style at different holes. I remained on the 8th and played with each group as they came through. It was a mixed-ability crowd, which made it all the more fun (the four pros who attended the wedding all decided that this was too much like a busman's holiday and were more than happy to enjoy a lazy morning at the hotel) and the set-up provided me with a great opportunity to meet some of the guests I didn't know.

The second to last group coming through the 8th included my brother Douglas, while Dad was in the last. Walking off with him by my side was one of my most cherished moments of the day.

The golf was followed by a presentation back at the clubhouse, conducted by my daughter Olivia and myself, where a variety of prizes were handed out for the longest drive, nearest the pin, etc., all engraved with a C and G. The major winners walked off with engraved silver salvers from Asprey's, and then it was a quick bite to eat before retiring for the afternoon in preparation for the big moment.

The wedding ceremony itself was conducted in a marquee that had been erected by the clubhouse and commanded a never-to-be forgotten view across the loch. Gaynor's son gave her away and he did a fantastic job, proudly walking his mum down the aisle. Gaynor looked, well, incredible.

Next came dinner and speeches at which Gaynor's brother Fraser spoke eloquently, followed by Guy Kinnings, who told some scandalous tales, and, finally, me, with a few short words and flowers for Marion and Isabel. After that, it was time for the party – and what a party it was.

We kicked off with the brilliant ABBA tribute band Björn Again. Gaynor and I had decided on 'Waterloo' as our first dance because it is impossible not to smile when you hear that song. Now, I am no dancer and, as much as I love ABBA, this was the one moment of the whole day that I had been dreading. But, 'Waterloo' being 'Waterloo', it was only a matter of seconds before the dance floor was full.

Once Björn Again had finished their act there was a fireworks display, part of which involved rockets trailing a stream of sparkling light behind them that formed the shape of a heart over the loch. Soppy, I know, but I'm an old-style romantic. After that, it was back to the party, this time to the accompaniment of The All-Star Band, musicians who had backed the likes of Madonna, Rod Stewart and George Michael on tour. They were brilliant, keeping the party going until the wee small hours with everything from Frank Sinatra to Queen. Thank goodness there were no neighbours.

Gaynor and I had wanted the day to be a celebration, full of light and happiness, and we had our wish. It was beyond our wildest expectations.

Meeting Gaynor turned my life around. We have built a home together, literally. I moved in to Gaynor's place in Perthshire after we were married, the house where she had lived with her husband, George. However, since this was a new beginning for us both, we decided that we needed to create our own memories in a home that was our own.

The building work took a good eighteen months, but it was worth every second of the disruption.

From my perspective, I have a front door and a family again and a place my kids can call home. The impact that has had on my life is beyond measure. It is no longer all about golf; in fact, at home, it is a four-letter word that is seldom mentioned. Gaynor is interested in my career, of course she is, but it was never a factor in her life before and, me aside, it still isn't. That is perfect as far as I am concerned. Our home is just that – a home with teenagers. We discuss school work, who is doing the dishes, what we are watching on television and who is going to walk the dogs. At times it reminds me of days with Mum and Dad. Happy and stable.

I am no longer consumed by my missed putt on the 1st or my poor approach at the 5th. I pull into my driveway, get out of my car, walk through the front door and I am home. Golf is a long way away.

16 | RYDER CUP REGRETS

Every Ryder Cup captain approaches the job from a different angle, one that reflects his personal ideas of what constitutes ideal preparation.

Take, for example, Ian Woosnam in 2006. Woosie is a lovely, honest man who believes in loyalty and close bonds. As a player he took this approach into the Ryder Cup with a 'brothers-in-arms' attitude, always prepared to put himself on the line if it would help the team's cause, but never one to point the finger of blame if things were not going well. Off the course, he was laid-back, happy to enjoy a pint or two without having to be front of stage.

So how did he marry these two aspects of his character in his role as captain? He engaged the services of a psychologist. Ian knew what he wanted – an incredibly strong unity within the team – and with the help of Jamil Querishi he felt more confident about getting that across to the players. I admired Woosie's foresight in recognising this was an aspect of his captaincy that could be strengthened. He was willing to do whatever it took to help the team.

The fact that in 2010 I chose not to bring in a psychologist does not mean I thought it was a bad idea. Jamil was a magician as well as a psychologist, and, during the week at the K Club, he performed tricks and devised a variety of exercises designed to help the team bond.

I took something from that experience when my turn came, employing a table magician for dinner times because I had seen it was a good way to bring people together, besides serving as a welcome distraction at a time when nerves were elbowing their way to the fore.

In the summer prior to the 2008 Ryder Cup, Nick Faldo arranged for a group of the players most likely to make the team to attend a high-tech gym facility to help them with their fitness. Once again, I think this illustrates how the character of the captain is reflected in his preparation.

Throughout his playing career, Nick prided himself on being in the best condition of anyone on the Tour – both physically and in the technical aspects of his swing. It worked for him, that's for sure, so why wouldn't he give his players the same opportunities? It makes sense, especially when you remember that Nick's team had to battle the potentially debilitating heat of Kentucky.

Monitoring various aspects of a player's conditioning might have highlighted a problem which could then have been remedied in advance.

Needless to say, I had no such concerns about temperature in Wales and decided it was better to leave the fitness of individuals to the individuals themselves. Let's face it, it would hardly have rung true had I insisted on gym work for my players. I would have come across as a fraud and it would have undermined my role. In Nick's case it would have been quite the opposite. It was through just such preparation that Nick won six Majors, so who wouldn't listen to what he was saying?

To reiterate: there is no right or wrong approach to being Ryder Cup captain. There is no rule book; no job description; you just have to do the best you can in the way that suits you. All three of us – Woosie, Nick and myself – went about our business in different ways, but each of those ways was equally valid.

As with the preparations, every captain also has a different view of what constitutes his best team – the balance between experience and youth, the mix of personalities, the different playing styles. That's why the captain's picks are never straightforward.

My European Open win in 2007 came just before the qualifying process for Nick Faldo's 2008 Ryder Cup began but, even so, I was confident my form that week would help to make me one or other of an automatic choice for his team, via the Order of Merit, or a pick. After all, the match was in the US, a happy hunting ground for me in a Ryder Cup context. At that point, I felt sure that if anyone was to write down the twelve most likely players for Valhalla, I would have been among them.

Good in theory, but I wasn't banking on my game taking a severe dip. Whether it was because I wanted to play in the 2008 team too much and put myself under pressure, I don't know, but something happened and the confidence I had enjoyed since 2004 all but evaporated. I was doing okay – a second place in the French Open in June 2008 showed I still had something in the tank – but no better than that.

Eventually it became clear that Nick's two selections were going to come from a quartet comprising myself, Paul Casey, Ian Poulter and Darren Clarke, and of the four I had to accept that in golfing terms I was definitely last. Throughout 2008 I had not performed to the best of my ability, there is no question about that, so I had to hope that Nick would adopt a Langeresque view about America and give Darren and me the wild cards on account of our experience.

D-Day fell, as in 2010, on the Sunday evening of the Johnnie Walker championship at Gleneagles. Both Darren and I were there, although well down the field, and I decided to head home before the tournament ended. It was only a short drive and I knew Nick would phone with the news, whichever way it went.

I was on another call when Nick rang, so in the end I learned my fate from a well-worded voicemail. 'Unfortunately on this occasion I can't select you, Colin. Your performances through the year just haven't been "Monty" enough to make you a pick. I'm sorry.'

It hit me hard. After almost twenty years I thought, is this it? I knew making the 2010 team would be a long shot, so had my Ryder Cup life just come to an end courtesy of a recorded message? It was no one's fault, but somehow that did not seem appropriate and it hurt.

I immediately phoned Darren to see if he had heard. Having won the previous week at the KLM Open, and earlier in the year in Asia, I felt sure he would have made it. He hadn't. Nick had decided to go for Casey and Poulter. Fair enough: it was his decision, based on what he thought would work best in America and, as it turned out, the two of them both performed well.

Conspiracy theories abounded. Had Nick tipped off Ian in advance? Was that why he had decided not to play Gleneagles and plumped instead for the Deutsche Bank championship in Boston? Earlier in the week I had, perhaps rather injudiciously, remarked that Ian had 'a hotline' to Nick, but in truth I had no idea whether he did or not.

Another of the rumours going the rounds was that Nick had not picked me because he was still annoyed at what he regarded as my 'disappointing' behaviour at the Seve Trophy in 2007. Nick was captain of the Great Britain and Ireland team, as a dry run, I guess, for the Ryder Cup, and told the press that I had only attended two of the five team meetings and that he had to deal with my 'emotions'.

Nonsense. The Seve Trophy hullabaloo was blown out of all proportion. Nick spoke out of turn when he went public. If he had any concerns, he should have raised them with me. I have no doubt he regretted saying what he said and that was it as far as I was concerned. He can hardly have been holding a grudge against me when you consider he put me out first in the singles and I won him a point against Robert Karlsson to set the team on its way to victory.

Finally, I heard suggestions that Nick had kept me out of the team to make sure he retained his Ryder Cup record of most points won – 25 to my 23½. Nonsense again, surely.

Nick cares about the Ryder Cup as much as I do. He wants Europe to win every time. I know that Mark James threw his good luck note in the bin in 1999 but I think James got that wrong.

I think Faldo genuinely wanted us to win and, by the same token, I believe he opted for Poulter and Casey because he thought they would serve him best.

I was devastated at being left out of that side of 2008. I lay on my bed at home trying to work out what had just happened but I failed. I couldn't quite take in that my Ryder Cup playing days were at an end.

Once I had come to terms with that, another disappointment took its place. Why did Nick not offer me a role as vice-captain?

After his text, I had expected a follow-up message along the lines, 'Come on, Monty, get on board, help us win.'

I would have been in there like a shot. But my phone never rang, and that was truly upsetting. I think I should have been there, and Darren as well, especially since Paul McGinley had withdrawn from the position of vice-captain a year previously, leaving Nick with only José Maria Olazábal.

Why did Nick not turn to Darren and me for assistance? On the playing side, absolutely fine, I could understand his thinking there, but his refusal to have us along in a non-playing capacity simply did not make sense. I can only put it down to the fact that it was his show, his team and he didn't relish the idea of having personalities like Darren and me getting in the way. In this respect, I do believe Nick put himself ahead of the overall good of the team.

How can I explain why my absence hurt so much? How do I put into words what the Ryder Cup means to me? The only way, I think, is to go back to 1991 and Kiawah Island.

I was a rookie, mesmerised by everything around me, doing my best to take it all in, but not fully succeeding until I came back from four down with four to play against Mark Calcavecchia.

That was the spark. As I explained earlier, winning that half-point had a profound effect. It was the moment I properly understood that this was all about the team, not the individual. That scrambled half was what allowed Bernhard Langer to have a putt to win for Europe. Okay, he missed, but that is irrelevant. As a team, we had created an opening.

That spark turned into rather more in the locker room afterwards. I was sitting alongside the other rookies, Paul

Broadhurst, Steve Richardson, David Feherty and David Gilford, studying their sad faces in general and the mood in particular.

I looked from one end of the room to the other and that's when I saw Seve and Langer hugging each other and crying openly. I had never witnessed anything like that before. Here were two giants of the game, people I looked up to and admired, with tears flowing down their cheeks. Because of the Ryder Cup.

That is the moment Samuel Ryder's brilliant concept seeped into my soul, never to leave. I wanted to be part of this for ever. And in 2008 I wasn't. That's why it hurt as badly as it did.

17 | WHY STOP NOW?

I have already admitted that I plan to enter the 2013 British Senior Open at Birkdale and, having let that much slip, I might as well come clean and say that I am tempted by the idea of a Senior Grand Slam. A tall order, I know, but golfing dreams are not purely the preserve of the young.

In fact, it's an even taller order than I first thought. Up until the turn of the year, I was thinking that the Senior arena had four Majors. Then I had this shock to my system. There are *five* – the Tradition, the Senior PGA, the Senior Open, the US Senior Open and the Senior Players' championship.

Jack Nicklaus, who holds the record with his eighteen regular Majors, has won eight Senior Majors and completed a career 'Senior Major Grand Slam' in the days before the British Senior Open was added to the list. By the time it was recognised – in 2003 – he had retired.

I turn fifty a month ahead of the 2013 Senior Open and I will see how I enjoy the atmosphere that week – the locker room, the companionship, the chat and the camaraderie. I'm beginning to suspect that I will like it a lot. I will be in the class of '63 which will include players like Vijay Singh and Davis Love. (Miguel Ángel Jiménez, in case you are wondering, is about six months younger than I am and will not make the switch until January 2013.)

But first things first ...

Because of my eighth and last win in the Order of Merit, I am still an exempt player on the European Tour until the end of

2015. I love it on the main circuit and, in the time I have left, it's my ambition to become the Tour's oldest winner. At the moment, Des Smyth heads the official list thanks to his win in the 2001 Madeira Island Open at the age of forty-eight years and thirty-four days.

If I am to improve on Des Smyth's feat, I have to be able to beat the increasing number of players on the European Tour who are young enough to be my sons – players like the twenty-one-year-old Tom Lewis and the eighteen-year-old Matteo Manassero. And players like Álvaro Quirós, for whom a 300-yard drive is the norm. There are courses where I simply cannot compete with fellows like him who are bombing their drives over the bunkers and taking a six-iron to a green where I need a wood.

Because of this, I have to pick my courses with care. Wentworth is a good venue for me, Hong Kong another. Both are less about length than testing every shot in the bag.

I also have to keep reminding myself of how Luke Donald came to lead the Order of Merit on both sides of the Atlantic. Luke is longer than people think but he is certainly not among the longest. It is his short game which has taken him to the top and there's absolutely nothing to stop me from polishing that side of my play.

If, or rather when, I start moving in senior circles, the length side of things will no longer be the issue it is at the moment.

The Over 50s don't go in for back, back tees and, in such circumstances, my swing should serve me better than it does at the moment.

Quite often, when I go to the range, I am telling myself I've got to hit the ball that bit harder if I am to give myself a chance. As a senior, I won't have to think about hitting hard. I will be back swinging within my comfort zone, which will in itself help me to rediscover my old rhythm.

Always assuming my short game is up to scratch, which it has to be, I could have some good early senior years, though I am no less aware of the opposition already in place than I am of such fine champions as Vijay Singh and Davis Love.

Peter Fowler of Australia led the European Senior Order of Merit in 2011; my old friend Barry Lane finished second; Andrew Oldcorn third; Gary Wolstenholme fourth and Ian Woosnam fifth.

Gary Wolstenholme is an interesting case. As an amateur, he won all over the world, including a couple of Amateur championships. (More famously still, he defeated Tiger Woods in the 1995 Walker Cup at Royal Porthcawl.) But because he felt he was not a long enough hitter to make it as a professional on the regular Tour, he waited to make the switch until he was on the verge of turning fifty.

It was a long wait but his suspicion that his shorter hitting would not be a problem on the senior circuit proved to be well founded.

He was given just one invitation to play a senior event when he turned fifty – namely, to the Travis Perkins event at Woburn. He finished third that week and went on from there to win the Casa Serena Open and thereby avoid having to go to the Senior Qualifying School. In 2011, his first full season, he won the Australian Senior Open and finished fourth in the Senior Order of Merit. Well done indeed.

I like the idea that I might do what I did in 1988 and be a Rookie of the Year again! And even if I don't succeed on that front, I like the idea of going from being the oldest player on the PGA European Tour with a players' card to being one of the youngest among the Over 50s.

So herewith my vision for 2013 ...

From the start of the season, I will be aiming my game at the Senior Open at Birkdale. I will have at least ten practice rounds over the links in the months leading up to it and, if you think I am putting pressure on myself by revealing as much, you are absolutely right. I actually want that pressure.

Ideally, I would want to play in the Open at Muirfield the week before because that would add up to the best possible preparation.

For years, I said I would not consider playing senior golf and would instead concentrate on my mother's charity, on course design and on expanding my commentary work for Sky.

My mother's charity will always be an integral part of my career; it's an area where I can use my golf for the good and I love the fact that the Maggie's Centres can make such a difference to people's lives. I meet a lot of these people and I hear their stories first-hand.

The course design work slowed in the recession but this, too, is something I find hugely challenging. I enjoy trying to do something to balance the ledger; to getting away from that mentality where courses have to be longer to be better.

I also like doing commentary and, at least so far, I haven't put my foot in it to the point where they don't want me back.

I was part of the Sky commentary team at the 2011 Masters and the fun was only interrupted by this nagging feeling that I was at that point too young to be sitting in the commentary box. The more I watched the competitors going about their business, the more I thought, 'Hang on, I can do that.'

True, I wouldn't have been hitting the eighth green with a drive and an eight-iron like Quirós did, but, given a bit of the belief which I lost while concentrating on the Ryder Cup captaincy, I would have been okay.

But in 2013, the Senior Tour could well be the place for me and, if the comradeship out there is everything the players say it is, I think I could be thanking my lucky stars at having a second lease of golfing life. The late Henry Cotton was a great one for saying that the best thing about golf was that it was a game for everyone – of all ages and both sexes – and I think he got it absolutely right.

Who knows, in 2030 I could be taking aim at Neil Coles's record as the Oldest Winner on the Senior Tour. (For the record, Neil was sixty-seven years and 276 days when he won the Lawrence Batley Senior Open at Huddersfield.)

There is always the chance that my competitive instincts might have been assuaged before then, but the longer I go on the more I recognise that I am a competitor.

Through and through.

18 | Q&A

INTRODUCTION TO Q&A

Like every other professional golfer, I am asked a lot of questions on my travels, probably the most common of which is 'Where are you going next?'

The answer to that is that the professional golfer can visit as many as twenty different countries a season without seeing anything like as much of any of those lands as he would wish. I have an inquiring mind but, quite often, it's a matter of flying into an airport, getting a courtesy car to the hotel and travelling back and forth from the hotel to the course for six days before heading back to the airport and home.

Mind you, all that has changed somewhat since I have become involved in course design. In my designer's guise, I need to see and understand more of a surrounding area to get a feel for what is appropriate.

As you would expect, the name which crops up the most often in any 'Golfer's Question Time' is that of Tiger Woods. Most people find him fascinating and want to know what the next few years have in store.

To be honest, I think everyone has his own take on the subject. All I can say for sure is that Tiger will be every bit as interesting to follow over the next few years as he has been since word first came that there was this richly gifted teenager who had won three US Junior championships in a row.

Players, writers and golfing fans are all lucky to be around in Tiger's time because there has been never been anyone quite like him, anyone who has created a similar all-round stir.

I love the fact that people are so interested in what we do: it makes me feel good about my choice of career. People may see golf as a selfish game but there's no question that it gives a lot of pleasure to a lot of people – and not least to those whose golfing days are done and who want to stay in touch.

It's fun to follow a player having a great round and, though I have to admit that I can't see too many positives in my bad days, I can appreciate that it's equally compelling to watch a professional making a hash of things.

There is no other game in the world in which players – amateurs and professionals – are able to 'connect' as well as they can in golf, and nothing to beat the way the sport lends itself to the pro-am format. Heaven knows how many sponsorship deals have their origins in a tournament pro-am day.

Away from the business potential of a pro-am, we can see how the amateurs play and, as Padraig Harrington has often said, we can learn from analysing what they are doing. At the same time, they can learn from us while plying us with the kind of questions I have listed below.

As we all know, a pro-am round can take comfortably over five hours so there is plenty of time to ponder the problems, the positives and the mysteries of golf.

The first question, 'Are Asian golfers set to overtake their Western counterparts', is one of the more compelling in my eyes.

Scotland introduced the game to the world before the Americans became dominant. The Europeans, with specific reference to the Irish, have been to the fore in the last few seasons – and now I believe things are about to swing Asia's way.

It is a truly arresting state of affairs.

Are Asian golfers set to overtake their Western counterparts?

Yes, they are. At the time of writing, we have just the one Asian winner of a men's Major in Y. E. Yang, who captured the PGA championship of 2009. My prediction, for what it's worth, is that between six and ten of the next thirty-six Major winners – that takes us to the end of 2020 – will come from the Far East.

I remember a conversation I had with Peter Dawson, the R&A's CEO, before the start of the 2011 Open. When the subject came up as to who might win, he said he was expecting an Asian winner at any moment and I can't see him changing his mind.

We have been slow to pick up on the fact that the Asian contingent is getting better and bigger all the time. The Asian Amateur championship, where the winner gets to play in the Masters, is an interesting showcase for how the game is developing in those parts. At the 2011 edition in Singapore, there were competitors from Outer Mongolia, from Nepal, from Bhutan – places which had never previously been mentioned in a golfing context.

The game has, quite literally, spread to all corners of the earth.

Indonesia, with its population of 240 million, is becoming a keen golfing land, while China is expecting to have twenty million golfers by 2020. In India, players like Shiv Kapur, Jeev Milkha Singh and S. S. P. Chowrasia are at the helm of what could be a massive wave of Indian winners, with the interesting thing here that they are coming from every background.

Chowrasia, who has won the co-sanctioned (European and Asian Tours) Indian Masters a couple of times, started off as a caddie, as did so many of the great Spanish golfers. Today, there are lots of would-be Chowrasias being given a chance, with the amateur officials in India making it their business to seek out the more talented caddies for their junior coaching squads.

When I first started out on the European Tour, we would go to all sorts of destinations in the Far East but the winner would invariably come from European Tour regulars rather than the locals. Now, Europeans no longer head east expecting easy money. The competition is tough wherever you go.

I remember causing a few raised eyebrows when I spoke to a gathering of juniors at Royal St George's during last year's Open. I told them that, while they were sleeping, there were hundreds and thousands of Koreans out practising at the start of what are far longer days than we put in over here.

The work ethic in the Far East is completely different from ours. Whereas in the UK the average working day for a man making cars is nine to five, with a break for lunch, in Japan or China his counterpart will put in a twelve-hour day. Not just because the workers have families to support but because they want to do the best thing by their leaders and their countries. They see things differently and, when they apply that kind of attitude to their sport, it shows.

Just look at the way the Korean girls have taken off on the LPGA Tour. They won't be the longest hitters out there but I think you can safely say that they will be outworking their sister players. Not just by an hour or so but by about three or four.

They are doing a lot right but, just as there are those of us over here – yes, me included – who could do with working harder, they probably need to make sure that they are not overdoing things. You hear stories of promising young girls burning themselves out and having injury concerns long before they are fully into their golfing stride.

The Olympics are going to add to golf's stature in lots of the Eastern countries, with much the same applying in the Middle East, where the game's growth in the desert regions has to be seen to be believed. In my role as an HSBC ambassador, I visited Bahrain, Oman, Kuwait, Qatar, Abu Dhabi and Dubai at the end of 2011 and there is a real golfing buzz in the Gulf region.

A new circuit, the MENA Tour – Middle East and North Africa – got under way last year and that will provide a perfect launching pad for players aiming their games at the Asian and European Tours.

Are you for or against the various tours making exceptions for very gifted young amateurs and allowing them to turn professional early?

Personally, I don't think any of the Tours should be making exceptions for anyone, however talented the player might be. I don't think anyone – boy or girl – should be allowed to turn professional before the age of eighteen.

Only one player in 10,000 is going to make it in this game, so for heaven's sake let's encourage teenagers to finish their schooling.

I receive any number of emails from parents telling me that their twelve-year-old is playing to, say, a handicap of five and asking what the child should do to prepare for the professional ranks. Usually, I come up with a counter-question: 'That's very good but how is he getting on at school? Is he getting good marks in Maths and English, etc.?'

I have said earlier in this book that I am convinced that my golfing results are all down to the fact that I had an education, a Plan B if you like. I had O-levels, A-levels and a degree. I didn't turn professional until the age of twenty-four and that was quite soon enough.

A lot of parents will have been influenced by Tiger Woods and how he started the game at much the same time as he was learning to walk. Brilliantly though Tiger has done, I think things might well have gone more smoothly for him over the last few years had he had a more run-of-the-mill childhood, one in which he wasn't appearing on *The Mike Douglas Show* at the age of four.

I'm also thinking of tennis players like Andrea Jaeger and Jennifer Capriati. There was huge excitement all round when these youngsters first came on the scene but Andrea got injured and could not get out of the game quick enough, while Capriati got herself into more than a spot of bother.

I see beauty pageants involving seriously young children as particularly hideous and I don't mind saying as much.

The children aren't to blame. It's the parents who are doing the pushing. Golf is a more obviously healthy pursuit but it, too, can get seriously out of hand where parents start putting their children's golfing progress above all else.

To take kids out of school early, or to have them cutting down on the academic side of things and being home-schooled, is tantamount to playing games with their lives.

Home schooling is usually approached with the attitude, 'Let's just pass, let's get the exams out of the way'.

I've got seven kids, three of my own and four of Gaynor's, and just passing doesn't get you anywhere these days. If you don't make it in golf – and even if you do – an education is important. I have added the rider 'and even if you do' because sponsors today want rather more from a player than merely good golf results. They need people who can interact with their clients on and off the course.

There really isn't this hurry to get good that people think there is. What is the point of turning pro in your mid-teens? An eighteen-year-old is still a talented youngster in a game where you have players winning Majors at forty-plus.

Take Darren Clarke. He was forty-two when he won the 2011 Open. Personally, I don't think he could have done that had he played too seriously through pre-teen and teenage years.

At this point, everyone will be thinking, 'What about Matteo Manassero, surely he is in the right place?'

Of course I am aware that Matteo turned professional when he was barely seventeen and that he won his first tournament at that age. Though not many people know as much, Matteo is still going back to Italy each summer to sit his school exams because he says it is important to him that he gets his leaving certificate. I admire him a lot for that, along with the fact that he is fluent in about five languages.

But I still do not think there should be exceptions, not least because of the effect it has on all those families who think they have the next Matteo Manassero or Tiger Woods on their hands.

I know there is pressure on youngsters in Asian countries to turn professional early. Sometimes it will be because their families are hoping that their offspring might provide them with an income; sometimes it might be because there is no amateur tour where they can hone their games.

Maybe the Federation of Tours should get together to thrash out this side of things; in fact I'm sure they should. More financial support should be given to amateurs who need it – and all the Tours should agree that no one can turn professional before eighteen, regardless.

A professional sportsman needs to be an adult. At fifteen, sixteen and seventeen, kids are not adults and good parenting – and in this case good officiating – is about allowing children to enjoy their childhood years.

What's different about the chat in the professionals' locker room and the amateurs?

Initially, when a young lad turns professional he might still be boasting about how well he did to reach such and such a green with a drive and a wedge. After a bit, he will be aware from the look on the professionals' faces that that kind of talk does not begin to impress. The top players are not remotely interested in the clubs they took. They are only interested in the figures that go down on the scorecard.

Now that golf has spread to the extent it has, should players in the UK be putting themselves out a bit and learning other golfers' languages instead of expecting everyone to speak English?

Definitely. I had a practice round with a fellow Scot, Colin Byrne, shortly after he turned professional in 2011 and one of his first observations was that there is an awful lot of time to kill on Tour.

It's because you can't play and practise all day that I think we should be given the opportunity to attend language classes in the evenings. I upload lots of DVDs to take with me when I go away, but I know I would feel a whole lot better about myself if I could polish up my French or Spanish. That way, I would really feel I had accomplished something.

We are the laziest nation on earth. All we do when we go overseas is to speak slower and louder – and get irritated when people cannot understand us. In this day and age it's appalling and I often wonder what our overseas sponsors think of our lack of effort in this regard.

Wouldn't it be good – for us and for the image of the European Tour – if we were able to make winners' and other speeches appropriate to the countries hosting our events? Phil Mickelson has learned a bit of Mandarin and I respect him hugely for that.

We pride ourselves on our team spirit in Europe and, were we to get together for language classes, it would help to foster these good relationships. I am not suggesting for a minute that the Tour should foot the bill. We could all chip in £20 per lesson and it would be £20 well spent.

It is probably not just the players who would want to get involved. I think there would be a good take-up from the caddies who, after all, work much the same hours as their employers.

I am sure I am not alone in saying that it would be a good move if we could have some kind of computer training on Tour as well. There may be some computer geeks among the golfers but most of us probably know no more than 5 per cent of what there is to know about the workings of our laptops.

What struck you most about Tiger Woods in his heyday?

Elsewhere in this book, I have made a couple of mentions of the day I played alongside Tiger in the 1987 Masters. He was twenty-one at the time and, as he shot a 65 to my 74, I was totally in awe of what I was seeing.

I studied the way he worked with his caddie and I studied the look in his eye as he stood over a putt. He 'stared' the ball into the hole in a way that went fathoms deeper than anything I had seen before. He holed the six- to ten-footers like no one else.

Because of that round at Augusta, I was probably as quick as any of the players to face up to the truth about Tiger. Besides looking at him from the position of a fellow player, I was also considering things from that of the marketing man I might have become with my degree from Houston Baptist.

I thought that he would turn the game upside down and that the prize money in the States and elsewhere would shoot through the roof for a bit, which is what it did.

After Tiger had waltzed off with that year's Masters, I remember wondering if anyone else would get a look-in at the event in his time. Only then, of course, we had three different winners in Mark O'Meara, José Maria Olazábal and Vijay Singh before Tiger won again in 2001 and 2002.

I wrote a column shortly before the 2002 Masters in which I said that he was still by tenfold the best player of us all. We had had other world No. 1s whose skills, when you put them together, were just enough to have them ahead of the next person. Tiger, though, got to the top by being the best in virtually every department.

At the 2002 Deutsche Bank SAP Open at St Leon-Rot, where I lost to him on the third play-off hole, one of the journalists asked me how you should think when going head-to-head with Tiger. I replied that, since Tiger did everything so much better than the next man, you could only think about scoring better than him on the day. Simple in theory but, unfortunately, you then have to put it into practice.

Seven men have changed the course of world golf. My list would start with Arnold Palmer and it would then take in the late Mark McCormack, who founded IMG, my management company. McCormack turned Palmer into the kind of star the game had never known before. After them, the players on my list of seven would be Jack Nicklaus, Gary Player, Greg Norman, the late Seve Ballesteros and then Tiger.

Do you think Tiger Woods will win more Majors?

I think he will but, through being as good as he has been, he has made life harder for himself. He left no stone unturned in his bid to get to the top and others have watched his every move in their efforts to do the same. He furnished the rest of the world with the ultimate in golfing models.

Is the life of the professional golfer as glamorous as it looks?

Don't get me wrong. Our Tour and the other golfing Tours offer marvellous opportunities and we are hugely lucky that these opportunities exist. Yet nothing is quite as glamorous as it is made out to be and I think I am speaking for everyone who turns his or her hobby into a job.

I've done a bit of filming for adverts and that world is much the same: it looks exotic and probably is at times but, as in golf, there is a lot of hanging about.

Everyone who plays golf for a living has to love it but, when you've been around for a bit, you love it in a different way from how you did at the start. It's a bit like playing your favourite record again and again and again; you lose what you once had with the song.

For me, the game today is mostly about the competition.

Yes, I still marvel at some of the hotels and venues on my schedule but, especially when you are a family man, you are more conscious of what you are missing at home.

I have to say 'No' to around 80 per cent of the invitations which come Gaynor's way and mine. Gaynor spent three or four years having to go to things on her own following the death of her first husband and I have so much admiration for the guts she showed in continuing to get out and about.

Now she is married again, she shouldn't have to be going solo. However, with my job as it is, not too much has changed for her and I just count myself lucky that she is so self-sufficient. I love it when we can go out together but it's comforting to know that her social life doesn't come to a full stop in the weeks when I'm away.

Her four children are still living at home, we have a couple of lively dogs and the house is busy with me or without me.

Gaynor fills me in on what's happening when I'm away playing golf, which is usually more entertaining than what I have to tell her. She did see me win the 2007 European Open but nowadays there are not too many occasions when I can report that I've scored in the mid-60s and that I'm on the verge of winning. Though I'm hoping to change this in 2012, the chances are that she will continue to hear more about the course design and other business activities I usually incorporate in my tournament sorties.

Back to the question about glamour ... By way of summarising my answer, I would say that there is a glamorous element to Tour life which can be particularly spell-binding at the start. You carry on appreciating that side of things but, little by little, you learn that it's lovely but not important.

The more you are away and the more glamorous the venues, the more it is brought home to you that family comes first.

Does losing at Winged Foot still haunt you?

I have mentioned Winged Foot several times in the book and, yes, it really does hurt. Yet I had a letter shortly after that week which helped me to put it in perspective. I had said to Padraig Harrington on the Sunday night, 'Why do we put ourselves through this?' and my remark had been reported in the *New York Times*.

The letter I mention came from a reader who was suffering from cancer and whose wife had multiple sclerosis. In answer to my question, he said, 'The reason you put yourself through it is because the alternative is unacceptable.' He went on to say that I provided him with a three- or four-hour escape from what he and his wife were going through. And that the battle I fought under the media microscope in the week of a Major helped me to give people like him, who were fighting their battles in private, a bit more courage.

Of all the wonderful messages I received after that US Open loss, that was the most poignant, especially with my own mother having suffered from cancer.

It also opened my eyes to the fact that double bogeys, no less than birdies and eagles, are all part of the entertainment as far as the viewers are concerned. If we all played 100 per cent all the time, no one would want to watch.

Is there anything about golf which infuriates you?

Yes, the pace at which it's played. Like most guys of my age, I was brought up on rounds of golf taking no more than three hours. When I play with my dad, who is in his eighties, he would consider we had been very dilatory if we didn't make it round in two and a half hours.

Nowadays, though, spectators have to suffer tournament rounds which can take in excess of five hours. Unfortunately, there are repercussions for youngsters who watch on television. When they see their favourite players taking for ever over everything from their routines to their putt-reading, they decide that they should be doing the same. It's crazy as far as I am concerned and it's also doing damage to the game overall.

In the days when people played at a decent speed, they would have a morning and an afternoon in their lives. Now, if they go out for a game of golf, it takes all day. Someone with a job and a family simply doesn't have that kind of time at his disposal, so no wonder people are thinking twice about joining clubs.

Should the belly putter be banned?

Yes, I think it should, and I say that from the standpoint of someone who used it successfully for a couple of years and is still tempted to work with the implement today.

As with other clubs, the putter should be held and steadied by the hands alone. With the belly putter or the chest-high putter, you have another point where the club is anchored and that can give too much of an advantage when you are under pressure. Your club is less likely to wobble.

Ernie Els pretty much sums it up. When he was asked if he planned to stay with the belly putter he started using last year, he said, 'As long as it is legal, I will keep cheating like the rest of them.'

Whether or not it will eventually be banned I would not like to say. The authorities have had a couple of looks at the issue but, at least as yet, they have made no decision to alter the current regulations.

The reason I discarded my original belly putter was that I grew to dislike the look of it. Heartily. I guess it was a psychological thing. When I pulled it out of the bag, it just didn't feel right, not like a real golf club. 'What on earth is this?' I would say to myself.

As soon as I started talking about it like that, the relationship went rapidly downhill and I reverted to a more traditional club. Now, I feel that my belly putters don't even deserve a place among the hundreds of discarded putters in my garage.

In reality, you could go back forty years to the Ping Anser putter and be just as well off with that as any of the latest implements. In all that time, the technology of the putter has barely changed, at least not in any significant way. Where other clubs in the bag have developed over the years, giving, say, more whip in the shaft or having larger heads, the putter has remained pretty much a putter.

Sir Bob Charles is one of the best putters of them all and he used the same stiff-wristed putting stroke and the same Bull's Eye putter for fifty years. He has explained that he was able to build up a store of good memories with the clubs, all of which played their part in keeping his confidence intact.

It could also be the case that he benefited from being left-handed. Where the manufacturers put out rows and rows of right-handed putters to tempt the right-handed professionals at every tournament venue, the left-handers are forgotten.

I think that could work in their favour.

What has been your most interesting challenge in the realm of course design?

Designing my course in Vietnam where the drainage asked a host of difficult and different questions. Vietnam experiences the monsoon from May to September and you have to accommodate that natural phenomenon and work around it. In addition, we were developing a tract of land that had once been a paddy field, which, by definition, is going to collect pools of water.

It was quite an undertaking but we had some fantastically talented people on board, some of them locals, which made all the difference. They understood the environment and used their knowledge to ensure we maintained the character of the land in what is a very special country with very special people.

The other unusual aspect of this project was that there were old pillboxes still dotted round the area, remnants from the Vietnam War. As dreadful as that conflict was, we felt it was important not to wipe out history and instead to recognise what had happened and demonstrate how the region has moved forward.

With the agreement of the local owners, we decided to turn the pillboxes into drinks huts – a reminder of the past and a nod to the future.

What do you think about golf's inclusion in the 2016 Olympics?

I am all for it. As far as I am concerned, having golf as part of the Games can only be a good move because it will introduce a compelling new contest and one which will bring in a new audience. The latter, of course, is critical to the health of the sport.

I am not saying that a gold medal would take over from a Major. It hasn't in tennis and I don't think it will in golf. But I believe it could slip into fifth place in the rankings behind the Masters, the Open, the US Open and the PGA. Winning an Olympic medal for your country would be something very, very special.

I was there at the presentation at Lausanne when the International Olympic Committee decided to accept golf. That was quite an experience. I had been approached by George O'Grady, the European Tour CEO, Peter Dawson from the R&A and Ty Votaw, the Executive Vice-President of the PGA Tour, to say a few words on my view of what it would mean were golf to become an Olympic sport.

Annika Sörenstam was representing the women's game, while Padraig Harrington, as a three-time Major winner, and Matteo Manassero, still in his teens, similarly had an input. There was also a video-link to Jack Nicklaus and Tiger Woods.

It was all a bit daunting. There I was representing golf alongside some of the world's greats in the IOC building which is a bit like something from a James Bond set.

It was a big ask for golf to get in when you think about the logistics – sixty competitors in the men's division, sixty in the ladies'.

Frankie Fredericks, the Namibian athlete who is on the committee, asked a very pertinent question: 'So we have one hundred and twenty rooms to find in the Olympic Village, but what about caddies?'

I was glad Peter Dawson fielded that one. He thought on his feet and indicated that the caddies, like coaches, would fall into the category of staff members and would therefore not require accommodation under the same roof as the athletes. Even so, when you add it all up, you are probably talking about an additional 350 people who will need to be looked after one way or another.

As I said, that's asking a lot but it will be worth it. It will make for an incredible spectacle and I can't wait to watch from my sofa at home.

If you could give just one piece of advice to your average club golfer, what would it be?

Loosen your grip. Too tight a grip is the most common fault in the amateur game and the one with the most severe repercussions. If you try to throttle the club because you are under the impression you will be able to belt the ball harder, you are on a hiding to nothing. You need to soften your hold on the grip in order to create a smooth swing; that's how you generate power and direction.

My recommendation would be that, when you are ready to swing the club away, you take a deep breath and relax your grip. Give it a try.

Any tips for winter golfers?

My first recommendation would be to leave it to everyone else to get in a state about temporary greens. Accept from the start that you will miss putts you expect to hole and that you will hole putts you expect to miss – and that the same will apply to your playing companion or opponent.

Also, make a deliberate effort to swing slowly. Most people going out for a winter round open with a couple of lightning-fast swings on the first tee, maybe in a bid to keep warm. Almost every time I play with amateurs, and this applies at any time of year, I have to suggest that they would do better to slow down. In all my years, I have never had to tell anyone to swing more quickly.

Bearing in mind that in winter the ball does not compress as much on the club face and therefore does not fly as far as it does in summer, it makes sense to take a club more than you think you need for shots to the green. Before you dismiss that suggestion out of hand, take a mental trip round your own course with reference to the positioning of the bunkers. Almost all the time, they are guarding the front of the green rather than the back.

Which do you prefer out of foursomes and fourballs – and why?

Although I have talked a lot in this book about my need to feel in control, the funny thing is that I prefer foursomes to fourballs because my game is naturally suited to that format. Foursomes is the more difficult because you are only playing every other shot but I love the challenge of marrying my game to someone else's and trying to get the best out of both of us.

In fourball golf, you have more freedom; you are playing your own ball and your own hole and it's all about how many birdies you can make. That, though, has never really been my style of play. I am more of a percentage golfer, hitting fairways and making pars, which is the kind of mentality you need for foursomes. You let your opponents be the more ambitious while you focus on keeping the ball safely in play.

After being asked this question, I checked on my Ryder Cup record. Interestingly, my points' tally in foursomes is 9½ in foursomes to 7 in fourballs.

How much do you practise before a round?

I know I'm guilty of sending out mixed messages here. In 1997 at Valderrama, I remember one of the press compared the number of divots I had taken on the practice ground to those of whoever was next to me. I had taken no more than a dozen whereas my neighbour had worn a patch of about two foot by two foot completely bare.

The explanation here would have been that I was feeling comfortable with my game that week and, when that is the case, I tend to see the practice ground more as a place to relax and loosen up rather than one to be hitting hundreds of balls.

The 1997 US Open at Congressional was an interesting week. Having had a tiring time at Slaley Hall the week before, winning the event and taking twice as long as I had expected to get home on the busy roads, I knew I needed to conserve energy insofar as that was possible.

I only played nine holes on the Tuesday at Congressional and nine holes on the Wednesday. I was hitting the ball as well as I have ever hit it and all I needed was to stay in the groove.

When it came to the Thursday morning, I arranged to meet Alastair, my caddie, on the practice ground an hour ahead of my starting time. It was only as I emerged from the locker room that I realised I did not have a clue where the practice ground was!

It hit me equally forcibly that this was not a question I could be asking anyone at this stage of the proceedings.

I didn't practise that morning at all other than on the practice putting green but I handed in a 65 on my way to finishing second. Even now, there will be readers who are saying, 'Well, that serves him right', but I remain convinced that my approach was right. I was shattered and to have practised any more than I did would have been to risk losing what I had.

In my earliest years, I would spend long hours on the range simply because that was what everyone else was doing and I didn't want to be the odd one out. Particularly in team situations, I didn't want to be accused of taking things too lightly.

The truth is that I have learned over the years that I am more likely to have a successful day when I limit myself to what I feel like doing.

What is important to me is that I should do everything I can to be in the right mood for a round.

On those days when, say, I have a ten o'clock tee-off time, I do not want a hotel breakfast. If the service is slow and I have to keep checking my watch to make sure that I am not running behind, that can start the agitation process, quite apart from ruining the breakfast. Similarly, if I am relying on a courtesy car and it is not outside the door on time, that could be another thing to get me in a state. It's only when I'm at the wheel of my own car that I feel I have things totally under control.

If you think about it, most of the above applies to anyone wanting to get off on the right foot with his or her job. The person who has to be sharp for a meeting at nine o'clock does not want to find himself stuck on a Tube half an hour beforehand.

I only start to relax when I walk into the clubhouse, hopefully about an hour and a half before my tee-off time. When I am in Europe, my next port of call is the Caddieshack restaurant where I can have something to eat and catch up on the football results at the same time.

Next on the agenda is the practice ground, where the first thing to get my attention is whether or not I have a golf glove which fits. Before someone chips in to suggest that I should see to that the night before, that does not work. Your hand is a very different size in an air-conditioned hotel room from how it will be in the heat of the following day. In all, I have about twelve gloves in the bag and can often go through half a dozen or more before finding one that is 100 per cent.

I will spend forty minutes running through my irons and woods, hitting a couple of shots with each before heading for the chipping area. After that, I have ten minutes on the putting green prior to heading for the first tee.

Apart from making sure I never have to rush at that point, I am not too different from most golfers in adhering to a couple of superstitions. In the first place, I would not dream of teeing up with anything other than a white tee. In my mind, red and yellow tees denote water hazards and, as such, are bad news.

My other little idiosyncrasy concerns the finish to my putting green practice. My preference is to miss three putts in a row before I sign off. Why? Because, by the law of averages, I am telling myself that I am bound to make the next one!

I attach a lot of importance to my first drive in that it is the shot which will often have most to do with how I play that day. Always, I try to focus on where I want the ball to land.

If I dispatch one down the middle, I will have a spring in my step as I follow it down the fairway.

The world's a wonderful place when you get off to a good start.

All of the above are how things go when I am in the throes of a good spell.

When I am having problems on some front, I will fit in more practice in the days leading up to the tournament. Sometimes, for example, I will go back to the putting routine I learned in university days – the '100-ball drill'. Though it sounds like something from the New Mexico Military Institute from which I made such a hasty exit, it is in fact an exercise I learned from Dave Mannon at Houston Baptist.

I put a marker down two or three feet from the hole and hit a hundred consecutive putts. If one misses, I have to begin all over again. The key here is to get into a rhythm that is comfortable and produces a smooth stroke that will stand up under pressure.

The exercise in itself puts you under pressure. Putts 1–85 are fairly straightforward but the last fifteen take on a very different slant if you have to make every one of them in order to finish on the right note. It is strange, but the nerves really do kick in and you can feel yourself tightening up.

Suddenly, it is all about mind over matter. Excellent training and all very much in accord with the 'pressure practice' which took Luke Donald to the top of the Order of Merits.

How important is drug-testing in golf?

My view on this has changed in the last few years. Not that long ago, my feeling was that it wasn't necessary as golf does not lend itself to one particular style of play and, as far as I was aware, there was no drug available that could help you to hit some extra yards off the tee before manufacturing the most delicate of chips and following it up with a nervy, downhill putt.

Now, having been involved in the Olympic bid, I can see that my previous view was not very well informed. We do need testing. Regardless of the efficacy of a particular drug in terms of a player's overall game, if it gives a player an advantage in just one of the areas mentioned it is unfair. The game cannot, and should not, allow that. A level playing field is what golf is all about and that has to be maintained at all costs.

Positive thinking versus realism?

Positive thinking, though you can't kid yourself that you're something you don't begin to be, is a big part of the equation, and maybe still more obviously so in a team situation than it is for the individual. The best lesson I ever had in this regard came from Ian Woosnam in the Ryder Cup of 2006 at the K Club.

That week, our team's secret was the way we boosted each other's self-esteem at every possible opportunity. It was Woosie's idea and every time one of us was teeing off, Woosie, or one of his assistants, would be there to say, 'You're a great champion', or something along those lines.

You may think that a Ryder Cup player doesn't need anything extra in the way of confidence but the truth is that we can all feel an element of self-doubt on the first tee.

As well as the above, we all talked in the team room as to how our twelve players were better than the Americans' twelve. I don't suppose there was any evidence to back that up but we talked ourselves into believing that that applied.

On a day-to-day basis, you have got to be positive but it works much better if you know what you are doing. Tiger Woods could force himself into making putts when he needed them, but only because he had a background of spending hours on the practice putting green grooving his stroke.

If the average punter comes along and says, 'Right, I'm going to hole everything today', he could well start off by holing a long putt and carry on like that, but it's hardly going to work long term. At least, not unless he practises.

You must have become quite a connoisseur on the food front thanks to your travels. which country's cuisine appeals the most?

I can actually narrow this down to a single restaurant as opposed to a country. My favourite place to eat would be Charnock Richard which is the M6 service station halfway between London and Perth. The Little Chef serves this All Day Breakfast, and as I tuck in, I could not be happier if I were sitting in a seven-star hotel in Abu Dhabi.

Appendix
CAREER STATISTICS

compiled by Tony Greer

AMATEUR RECORDS

1983   Scottish Youths Champion

1984   Represented Scotland in the Eisenhower Trophy
        Runner Up British Amateur Championship

1985   Scottish Strokeplay Champion
        Represented GB & Ireland in the Walker Cup

1986   Represented Scotland in the Eisenhower Trophy

1987   Scottish Amateur Champion
        Represented GB & Ireland in the Walker Cup

40 PROFESSIONAL VICTORIES
(European Tour unless otherwise stated)

1989   Portuguese Open TPC

1991   Scandinavian Masters

1993   Heineken Dutch Open
        Volvo Masters Andalucia

1994   Peugeot Open de España
        Murphy's English Open
        Volvo German Open

1995   Volvo German Open
        Trophée Lancôme

1996   Dubai Desert Classic
        Murphy's Irish Open
        Canon European Masters
        Nedbank Million Dollar Challenge (RSA)

1997   King Hassan II Trophy (MOR)
        Compaq European Grand Prix
        Murphy's Irish Open
        World Cup of Golf (individual) (USA)
        Andersen Consulting World Championship of Golf (USA)

1998   Volvo PGA Championship
        One 2 One British Masters
        Linde German Masters

1999   Benson & Hedges International Open
        Volvo PGA Championship
        Standard Life Loch Lomond
        Volvo Scandinavian Masters
        BMW International Open
        Cisco World Match Play Championship

2000   Novotel Perrier Open de France
        Volvo PGA Championship
        Skins Game (USA)

2001   Ericsson Masters (AUS)
        Murphy's Irish Open
        Volvo Scandinavian Masters

2002   Volvo Masters Andalucia (tied)
        TCL Classic (ASIA)

2003   Macau Open (ASIA)

2004   Caltex Masters Singapore (Asia/Eur)

2005   Dunhill Links Championship

2006   UBS Hong Kong Open (Asia/Eur)

2007   Smurfit Kappa European Open

RYDER CUP RECORD

Singles: **8 Played: 6 Won, 2 Halved, None Lost**

1991	Halved	v Mark Calcavecchia
1993	Won (1 hole)	v Lee Janzen
1995	Won (3&1)	v Ben Crenshaw
1997	Halved	v Scott Hoch
1999	Won (1 hole)	v Payne Stewart
2002	Won (5&4)	v Scott Hoch
2004	Won (1 hole)	v David Toms
2006	Won (1 hole)	v David Toms

Foursomes: **14 Played: 8 Won, 3 Halved, 3 Lost**

1991	Lost (4&2)	(with David Gilford) v Lanny Wakins & Hale Irwin
1993	Won (4&3)	(with Nick Faldo) v Ray Floyd & Fred Couples
	Won (3&2)	(with Nick Faldo) v Lanny Wakins & Corey Pavin
1995	Lost (1 hole)	(with Nick Faldo) v Corey Pavin & Tom Lehman
	Won (4&2)	(with Nick Faldo) v Curtis Strange & Jay Haas
1997	Won (5&3)	(with Bernhard Langer) v Tiger Woods & Mark O'Meara
	Won (1 hole)	(with Bernhard Langer) v Lee Janzen & Jim Furyk
1999	Won (3&2)	(with Peter Lawrie) v David Duval & Phil Mickelson
	Lost (1 hole)	(with Peter Lawrie) v Hal Sutton & Jeff Maggert
2002	Halved	(with Bernhard Langer) v Phil Mickelson & David Toms
	Won (1 hole)	(with Bernhard Langer) v Scott Verplank & Scott Hoch
2004	Won (4&2)	(with Padraig Harrington) v Davis Love III & Fred Funk
2006	Halved	(with Lee Westwood) v Phil Mickelson & Chris DiMarco
	Halved	(with Lee Westwood) v Chad Campbell & Vaughn Taylor

Fourballs: **14 Played: 6 Won, 2 Halved, 6 Lost**

1991   Won (2&1)   (with Bernhard Langer) v Steve Pate & Corey Pavin

1993   Halved   (with Nick Faldo) v Paul Azinger & Fred Couples
        Lost (2 holes) (with Nick Faldo) v John Cook & Chip Beck

1995   Lost (3&2)   (with Nick Faldo) v Fred Couples & Davis Love III
        Lost (4&2)   (with Sam Torrance) v Brad Faxon & Fred Couples

1997   Lost (3&2)   (with Bernhard Langer) v Tiger Woods & Mark
                       O'Meara
        Won (1 hole) (with Darren Clarke) v Fred Couples & Davis Love
                       III

1999   Halved   (with Peter Lawrie) v Davis Love III & Justin Leonard
        Won (2&1)   (with Peter Lawrie) v Steve Pate & Tiger Woods

2002   Won (4&3)   (with Bernhard Langer) v Scott Hoch & Jim Furyk
        Won (2&1)   (with Padraig Harrington) v Phil Mickelson & David
                       Toms

2004   Won (2&1)   (with Padraig Harrington) v Phil Mickelson & Tiger
                       Woods
        Lost (3&2)   (with Padraig Harrington) v Stewart Cink & Davis
                       Love III

2006   Lost (1 hole)   (with Padraig Harrington) v Tiger Woods & Jim
                       Furyk

Results overall: **36 Played: 20 Won, 7 Halved, 9 Lost**

Total points won: **23½**

CAPTAIN: 2010   **WON Europe defeated United States 14½ to 13½**

EUROPEAN AND WORLD RANKINGS

Year	European Tour		Worldwide		
	Order of Merit		World Ranking	Total Prize Money*	
	Position	Euro		Position	$
2011	102	300,287	306	-	435,615
2010	1219 ##	148,216 ##	417 ##	- ##	227,049 ##
2009	87 ##	354,303 ##	254 ##	- ##	447,188 ##
2008	27	815,153	121	110	1,301,053
2007	12	1,403,293	57	27	3,050,694
2006	9	1,534,748	17	31	2,617,698
2005	1	2,794,223	8	11	4,175,810
2004	25	767,249	81	63	1,538,155
2003	28	730,773	41	80	1,188,607
2002	4	1,980,720	10	13	2,856,124
2001	5	1,578,676	14	28	1,912,941
2000	6	1,740,917	6	15	2,328,358
1999	1	1,822,879	3	4	2,988,543
1998	1	1,390,308	7	8	2,206,532
1997	1	1,118,527	7	1	3,366,900
1996	1	1,225,204	3	1	3,071,442
1995	1	1,169,073	6	3	2,153,211
1994	1	1,067,807	8	8	1,739,349
1993	1	859,156	14	15	1,219,710
1992	3	622,598	20	16	1,098,732
1991	4	481,006	36	25	827,938
1990	14	244,793	81	85	356,700
1989	25	152,718	162	184	178,951
1988	52	54,881	308	-	105,164
1987	164	2,731	-	-	3,941
TOTALS	(Euro) No.3	24,360,244	World Career Total ($) No.11		41,396,405
	(1987 to 2011)		(1987 to 2011)		

2009 and 2010 Play restricted during tenure as Ryder Cup Captain

**Progressive improvement year by year in Order of Merit,
World Ranking and Worldwide Earnings from 1987 to 1996**

Entered World Top-200 on 15 October 1989   Moved out of World Top-200 on 21 June 2009

In World Top-200 continuously for over nineteen and a half years

* World career earnings taken from *The World of Professional Golf*, founded by Mark H. McCormack

WORLD MATCH PLAY RECORD
(Won title in 1999, Finalist in 1994 and 2000)

Hole	1	2	3	4	5	6	7	8	9	Out	10	11	12	13	14	15	16	17	18	In	Total	Par	State After holes	holes
Par	4	3	4	5	3	4	4	4	4	35	3	4	5	4	3	4	4	5	5	37	72			
1991 1st Round	4	3	4	5	3	4	4	4	5	36	4	4	4	4	3	4	4	4	4	35	71	-1	1 Up	2 Up
v M Calcavecchia	5	3	4	4	3	5	4	4	3	35	3	4	5	6	3					-	-	+2	8 Up	**Won 7&6**
1991 2nd Round	4	2	4	c	3	5	5	3	4	-	3	4	3	4	3	4	4	5	5	35	-	-2	1 Down	a\s
v N Faldo	6	4	4	4	3	4	3	4	5	37	3	4	4	4	3	4	4	6	4	36	73	+1	a\s	a\s
	4	4								-										-	-	+1	-	**Lost 38th**
1993 1st Round	4	3	4	5	3	4	4	4	4	35	3	4	4	4	3	5	4	6	4	37	72	0	1 Up	1 Down
v Y Mizumaki	4	3	3	3	3	4	5	4	5	34	3	3	5	4	3	4	5	5	4	36	70	-2	1 Up	a\s
	3									-										-	-	-1	-	**Won 37th**
1993 2nd Round	4	5	4	4	3	3	4	4	4	35	3	4	3	5	3	4	5	4	4	35	70	-2	2 Up	2 Up
v B Langer	4	2	4	3	3	5	3	4	4	31	3	3	4	3	3					-	-	-6	4 Up	**Won 6&4**
1993 S-Final	4	3	4	4	3	5	5	4	4	34	3	4	4	4	3	5	4	5	4	36	70	-2	1 Up	a\s
v C Pavin	5	4	4	4	4	5	4	4	4	37	3	4	4	4	3	4	3	4	5	34	71	-1	3 Down	a\s
	5									-										-	-	+1	-	**Lost 37th**
1994 1st Round	4	3	3	3	3	4	4	4	3	33	3	4	4	3	3	5	5	4	4	35	68	-4	1 Down	1 Up
v Y Mizumaki	4	3	3	3	3	4	5	4	4	35	3	4	4	4	3	5	4			-	-	-2	a\s	**Won 2&1**
1994 2nd Round	5	2	4	4	3	4	3	4	4	33	3	4	4	4	3	4	3	4	3	32	65	-7	2 Up	3 Up
v N Faldo	4	2	5	4	3	4	4	4	5	35	3	4	4	4	4	4	5	4	4	35	70	-2	1 Up	**Won 1 Up**

Match	1	2	3	4	5	6	7	8	9	Out	10	11	12	13	14	15	16	17	18	In	Tot	+/-		Result
1994 S-Final	4	4	4	3	4	4	4	4	4	35	3	4	3	5	4	4	5	3	4	35	70	-2	2 Down	a\s
v V Singh	4	3	4	2	5	4	5	4	3	34	4	3	5	4	4	4	4	3	5	36	70	-2	2 Up	**Won 1 Up**
1994 Final	4	3	5	3	4	4	5	4	5	37	3	3	3	5	3	4	5	3	4	33	70	-2	3 Down	a\s
v E Els	4	3	4	3	4	4	4	4	4	34	3	5	4	4	3	4	4	3	4	—	—	-1	2 Down	**Lost 4&2**
1995 1st Round	4	3	4	3	4	4	3	4	4	33	3	4	3	4	4	4	4	3	4	33	66	-6	2 Up	5 Up
v D Duval	4	3	5	2	4	4	4	4	4	34	3	5	3	5	4	4	4	3	c	—	—	-2	5 Up	**Won 2 Up**
1995 2nd Round	4	3	4	3	4	4	3	4	4	34	3	4	3	4	5	4	4	3	3	35	69	-3	a\s	2 Down
v S Elkington	4	2	4	5	4	4	3	4	4	34	3	5	3	5	4	4	3	2	4	—	—	-4	2 Down	**Lost 3&1**
1996 1st Round	4	3	4	3	4	3	4	4	4	35	3	4	3	4	4	3	4	3	4	33	68	-4	1 Down	1 Up
v I Woosnam	4	3	3	3	4	4	4	3	4	32	3	4	4	4	4	4	4	3	3	—	—	-4	4 Up	**Won 4&3**
1996 2nd Round	4	3	4	4	4	4	3	4	5	37	3	5	2	4	4	4	5	3	4	35	72	0	a\s	1 Down
v M Brooks	4	2	4	3	4	4	3	4	5	34	2	5	3	4	4	3	5	2	4	33	67	-5	a\s	**Lost 1 Down**
1997 2nd Round	4	3	3	4	5	4	3	5	4	35	3	4	3	5	4	4	4	3	5	35	70	-2	1 Up	a\s
v B Faxon	5	3	4	2	4	4	4	4	4	34	4	5	3	4	5	5	4	4	4	—	—	+1	2 Up	**Lost 2&1**
1998 1st Round	5	3	3	5	2	4	5	4	5	36	3	4	2	4	4	4	3	3	4	36	72	0	2 Down	1 Up
v T Björn	4	3	5	3	3	4	4	4	4	33	4	5	3	4	5	3	4	4	3	—	—	-2	3 Up	**Won 4&3**
1998 2nd Round	4	2	4	3	4	5	4	5	4	34	5	4	3	4	4	3	4	3	4	34	68	-4	1 Up	1 Up
v M O'Meara	4	3	4	4	4	4	4	4	4	37	4	5	3	4	4	3	4	4	4	—	—	+1	5 Down	**Lost 5&4**
1999 2nd Round	4	3	4	3	3	4	4	4	4	33	3	4	3	4	4	3	4	2	4	32	65	-7	2 Down	1 Up
v N Begay III	4	2	4	3	4	4	4	4	4	32	3	4	3	5	4	3	4	3	4	—	—	-4	3 Up	**Won 2 &1**

Hole	1	2	3	4	5	6	7	8	9	Out	10	11	12	13	14	15	16	17	18	In	Total	Par	State After	
Par	4	3	4	5	3	4	4	4	4	35	3	4	5	4	3	4	4	5	4	37	72		holes	holes
1999 S-Final	4	3	4	4	2	5	4	4	4	34	3	3	4	4	3	3	4	4	4	32	66	-6	2 Up	5 Up
v P Harrington	4	3	4	4	3	4	4	4	4	33	3	3	4							-	-	-4	5 Up	Won 7&6
1999 Final	3	2	4	4	3	3	5	4	4	32	3	3	4	3	3	4	4	5	5	34	66	-6	2 Up	3 Up
v M O'Meara	4	3	4	4	3	4	4	5	4	35	3	3	4	4	3	3	4			-	-	-2	3 Up	Won 3&2
2000 2nd Round	4	3	3	3	2	3	3	4	4	30	3	3	4	3	3	3	3	5	4	31	61	-11	1 Up	5 Up
v P Harrington	4	3	5	4	3	3	4	3	4	33	2	4	4	4	3	w	4			-	-	-4	4 Up	Won 5 &3
2000 S-Final	3	3	5	3	4	3	3	4	3	31	2	4	4	4	3	3	4	5	4	33	64	-8	3 Up	4 Up
v V Singh	4	3	4	4	4	4	4	4	4	34	2	4	4	4	3	3				-	-	-3	3 Up	Won 5&4
2000 Final	4	2	4	4	3	3	4	4	4	32	3	4	4	4	3	4	3	5	3	33	65	-7	1 Down	2 Down
v L Westwood	4	3	4	4	3	3	4	3	4	32	3	4	4	5	4	4	4	4	4	36	68	-4	1 Up	a\s
	4	3								-												0	-	Lost at 38th
2001 2nd Round	3	3	4	4	3	5	3	4	5	33	3	4	4	4	3	4	4	4	4	34	67	-5	2 Down	3 Down
v I Woosnam	4	3	4	4	4	3	4	4	5	34	3	4	4	5	3	5				-	-	0	4 Down	Lost 4&3
2002 1st Round	4	4	4	2	4	4	4	4	4	34	2	5	3	4	2	4	5	5	4	33	67	-5	1 Up	2 Up
v F Funk	5	3	5	3	3	4	4	4	4	35	4	4	4	4	3	5	4			-	-	+1	3 Up	Won 3&2
2002 2nd Round	5	3	3	5	2	3	4	3	4	32	2	5	4	3	3	5	3	4	4	33	65	-7	1 Down	4 Down
v E Els	4	3	5	3	4	4	3	4	5	36	3	4	4	c						-	-	0	5 Down	Lost 6&5
2005 1st Round	4	2	4	4	3	4	4	4	4	33	3	4	4	4	4	5	4	3	4	35	68	-4	3 Up	3 Up
v M Hensby	5	3	5	4	4	4	4	4	5	38	3	4	4	4	3	4	4	4		-	-	+1	a\s	Lost 2&1

Round	1	2	3	4	5	6	7	8	9	Out	10	11	12	13	14	15	16	17	18	In	Total	+/-	Result	Result
2006 1st Round	4	3	5	3	3	4	4	4	5	35	3	4	4	5	4	4	4	4	5	35	70	-2	1 Up	a\s
v D Howell	3	2	4	4	2	5	3	4	4	31	3	4	5	4	3	5	3	4	4	34	65	-7	1 Up	Won 1 Hole
2006 2nd Round	4	3	4	c	4	4	3	4	c	–	3	4	5	4	2	4	3	5	4	34	–	-3	2 Down	a\s
v M Campbell	4	3	3	4	3	4	4	3	c	–	3	4	5	3	4	4	4	4	5	36	–	-4	1 Up	Won 1 Hole
2006 S-Final	4	4	4	5	5	5	3	5	4	38	3	4	4	4	3	5	4	5	4	36	74	+2	4 Down	5 Down
v P Casey	4	3	5	3	4	4	4	4	c	–	3	4	4	4				3	4	–	–	-1	5 Down	Lost 6&5
2007 1st Round	5	2	4	5	4	4	5	5	c	35	3	3	5	3		3			5	–	–	-2	3 Down	5 Down
v E Els	w	4	5	5	4	5	3	4	4	–	4	5	4						4	–	–	+2	5 Down	Lost 6&5

Montgomerie's Summary Appearances 14, Matches Played 30, Won 17, Lost 13

Hole	1	2	3	4	5	6	7	8	9	10	11	12	13	14	15	16	17	18	Total	Par
Par	4	3	4	5	3	4	4	4	4	3	4	5	4	3	4	4	5	5	72	Par
Eagles				6								3					1	2	12	-24
Birdies	5	13	9	37	11	15	12	10	4	9	8	48	11	5	5	14	18	30	264	-264
In Par	47	43	36	14	40	34	39	46	42	44	46	9	40	47	32	34	22	8	623	0
Bogeys	10	6	15	9	11	8	3	13		7	5	6	4	13	1		3		114	+114
Double-Bogeys			1										1					1	3	+6
Won / Conceded	1		3				1	1		1			1			2	1		11	0
TOTAL	64	62	60	60	60	60	60	60	60	60	60	60	59	56	52	49	45	40	1027	-168
+/-	+	-	+	-	:	:	+	-		-	-	:	+	-	:	-				
Par	7	7	6	49	2	4	2	7	9	2	3	54	3	1	8	13	17	34		

MAJORS AND FLAGSHIP EVENTS

| Year | Major Championships | | | | | World Golf Championships | | |
	Masters	US Open	Open	US PGA	BMW PGA	WGC Accenture	WGC Cadillac	WGC Invitational
1989					m\c			
1990			t48		9			
1991			t26		2*			
1992	t37	3	m\c	t33	t10			
1993	t52	t33	m\c	m\c	t2			
1994	m\c	t2*	t8	t36	t37			
1995	t17	t28	m\c	2*	t9			
1996	t39	t10	m\c	m\c	t7			
1997	t30	2	t24	t13	5	# Won Andersen Consulting		
1998	t8	t18	m\c	t44	1	WC of G before it became a WGC		
1999	t11	t15	t15	t6	1	t33	t20	t30
2000	t19	t46	t26	t39	1	t17	t25	t8
2001	m\c	t52	t13	t76	t17	-	-	4
2002	t14	m\c	t82	m\c	t2	t33	t31	78
2003	m\c	t42	m\c	m\c	t9	t33	t51	t23
2004	m\c	-	t25	70	t47	t9	-	t58
2005	-	t42	2	m\c	t11	-	t3	t9
2006	m\c	t2	m\c	m\c	t53	t17	t41	-
2007	m\c	m\c	m\c	t42	t30	t17	t55	t41
2008	-	m\c	t58	m\c	m\c	t9	t65	77
2009	-	-	m\c	m\c	t35	-	-	-
2010	-	-	t68	m\c	t48	-	-	-
2011	-	-	-	-	t7	-	-	-
Total Played	15	16	21	19	23	8	8	9
Best Result	t8	2	2	2	1	t9	t3	4

* Lost in play-off

ALFRED DUNHILL CUP FOR SCOTLAND

10 Appearances, 34 Matches played, 19 Wins, 13 Losses, 2 halved

1988	72	Beat Suthep Meesawad (80) (Thailand)
	71	Lost to Mark James (69) (England)
1991	67	Beat Giuseppe Cali (71) (Italy)
	73	Beat David Feherty (74) (Ireland)
	72	Lost to John Bland (69) (RSA)
	69	Beat Philip Parkin (70) (Wales)
1992	71	Beat Brent Franklin (72) (Canada)
	71	Beat Thomas Levet (78) (France)
	70	Beat Per-Ulrik Johansson (74) (Sweden)
	68	Beat Ian Baker-Finch (72) (Australia)
	69	Halved with Jamie Spence (68) (England)
1993	75	Lost to Raul Fretes (74) (Paraguay)
	67	Beat Ian Woosnam (74) (Wales)
	73	Lost to Fred Couples (69) (USA)
1994	78	Beat Carlos Franco (79) (Paraguay)
	70	Beat Chen Tze-Ming (75) (China)
	74	Lost to David Frost (71) (RSA)
1995	71	Beat Chung Chun-hsing (80) China)
	72	Beat Sven Struver (73) (Germany)
	69	Beat David Frost (71) (RSA)
	70	Beat Darren Clarke (72) (Ireland)
	74	Lost to Nick Price (68) (Zimbabwe) (Scotland won Cup)
1996	69	Lost to Jarmo Sandelin (68) (Sweden)
	79	Lost to Gaurav Ghei (78) (India)
	70	Lost to Mark McNulty (69) (Zimbabwe)
1997	67	Beat Sven Struver (73) (Germany)
	72	Beat Padraig Harrington (76) (Ireland)
	68	Halved with Ernie Els (68) (RSA)
1998	73	Lost to Zhang Lian-Wei (72) (China)
	72	Beat Paul McGinley (78) (Ireland)
	70	Lost to Miguel Ángel Jiménez (70) (Spain) at 1st extra hole
2000	70	Lost to Sven Struver (66) (Germany)
	69	Beat Brian Davis (70) (England)
	73	Lost to Ian Woosnam (73) (Wales) at 2nd extra hole

INDEX